Research Report on the Socialist Legal System with Chinese Characteristics

Research Report on the Socialist Legal System with Chinese Characteristics

Volume 1

Edited by Zhu Jingwen and Han Dayuan

Enrich Professional Publishing

Singapore • Hong Kong • Beijing • Honolulu

Published by

Enrich Professional Publishing (S) Private Limited
16L, Enterprise Road,
Singapore 627660
Website: www.enrichprofessional.com
A Member of Enrich Culture Group Limited

Hong Kong Head Office:
2/F, Rays Industrial Building, 71 Hung To Road, Kwun Tong, Kowloon, Hong Kong, China

China Office:
Rm 1800, Building C, Central Valley, 16 Hai Dian Zhong Jie, Haidian District, Beijing, China

United States Office:
PO Box 30812, Honolulu, HI 96820, USA

Translated by Zhang Xingquan

Edited by Glenn Griffith and Caren Ng

ISBN (Hardback)	978-981-4332-45-3
ISBN (ebook)	978-981-4339-63-6 (pdf)
	978-981-4339-64-3 (epub)

Enrich Professional Publishing is an independent globally-minded publisher focusing on the economic and financial developments that have revolutionized new China. We aim to serve the needs of advanced degree students, researchers, and business professionals who are looking for authoritative, accurate, and engaging information on China.

Printed in Hong Kong with woodfree paper from Japan

Contributors (in alphabetical order)

Chen Weidong	Professor, Renmin University of China Law School Director, Litigation System and Judicial Reform Research Center, Renmin University of China Vice Chairman, Criminal Procedural Law Research Association, China Law Society
Fan Wei	Lecturer, School of Labor Economics, Capital University of Economics and Business Doctor in Civil and Commercial Law, Renmin University of China Law School
Fan Yu	Professor, Renmin University of China Law School Director, Dispute Resolution Research Center, Renmin University of China Vice Chairman, Comparative Law Research Association, China Law Society
Feng Hui	Doctoral Student in Economic Law, Renmin University of China Law School
Han Dayuan	Professor, Renmin University of China Law School Dean, Renmin University of China Law School Chairman, Constitutional Law Research Association, China Law Society
Hu Jinguang	Professor, Renmin University of China Law School Deputy Dean, Renmin University of China Law School Vice Chairman, Constitutional Law Research Association, China Law Society
Huang Jingping	Professor, Renmin University of China Law School Executive Director, Research Center for Criminal Jurisprudence, Renmin University of China Vice Chairman, Criminal Law Research Association, China Law Society
Jiang Mengya	Doctoral Student in Economic Law, Renmin University of China Law School
Li Fenfei	Associate Professor, Renmin University of China Law School Doctor in Law
Li Jianfei	Professor, Renmin University of China Law School Executive Director, Social Law Research Association, China Law Society
Li Xiang	Doctoral Student in Economic Law, Renmin University of China Law School

Li Xiuqi	Editor, China Renmin University Press Doctor in Environmental Law
Li Yunping	Ph.D in Criminal Law, Renmin University of China Law School
Liang Shengyuan	Ph.D in Criminal Law, Renmin University of China Law School
Lin Jia	Professor, Renmin University of China Law School Party Committee Secretary and Vice Dean, Renmin University of China Law School Executive Vice Chairman, Social Law Research Association, China Law Society
Liu Chuntian	Professor, Renmin University of China Law School Executive Director, Intellectual Property Teaching and Research Center, Renmin University of China Law School Vice Chairman, Intellectual Property Research Association, China Law Society
Liu Mingxiang	Professor, Renmin University of China Law School Deputy Dean, Renmin University of China Law School Executive Director, Research Center for Criminal Jurisprudence, Renmin University of China
Qi Xiaoling	Ph.D in Criminal Law, Renmin University of China Law School
Qin Qiang	Doctor in Law Postdoctoral Research Fellow, School of Sociology and Population Studies, Renmin University of China
Shi Jichun	Professor, Renmin University of China Law School Director, Economic Law Research Center, Renmin University of China Vice President, Economic Law Research Association, China Law Society
Song Biao	Associate Professor, Renmin University of China Law School Doctor in Law
Sun Xiao	Ph.D in Criminal Law, Renmin University of China Law School
Tang Weijian	Professor, Renmin University of China Law School Vice Chairman, Civil Procedural Law Research Association, China Law Society

Wang Liming	Professor, Renmin University of China Law School Deputy Secretary and Vice President, Renmin University of China Chairman, Civil Law Research Association, China Law Society
Wang Taiping	Professor, Xiangtan University Law School
Xu Wenxing	Postdoctoral Research Fellow in Administrative Law, Renmin University of China Law School
Yang Lixin	Professor, Renmin University of China Law School Director, Civil and Commercial Law Research Center, Renmin University of China Vice Chairman, Civil Law Research Association, China Law Society
Yang Wenlong	Ph.D in Criminal Law, Renmin University of China Law School
Ye Lin	Professor, Renmin University of China Law School Vice Chairman, Commercial Law Research Association, China Law Society
Yu Wenhao	Ph.D in Constitutional Studies, Renmin University of China Law School
Zhang Aixiao	Ph.D in Criminal Law, Renmin University of China Law School
Zhao Jian	Ph.D in Criminal Law, Renmin University of China Law School
Zhao Xianghua	Doctoral Student in Economic Law, Renmin University of China Law School
Zhou Ke	Professor, Renmin University of China Law School Vice Chairman, Environmental and Resources Law Research Association, China Law Society
Zhou Wang	Ph.D in Jurisprudence, Lecturer, China Executive Leadership Academy Pudong
Zhu Jingwen	Professor, Renmin University of China Law School Director, Research Center for Law and Globalization, Renmin University of China Vice Chairman, Jurisprudence Research Association, China Law Society
Zuo Xiuyang	Ph.D in Criminal Law, Renmin University of China Law School

Contents

Preface by Zeng Xianyi

In a modern society ruled by law, the formation of a legal system is a milestone as well as an achievement of a country's well-developed research on legal theory and legal institutions. The 15th and the 16th Party Congress of the Communist Party of China (CPC) proposed that the Socialist legal system with Chinese characteristics would be formed by 2010, and the 17th Party Congress further put forward the mission of perfecting the Socialist legal system with Chinese characteristics. Since it was the last year in the process of the formation of the Socialist legal system with Chinese characteristics, 2010 was, in a sense, a year of great significance in the development of the rule of law in China as it also brought new influential topics and issues to the surface for both the jurisprudential and law sectors.

From its birth to its gradual improvement, the development of the Socialist legal system with Chinese characteristics, as the important value connotation and a formal feature of the development of the rule of law in China, experienced three phases, including its "emergence" in the 9th National People's Congress (NPC), "basic formation" in the 10th National People's Congress, and "formation" in 2010. In March 2001, Li Peng, Chairman of the NPC Standing Committee, proposed in the fourth meeting of the 9th NPC that the Socialist legal system should be initially formed in his term; in March 2008, Chairman Wu Bangguo stated in the report on the work of the Tenth NPC Standing Committee in the first meeting of the 11th NPC that the Socialist legal system with Chinese characteristics — which constituted seven legal branches and three levels of laws with the Constitution as its core and laws as its backbone, including administrative regulations, local ordinances, and other regulatory documents — had basically taken shape; in March 2009, Wu Bangguo pointed out in the second meeting of the 11th NPC that 2009 was a crucial year to ensure the formation of the Socialist legal system with Chinese characteristics in 2010.

The Socialist legal system with Chinese characteristics is crucial to the development of Socialism with Chinese characteristics. It was a significant achievement in the legal system establishment during the past 30 years of reform and opening up, as well as a valued experience of new China's challenging exploration over the past 60 years since its founding. The Socialist legal system with Chinese characteristics contains the Communist Party of China's basic experience and political wisdom about exercising state power according to the law, and it is the basis and new starting point of building a Socialist country under the rule of law. As a milestone in the development of the country, the formation of the

Socialist legal system with Chinese characteristics would be of great theoretical and practical significance when reviewing the legal system that has already formed. The formation of the legal system also provides an opportunity to systematically analyze some related theoretical issues and a chance to objectively evaluate the characteristics of this legal system from different perspectives. In the modern era, China remains part of history and part of the world. The formation of the system also illustrates the law of formation, summarizes its development experience, assesses its structural deficiencies, and foresees the future development since its "formation" and other issues.

Based on the background mentioned above and problem awareness, in 2008, the Law School of the Renmin University of China began to include the subject entitled "Research Report on the Socialist Legal System with Chinese Characteristics" in the national 985 Project of the Ministry of Education "Innovation Platform for the Socialist Legal System with Chinese Characteristics." Through the joint efforts of scholars in more than two years, the report was finally completed. In the research process, the members of the research team always adhered to Chinese awareness, problem awareness, academic consciousness and open consciousness, strove to grasp the features of openness and saw the practical reason of the legal system from a dual perspective of both theory and practice, and tried to answer the following questions: First, what are the features of the basic idea and structure of the Socialist legal system with Chinese characteristics? What is its reasonable theoretical basis? How to understand the local and international features of this legal system in the context of economic globalization? Second, how does the Socialist legal system with Chinese characteristics form? What are its historical legitimacy and legality? What are the basic and major laws in each legal branch? How to establish a reasonable legislative environment? Third, what features of openness does the Socialist legal system with Chinese characteristics show? What is the main development pattern? Fourth, how can one objectively evaluate the problems in the Chinese legal system from a practical perspective? What is the future development of "the Socialist legal system with Chinese characteristics" after its formation? And how can we further improve this system in the future?

Supported by theoretical reflection and analysis, this five-volume report includes the discussion on the above issues and other important phenomena.

The "Overview" discusses the general structure and system of the Socialist legal system with Chinese characteristics. The structural separation of the legal system is the objective requirement for improving the quality of legislation, forming and perfecting the legal system, and promoting jurisprudential study. In this overview, the social basis of the legal system's formation is interpreted in the aspects of legislative practice and jurisprudential study. It also clarifies the historical development of the structure of the legal system, analyzes the quantity and the degree of systematization of legislation, and expounds the nature and type of the Socialist legal system with Chinese characteristics from various perspectives including public and private law, substantive and procedural law, international and domestic law. The discussion is not only based on the current environment in China, but is also focused on future development and it emphasizes the logic of the common development of the changing legal system.

The five volumes form an in-depth analysis of the internal structure of the Socialist legal system with Chinese characteristics. In accordance with the development logic of "history–current situation–tendency–perfection," it analyzes the seven legal branches: the Constitution and the Related Laws, administrative law, criminal law, civil and commercial laws, economic law, social law, and procedural and non-procedural laws. This report shows the panorama of the development course of each branch as well as its role in the legal system since the establishment of new China, objectively evaluates the specific content and legislative status quo of each legal branch, summarizes its development pattern, explores its development tendency, uncovers the problems, and puts forward suggestions and countermeasures for further improvement. The research report is basically organized according to the classification of "seven legal branches," affirming the basic structure of the legal system in form. It is aimed at identifying the contents of this report so as to combine the legislative system in political practice with the discussion of academic logic, and enhance the constructive academic position of the research. To be more specific, the style adopted in the report does not mean that it only demonstrates the legislature's classification of the legal system by putting forward countermeasures, while the problem awareness and academic awareness are always the principles that the report upholds. In the discussion of the specific legal branch, the research team members explore the interrelation and principles within the system. In particular, on the basis that the development and law of each legal branch are shown objectively, they try to offer theoretical answers to a number of major legislative and practical issues, such as the constitutional status of the NPC and its Standing Committee, the classification of the Constitution and the Related Laws, the compiling pattern of the Civil Code, the coordination of criminal law and its relevant branch laws, the selection of the modification mode of criminal procedure law, and the equilibrium of social law in the legal system.

In 2010, the goal of the formation of the Socialist legal system with Chinese characteristics had turned into a reality, which was a milestone in the development of the rule of law in China as well as a landmark of the era. The formation of the

Socialist legal system with Chinese characteristics was not an accomplishment of the legal construction in China, but it also opened up a new era. Yet, driven by the pursuit of scholarship, we understand that the "formation" of the legal system is not an end, but a beginning of a new stage of the development of the rule of law, or in other words, it was nothing more than a beginning. We have to be more conservative to face the new challenges and new issues arising from the formation of the legal system. Thus, we should regard it from a development perspective and develop it with a scientific attitude. For the future development trend of the Socialist legal system with Chinese characteristics, this report puts forwards some problems that deserve attention and exploration in four aspects in the academic world.

First is the long-term development of the legal system. The legal system cannot be built in a day, nor can it stop developing or improving once it has been formed, it needs to constantly respond to the needs of China's social development process and the process of the rule of law. China's social transformation is still in progress, thus the definition of "formation" of the corresponding legal system is just in a relative sense. The report argues that we should make corresponding adjustments to the situations since social relations constantly generate, shape, and change. Many technical or even conceptual issues within the legal system also need to be taken and handled seriously and carefully. As pointed out in the beginning of this report, in the sense of legislative initiation, the legal system has already been established; while in the sense of the generation of the legal order, the development of the legal system is an arduous task, which demands much effort to explore the principle behind the establishment of the legal order.

Second is the openness of the development of the legal system. Law is the product of practicing reason. This report holds that since China is experiencing social transformation, the legal system needs to constantly respond to the needs of the society in transition. It is meant to meet the requirements that there are sound and perfect laws to abide by, even to reflect the development needs of a transforming society. In the process of forming the legal system, the traditional operation mode, with the legislature in the dominant position and administrative departments as a subsidiary, has brought about different conflicts in practice. Therefore, we need to set up a comprehensive legislative mode to attain the power of social autonomy through a variety of forms, so as to extend its significance more than legal effectiveness. This would help the legal system to become a self-contained dispersion mechanism to cope with the complex and rapid changes in a transforming society.

Third is the value of the development of the legal system. In the last few decades of legislative practice, the formation of the Chinese legal system has shown characteristics in terms of phased development and practice. To cater to the needs of reform and opening up and social transformation, we do not have sufficient time to consider the principles of the legal system, and sometimes we are too focused on the needs of policy development. In the early stage of establishing the legal system, the choice of such a legislative development made this inevitable, but once the Socialist legal system had formed, the concept of "constructivism" would meet challenges and this would result in a demand for a legislative stage of reason, tolerance, and relativism. The organization of law enactment, law revision, and statutory interpretation would become the element to maintain the vitality of the legal system.

Fourth is the scientific nature of the development of the legal system. Scientific nature is the basic principle and law that the development of the legal system must follow. A sound legal system should reflect the essence of science and the times, and always stays scientific. On various aspects of the legal system, including the establishment of legislative planning, the formulation of draft legislation, the arrangement of legislative procedure, and the supervision of legislative effect, only by following the scientific legislative principles can we ensure the organic unity of the legal system. To ensure the scientific nature of the legal system, it is fundamental to take the Constitution as its basis to reflect the spirit of the Constitution in the internal structure of the legal system, so as to maintain a balanced development of different legal branches, and improve the legislative technique at the same time. At present, the development of China's rule of law is gradually transforming from the "legislation age" to the "interpretation age." Compared with frequent law revisions, it is more technical and practical to improve statutory interpretations, which make it possible to maintain the stability and adaptability of the law.

This report is a result of collective efforts. All the leaders of the research teams coordinate with their members to conduct special studies and to complete their sub-subjects in accordance with the content designed for this report. The report involves different disciplines with different characteristics and varied research methods, and scholars may hold different academic viewpoints towards the same issue. In order to maintain the overall framework and the organization of this research report, we tried to keep it in harmony as far as possible in respect of writing style and research framework. Yet, in terms of the specific academic point of view, scholars' academic freedom and individuality have been respected and encouraged to fully show the academic idea and style of this report.

The research report was finalized by the editors, Professor Zhu Jingwen and Professor Han Dayuan. All the members of the Editorial Board have made a great contribution to this publication, and I would like to express my heartfelt gratitude to them.

Zeng Xianyi
January 25, 2010

* **Zeng Xianyi** (1936–2011) was a Professor of Renmin University of China, the Honorary President of Renmin University of China Law School, the Honorary Director of the University's Law Teaching Committee of the Ministry of Education, and the Chairman of Legal Education Institute of the China Law Society.

Preface by Wang Liming

"An orange grown in the south of Huaihe River grows into a tangerine, while it turns into a trifoliate orange if it grows in the north of Huaihe River (橘生淮南為橘，生於淮北為枳)." This is one of the famous quotes from Yan Ying, a renowned statesman in the Spring and Autumn Period. It means that anything can change its nature in different environments. The law is no exception. As a cultural achievement rooted in specific historical periods and particular social circumstances, the law reflects the social needs and values in corresponding periods and contexts. The law is meant to be enacted for people, while people are not born for the law. Every system and institution reflects a country's history and culture, meeting the actual needs of the society. The legal culture, as an important component of Chinese civilization, is also one with a long history and profound traditions. As time goes by, the legal culture also undergoes constant self-renewal and evolution, reflecting the political and economic systems and providing institutional support for the dynamic political and economic establishment.

In the process of constructing Socialism with Chinese characteristics, the Socialist market economy and the Socialist legal system complement each other harmoniously and develop simultaneously, arousing worldwide attention. Socialism has become an important event in the history of human social development. Since the founding of new China, especially since the reform and opening up, the Socialist legal system of China is growing along with the development of the reform and opening up as well as the economy. The strategy of constructing a Socialist country under the rule of law contributes as the basic content of the *Constitution of the People's Republic of China*, laying the political cornerstone for the establishment of the Socialist legal system. It was proposed in both the 15th and the 16th Party Congress of the Communist Party of China (CPC) that the Socialist legal system with Chinese characteristics would be formed by 2010. In the 17th Party Congress, it was even suggested perfecting this Socialist legal system with Chinese characteristics. So far, the Socialist legal system has already been established in a sense, as is reflected by the gradual establishment of the Constitution and the basic laws in the legal system and legal life. Criminal law, civil and commercial laws, administrative law, and the traditional public and private basic laws that are used to adjust Socialist market economic activities have all been enacted; all kinds of new social laws, such as the *Law on Protection of Consumer Rights and Interests*, the *Anti-Unfair Competition Law*, the *Labor Law*, the social security law, and the environmental and resources law, have also been greatly improved; and

China participates in the bilateral, or multilateral, international treaties with other countries to become a rising superpower. Accordingly, the status and the role of law in social life are also becoming more prominent. The goal of establishing the Socialist legal system with Chinese characteristics has been realized in a sense so as to provide a strong institutional support for the Socialist market economy.

The Socialist legal system with Chinese characteristics cannot be formed in a day. The initial formation of the Socialist legal system with Chinese characteristics, the achievement of several generations of Chinese legalists' hard struggle in over half a century, embodies the efforts and wisdom of many people. Nevertheless, we should stay conscious of the fact that the negative factors from the thousands of years of feudal tradition and the disorder existing in the transforming society remain critical issues which urgently need to be resolved to accelerate the establishment of the legal system. A variety of social problems, such as power-money bargains, collusion between government officials and the business sector, twisting of the law and legal judgments, and the abuse of power for personal means, also show the deficiency of China's legal system. Undoubtedly, perfecting the legal system will not be a piece of cake. It is still too early to expect a flawless Socialist legal system that plays an important role in society. Facing these problems and solving them through further promoting the progress of the rule of law are inevitable in the establishment of the legal system. The improvement of the Socialist legal system and the exercise of its actual function require the efforts of the whole society. The legislature's active promotion and innovation, the judicial practitioners' enthusiastic exploration and accumulated experience, the legal theoretical research and academic contribution, and the participation in all walks of life are also essential to the progress of bettering the legal system. Therefore, all the legal practitioners should join hands to contribute to the constant development and improvement of the Socialist legal system.

The Socialist legal system with Chinese characteristics cannot be perfected once and for all. In order to further improve the legal system, thoughtful scientific planning is a must. This clear development map represents the goal of governing the country by law and building a Socialist country under the rule of law as stated in the constitution. To realize this grand blueprint, we need a strategic plan — a road map to the accomplishment of the rule of law. This road map is a strategic plan for the establishment of the legal system which sets a number of goals for different stages, and specifies the task and the indicatory system of each stage. Besides, to construct a more well-equipped Socialist legal system, it is necessary to further modify various laws of China, to accelerate the formulation and the enactment of the civil code, to improve the laws related to social insurance and social security, and to develop administrative procedure law and other related laws. In addition, the Socialist legal system with Chinese characteristics should be based on the actual environment of China. The establishment of the system can neither be a rote foreign experience nor a complete refusal of the experience from other countries. The system must be mapped out from the circumstance of the country, since any legal system in line with the current environment is the most suitable one. Last but not least, the Socialist legal system should be effective enough to regulate and protect the Socialist system and the market economy system, which means that it should not only strictly direct the exercise of the official power, but also effectively ensure the entitlement of private rights. Obviously, the initial establishment of the Socialist legal system is not equal to the realization of the rule of law, yet, it is only the groundwork for the governance by law. The true realization of the rule of law still requires successful implementation of various systems in the legal system as well as the promotion and the popularity of the concept of the supremacy of law.

The further improvement of the Socialist legal system raises challenging tasks for legal theorists. On the one hand, we need to summarize the valuable experience and profound lessons accumulated in the past 60 years of establishing the Socialist legal system, and grasp the basic law in the development of the Socialist legal system and legal institutions, so as to provide scientific reference for the further development of the Socialist legal system; on the other hand, we should review the newly-formed legal system. It is critical to pay attention to the unsolved problems in the existing legal system, and to find solutions to them. There are still numerous problems in the existing Socialist legal system, such as the disunity of legislative spirit, the incongruity between pieces of legislation, the duplication of legislation, and the inadequacy of the legal institution. These problems are difficult to solve in a short time. In this regard, legal theorists should continue to be devoted to academic studies. Based on China's actual environment, we learn from the traditional legal culture, take the advanced achievements from foreign legal culture as a reference, and actively commit ourselves to provide theoretical guidance and reference for the settlement of Chinese legal issues. Meanwhile, we need to actively advocate for the establishment of the Socialist legal theory with Chinese characteristics, as well as transform the simple comparison and reference to create a unique model, so as to increase Chinese elements in legal theory, and to highlight its Chinese characteristics. Only in this way can we provide the impetus for the establishment of a higher level Socialist legal system with Chinese characteristics.

"Research Report on the Socialist Legal System with Chinese Characteristics" is a national 985 Project of the Ministry of Education "Innovation Platform for the Socialist Legal System with Chinese Characteristics" undertaken by the Law School of the Renmin University of China. It embodies the efforts and wisdom of all my colleagues in the Law School of Renmin University of China Law School who have been dedicated to the cause of promoting the establishment of the legal system in recent years. This research reflects some of their thoughts on the establishment of the Socialist legal system with Chinese characteristics and insights into exploring the future development of the legal system. As one of the team members of this research report, I wish this publication to be a theoretical reference work for the further development and improvement of the Socialist legal system with Chinese characteristics which shows the great achievements of its establishment. I also would like to contribute to the advancement of the Socialist legal theory research with Chinese Characteristics.

* **Wang Liming** is the Deputy Secretary and Vice President, and a Professor of Renmin University of China, the Vice Chairman of the China Law Society, and the Chairman of the Civil Law Research Association of the China Law Society.

Overview

Framework of the Socialist Legal System with Chinese Characteristics

The Foundation of the Formation of the Socialist Legal System with Chinese Characteristics: Legislative Practice and Jurisprudential Study

In the 15th and the 16th Party Congress of the Communist Party of China (CPC), it was proposed that the Socialist legal system with Chinese characteristics would be formed by 2010, and the 17th Party Congress further put forward the mission of perfecting the Socialist legal system with Chinese characteristics.

The formation of legal system was a milestone as well as a product of the country's fully developed legislative practice and its corresponding jurisprudential research. Besides, the structural separation of the legal system was inevitable in the process of improving the quality of legislation, forming and perfecting the legal system, and undertaking jurisprudential study.

The legislative practice

The formation of a country's legal system depends on the maturity of legislative practice. China's 60-year experience in legislation has been an effective legislative basis for the formation of the Socialist legal system with Chinese characteristics.

In the early years of new China, i.e. the 1950s, society languished and legislation was the key to the stability of the country. The National People's Congress and its Standing Committee (entitled the Central People's Government before 1954) had formulated 114 sets of laws and relevant legal decisions in total, including the *Constitution*, the *Marriage Law*, the *Agrarian Reform Law*, the *Trade Union Law*, the *Regulations on Punishment of Counter-Revolutionaries*, and a series of other significant laws, which formed the foundation for the early legal system of the People's Republic of China (PRC). Under the impact of the Cultural Revolution and legal nihilism in the 1960s and the 1970s, the legal system came to a standstill and had even been seriously damaged. There were only 14 sets of laws and relevant legal decisions formulated in the 1960s, and 23 in the 1970s, of which 14 were only enacted in 1979. During the 10 years of the Cultural Revolution, from 1966 to 1976, there were only three sets of laws and relevant legal decisions: the *Constitution* in 1975, and two amnesty decisions in 1966 and 1975.

Since the period of reform and opening up, the legislation in China started from zero and gradually developed into a more comprehensive system. Its emphasis shifted from quantity to quality. During the early stage of reform and opening up, China's legal system remained imperfect, so it was urgent to review the areas without laws. Regarding the situation at that time, Deng Xiaoping expressed the idea that the legal system had not been established, with many laws yet to be enacted."[1] He also considered that once a law had been developed, the supplement had to be amended. It was not necessary to change the whole set of laws at once. In short, it was better to have some laws than none, and better to have them sooner rather than later."[2] In the 1980s, China formulated 148 sets of laws and relevant legal decisions among which 84 were laws, including the *Constitution* in 1982, the *Criminal Law* and the *Criminal Procedure Law* implemented since 1980, the *Marriage Law* in 1980, the *General Principles of the Civil Law* in 1986, the *Economic Contract Law* in 1981, and the *Administrative Procedure Law* in 1989, all these were landmarks. China's legislation reached a climax in the 1990s, formulating 220 sets of laws and relevant legal decisions, including 128 laws. The symbolic achievements during this period involved the constitutionalization of the "rule of law," the formulation of the Basic Law of the special administrative regions of Hong Kong and Macau, as well as administrative laws of various fields, such as the *Administrative License Law*, the *Law on Administrative Penalty*, the *Administrative Reconsideration Law*, and the *Administrative Supervision Law*. The legal procedural systems of criminal cases, civil cases, and administrative laws were also formed at this stage. Moreover, the 1990s was also highlighted for the progress of intellectual property laws including the *Trademark Law*, the *Copyright Law*, and the *Patent Law*, and the integration of the *Contract Law*. Since 2000, China has drawn up 191 laws, relevant legal decisions and legal interpretations, of which 140 are laws. The most representative achievements included the constitutionalization of human rights protection, private property protection, and the social security system; the *Road Traffic Safety Law*, the *Public Security Administration Punishments Law*, and the *Emergency Response Law*. On the civil and commercial aspects, the *Property Law*, the *Tort Law*, the *Marriage Law*, and the *Enterprise Bankruptcy Law* were completed. It was also the time when various types of enterprise income tax laws were integrated. Furthermore, the *Anti-Money Laundering Law*, the *Law on the State-Owned Assets of Enterprise*, and the *Labor Contract Law* were formulated. The laws on the environment and resources were also further improved. (Please see Fig. 1.1 and Fig. 1.2 for more information about the number of laws that the National People's Congress and its Standing Committee formulated since the establishment and the reform and opening up, respectively.) Yet, apart from the quantity, it is also important to improve the quality of legislation so as to ensure that laws, administrative regulations, and local enactments are in line with the *Constitution* and enhance the coordination and consistency between various legislations. The quality has gradually become the focus of China's legislatures at all levels, especially the National People's Congress and its Standing Committee. The quality of legislation is closely related to the Socialist legal system with Chinese characteristics. In order to improve the quality of legislation, the laws enacted must conform to the characteristics of China's current social relations; we also have to consider the full picture of China's legislation as well as the consistency between different kinds of laws. In other words, we should study the Socialist legal system with Chinese characteristics from an all-round perspective. Therefore, the 11th National People's Congress Standing Committee regarded improving the quality of legislation and forming the Socialist legal system with Chinese characteristics as a top priority.

Fig. 1.1 The number of laws and legal decisions formulated by the National People's Congress and its Standing Committee (1949–2009)

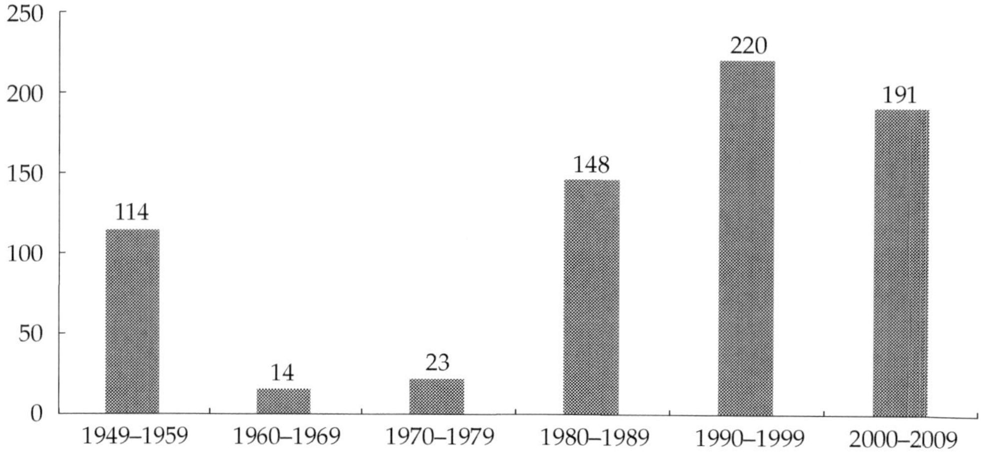

Source: Legislation Planning Office of the Commission of Legislation Affairs of the National People's Congress Standing Committee, ed., *Legislation Statistics of the People's Republic of China* (Beijing: China Democracy and Law Publishing House, 2008), 4–208.

Note: The number of laws and legal decisions formulated by the NPC and its Standing Committee since March 2008 can be retrieved from the official website of the NPC (http://www.npc.gov.cn/npc/).

Democratic legislation and scientific legislation are the key measures to improve the quality of legislation. The democratic legislation is aimed at ensuring people's participation in legislative activities through various ways, including seminars, demonstration meetings, hearings, and other means, to receive different opinions and promulgate important draft laws with consultation papers. In recent years, it has become more common to release consultation papers for the draft laws. According to the NPC statistics, since the release of the draft of the *Property*

Fig. 1.2 The number of laws formulated by the National People's Congress and its Standing Committee (the 5th to the 10th National People's Congress)

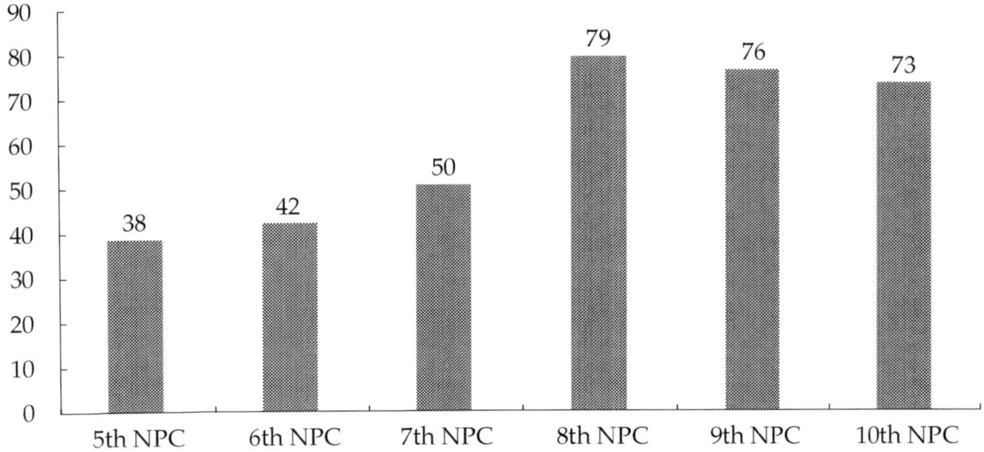

Source: Legislation Planning Office of the Commission of Legislation Affairs of the National People's Congress, ed., *Legislation Statistics of the People's Republic of China* (Beijing: China Democracy and Law Publishing House, 2008), 270.

Law and its consultation paper in 2005, there have been a total of 25 draft laws and the consultation papers released in China (see Table 1.1). Among all these draft laws, the ones of the *Property Law*, the *Labor Contract Law*, the *Food Safety Law*, and the *Social Insurance Law* have aroused extensive attention. Nearly 80,000 people participated in the discussion of the draft of the *Labor Contract Law* and 187,773 pieces of opinion were received; nearly 10,000 people participated in the discussion of the draft of the *Social Insurance Law* and 68,208 pieces of opinion were received. Before these two draft laws, the laws that China promulgated their drafts and consultation papers included the *Constitution* in 1954, the *Constitution* in 1982, the *Law on Industrial Enterprises Owned by the Whole People*, the *Administrative Procedure Law* in 1989, the *Law of Assemblies, Processions and Demonstrations* in 1989, the *Basic Law of the Hong Kong Special Administrative Region* in 1990, the *Basic Law of the Macao Special Administrative Region* in 1993, the *Land Administration Law* in 1998, the *Organic Law of the Villagers Committees* in 1998, the *Contract Law* in 1999, and the *Marriage Law* in 2001.

Table 1.1 National People's Congress statistics of draft laws and consultation papers (2005–2009)

Draft law	Consultation period	Number of participant	Number of opinion
Tort Law (Draft)	Novermber 6, 2009–December 5, 2009	340	3,468
Amendment to the Electoral Law (Draft)	Novermber 6, 2009–December 5, 2009	60	348
Oil and Natural Gas Pipeline Protection Law (Draft)	Novermber 6, 2009–December 5, 2009	23	489
Administrative Compulsion Law (Draft)	August 28, 2009–September 30, 2009	443	3,874
Amendment to the Renewable Energy Law (Draft)	August 28, 2009–September 30, 2009	79	254
Law on Guarding State Secrets (Amendment Draft)	June 27, 2009–July 31, 2009	171	2,112
Law on Diplomatic Personnel Stationed Abroad (Draft)	June 27, 2009–July 31, 2009	101	837
Island Protection Law (Draft)	June 27, 2009–July 31, 2009	25	244
National Defense Mobilization Law (Draft)	April 24, 2009–May 31, 2009	51	417
Law on the People's Armed Police Force (Draft)	April 24, 2009–May 31, 2009	56	411
Social Insurance Law (Draft)	December 28, 2008–February 15, 2009	9,924	68,208
Law on the Mediation and Arbitration of Rural Land Contract Disputes (Draft)	December 28, 2008–February 15, 2009	542	4,125
Statistics Law (Amendment Draft)	December 28, 2008–February 15, 2009	615	4,327
Law on Protecting Against and Mitigating Earthquake Disasters (Draft)	October 28, 2008–November 30, 2008	579	7,308
Amendment to the State Compensation Law (Draft)	October 28, 2008–November 30, 2008	346	1,966
Postal Law (Draft)	October 28, 2008–November 30, 2008	657	5,365

(Cont'd)

Draft law	Consultation period	Number of participant	Number of opinion
Amendment to the Patent Law (Draft)	August 29, 2008– October 10, 2008	304	1,530
Insurance Law (Draft)	August 29, 2008– October 10, 2008	257	2,756
Amendment (VII) to the Criminal Law (Draft)	August 29, 2008– October 10, 2008	850	3,238
Food Safety Law (Draft)	April 20, 2008– May 21, 2008	2,858	9,604
Fire Control Law (Amendment Draft)	May 4, 2008– June 5, 2008	505	2,180
Water Pollution Prevention and Control Law (Draft)	September 5, 2007– October 11, 2007	307	1,408
Employment Promotion Law (Draft)	March 25, 2007– April 25, 2007	3,469	7,647
Labor Contract Law (Draft)	March 20, 2006– April 19, 2006	79,904	187,773
Property Law (Draft)	July 10, 2005– August 20, 2005	2,249	9,605

Source: Website of the National People's Congress, December 31, 2009, http://www.npc.gov.cn/npc/flcazqyj/node_8195.htm.

In 2000, China passed the *Law on Legislation,* so as to standardize the legislative procedure of the NPC and its Standing Committee as well as the State Council. Before the 8th National People's Congress, the deliberation procedure was relatively simple and the number of times of instance was not clearly stated. A law, from being submitted by the State Council or other drafting institutions and explained to the NPC Standing Committee to being passed, was completed in one meeting or within a few days. Since 1998, a three-instance system had been adopted for the deliberation of draft law: In the first instance, proposer's interpretation of the draft law will be heard, and this is the preliminary deliberation; in the second instance, having fully investigated the draft law for more than two months, committee members will proceed to further deliberation on the main ideas, difficulties, and variations of opinions; in the third instance, the special committee will make amendments to the draft law and propose a report on the deliberation result based on the committee members' advice, on the basis of which the draft law will be reconsidered. The draft law will proceed to voting if there is no objection. The *Law on Legislation* in 2000 clearly defined the three-instance system. Among the 122 laws passed by the NPC and its Standing Committee between 2000 and 2009, 22 were passed in the first instance, 30 in the second instance, 59 in the third instance, and 10 in the fourth instance. The *Property Law* was even passed in the eighth instance. Seventy laws were passed in the third and upper instances, i.e. 57.3%, and 52 laws were passed in the first and the second instances, i.e. 42.7%. Between 1979 and 1989, most of the laws, 66 in total, were passed in the first and the second instances, accounting for 82.5%, and there were only 14 laws passed in the third and upper instances, accounting for 17.5% (see Table 1.2).

Table 1.2 The number of instances for the laws passed by the National People's Congress and its Standing Committee (1979–2009)

	1st instance	2nd instance	3rd instance	4th instance	5th instance	6th instance	7th instance	8th instance
1979–1989	21	45	13	—	—	1	—	—
1990–1999	7	89	32	5	2	—	—	—
2000–2009	22	30	59	10	—	—	—	1

Source: Legislation Planning Office of the Commission of Legislation Affairs of the National People's Congress, ed., *Legislation Statistics of the People's Republic of China* (Beijing: China Democracy and Law Publishing House, 2008), 4–90.

Another measure to enhance the quality of legislation is the shift of focus from the enactment of new laws to the amendment of formulated laws. During the early stage of reform and opening up, especially the 1980s, in order to efficiently improve the "lawless" situation, formulation of new laws was the top priority in legislation. By the 1990s, there had been a considerable number of laws that were amended. After the enactment of the most stable *Constitution* in 1982, there had been three amendments by the late 1990s, i.e. in 1988, 1992, and 1999; from the enactment of the law in 1979 to the amendment in 1997, the *Criminal Law* has been revised 25 times and had 107 accessory criminal norms in other laws. Since 2000, the scale of amendment of different branches has become larger, and over 50% of administrative laws, economic laws, civil and commercial laws, and procedural laws have been amended. Moreover, among the emerging social laws, the *Trade Union Law*, the *Labor Law*, and the social security laws of various organizations have been amended many times. During the 5th National People's Congress (1978–1982), 34 laws were formulated and four laws were amended. During the 10th

National People's Congress (2003–2007), 31 laws were formulated and 42 laws were amended. The ratio of formulation to amendment has decreased from 8.5:1 at the 5th National People's Congress to 0.73:1 at the 10th National People's Congress (see Fig. 1.3).

Fig. 1.3 The number and the ratio of the laws formulated and amended by the National People's Congress and its Standing Committee (the 5th NPC to the 10th NPC)

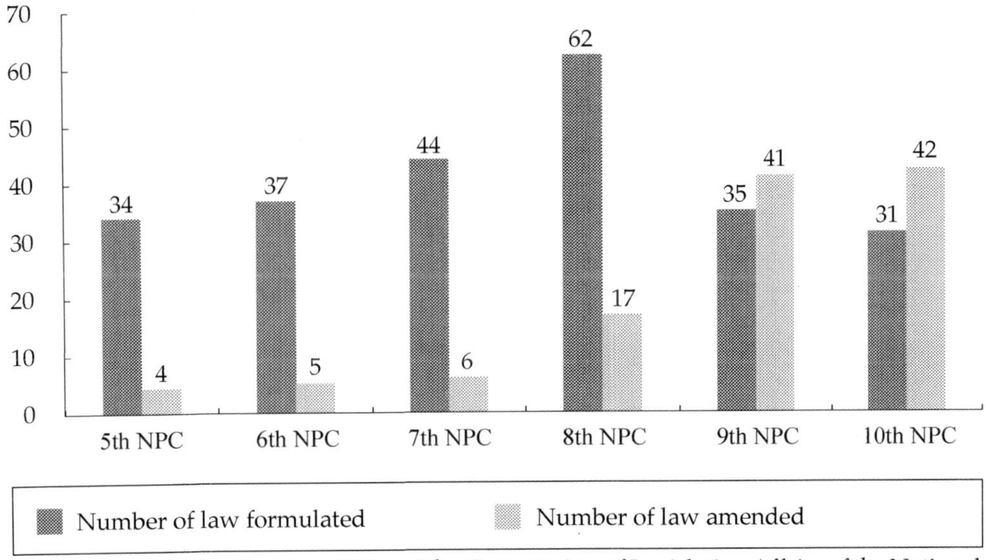

Source: Legislation Planning Office of the Commission of Legislation Affairs of the National People's Congress, ed., *Legislation Statistics of the People's Republic of China* (Beijing: China Democracy and Law Publishing House, 2008), 270.

Jurisprudential study

The legal system cannot be formed without the development of jurisprudential study. The development of legislation constitutes the foundation for the formation of the legal system. While the number of laws is increasing rapidly, the key to forming a legal system lies in the processing of the existing laws — eliminating internal conflicts, overlaps, and inconsistencies. This hardwork of organization and the urge of of truth require the reason of jurists in order to form a harmonious and integrated system.

This organization process consists of two aspects. One is from the vertical perspective, for the relationship between the legislation at different levels, i.e. the issues of the legislation system and the origin of the legal system. It is about the hierarchical structure of laws, such as the issue of the three levels of legislation. At the same time, numerous questions are also handled: What are the constituents of law? Are the statutes, the administrative regulations, and the local regulations included? Are the departmental regulations, local government regulations, or even some normative documents drafted by the offices below the provincial level included in the sphere of law? What kind of laws, regulations, and rules should be formulated by the National People's Congress? And what kind should be formulated by the State Council or local governments? These issues are related to the relations between different state organs or to the division of central and local government's legislative authority. The other aspect is a horizontal one, which is about the relations between different legal branches, i.e. the internal structure of laws in a country. This internal structure cannot be recognized only by the virtue of feeling but by reasonable thinking. The manifestation of laws, i.e. normative documents, and their internal structure may not be consistent with each other. A set of normative documents may contain regulations of different legal branches. For the convenience of codification, the legal regulations of different legal branches are often put in one document. Therefore, it is noticed that a legal document contains regulations of different legal branches when we look into those branches and explore their internal structure. For example, the *Administrative Procedure Law* is included in the documents of the *Administrative Compulsion Law*, the *Administrative Supervision Law*, the *Administrative Remedy Law*, and the *Law on Administrative Penalty*. Obviously, it is not comprehensive enough to include these documents into the substantive administrative law. Some legal documents should be included in different branches from different perspectives. For instance, it is reasonable to include the *Trade Union Law* in the Constitution and the Related Laws or social law. It is also reasonable to regard the market-regulating laws, such as the *Company Law*, the *Law on Industrial Enterprises Owned by the Whole People*, the *Law on Individual Proprietorship Enterprises*, the *Partnership Enterprise Law*, the *Law on Farmers' Professional Cooperatives*, the *Law on Chinese-Foreign Contractual Joint Ventures*, the *Law on Joint Ventures Using Chinese and Foreign Investment*, and the *Law on Foreign-Funded Enterprises* as a part of civil and commercial laws; on the other hand, they are also related to the subjects of economic law. The branch of criminal law is not only presented in penal code and specific criminal law but also in subsidiary criminal law, i.e. other legal branches including the intellectual property laws and the financial laws with criminal penalties involved. If we simply classify the legal branches according to the subjects of the normative documents, it is appropriate to have the penal code and specific criminal law included in the branch of criminal law. However, it will be obviously a problem if the intellectual property laws and the financial laws are classified into the branch of criminal law. According to the seven-branch classification system of the Commission of

Legislative Affairs of the NPC, the *Organic Law of the People's Courts* and the *Organic Law of the People's Procuratorates* are included in the Constitution and the Related Laws. In fact, however, they are closely related to litigation procedure law. Before the enactment of procedural law, they functioned like a procedure law, while they are regarded as one of the sources of China's procedural law after the enactment.

Reason is required in revealing the internal structure of the legal system. Yet, different people may vary in their understanding of the internal structure — One may think that the legal system consists of five branches while the other may believe that it consists of seven or nine or more branches. Different people analyze from different perspectives.[3] Some people may therefore claim that the division of the legal system is not necessary. Undoubtedly, it is true that theory can mislead the practice, but it is still too soon to conclude that the division of theories as well as legal branches is worthless. The foundation for the formation of legal system lies in a great number of legislative practices. This foundation requires more elaboration of the theories so that an immature legal system can become well-established. Otherwise, the legal system will never be a sustainable and healthy institution. It should be noted that legislation is always for the purpose of meeting social needs and addressing an emergency; it is so in both China and foreign countries in both ancient times and the modern world. In the initial stage, it is difficult to consider the consistency and the coordination among different legal regulations and branches. However, once legislation has been developed to a certain extent, the consistency and the coordination between legislations and the issues in the system cannot be ignored. This is not only for the theoretical progress but also for the practical requirements. In a sense, it is the duty and the compulsory responsibility of jurists to establish a mature legal system on the basis of legislative practice.

Historical Development of the Structure of the Legal System

The development of a country's legal system, like that of social relations, is always a process from simplicity to complexity.

In the time when a civilized society just began, social relations were very simple and the legal rules were rather simple accordingly. At that time, the rules were in the form of customary law and were not separated from practice. In addition, there was no obvious boundary separating legal regulations for social relations and other social norms. The law, morality, and religion were integrated with each other, not to mention a clear division of legal branches, resulting in a society of "no separation between civil law and criminal law and all laws integrated (*minxing bufen, zhufa heti* 民刑不分，諸法合體)." The relationship between people's actual behavior, norms of conduct, and law was in a chaotic situation.

Later, as the social relations get complicated, particularly with the development of the division of labor in society, a simple division of law started to emerge, such as the public law and the private law in Roman law, the canon law and common law in the middle ages as well as the common law and equity in the English legal system. These classifications conformed to the social needs at that time. All legal norms were classifiable. The public law and private law in the civil law system is an example of legal division. In the age of Ancient Rome, this kind of division met the need of the simple social relations at that time when all relations could be clearly classified into either the sphere of individual autonomy or the sphere of public power. The subjects were either nations or the public power representing the nation, or individuals. According to Justinian,[4] "The study of law consists of two branches: law public, and law private. The former relates to the welfare of the Roman State; the latter to the advantage of the individual citizen."[5] The common law and the equity are also something black or white. The equity is supplementary to the common law. If the remedy of common law was justifiable, the remedy of equity was not allowed. The jus gentium and the jus civil were also classified in this way. Those regulating the relations between Roman citizens belonged to the jus gentium, while those regulating the relations between Roman citizens and foreigners, and the relations between foreigners belonged to the jus civil.

With the codification movement in the eighteenth and the nineteenth centuries, the modern legal system gradually had been taking shape out of the civil law system, including five major legal branches: constitutional, administrative, criminal, civil (commercial), procedural (including civil procedural law and criminal procedural law, as well as administrative procedural law separated from administrative law afterwards). Then, every regulation and norm could be classified into these branches accordingly. To be more specific, constitutional law stated the basic rights and duties of state organs and citizens; administrative law regulated the relations between administrative state organs and the relations between these organs and citizens; criminal law clarified the definition of crime and the corresponding punishments; civil law acted as a code for the civil relations among citizens, including property right, creditor's right, infringement of rights, marriage and family, and inheritance, etc.; procedural law was meant to identify and protect rights through trial when substantive rights of subjects encountered disputes or were infringed. The characteristics of this kind of division, especially the characteristics of the legal adjustment, conformed to the social relations at that time. The division of legal branches was always connected with the code of laws. Since the code of laws and the division of legal branches were the products of reason, improving the confusing normative documents into the code of laws required jurists to eliminate the internal conflicts on the basis of the existing documents; while the division of branches extends the compiling of the code of laws from one branch to the whole legal system. The *Napoleonic Code* (*Code civil des français*) was an influential source in the development of legal branch code. Enacted in 1804, it was recognized as the first code of laws in modern capitalist society. It was commented that the French Revolution had fully pulled down feudalism and tyranny of the police. Based on the French Revolution, the jurists translated the economic life of the emerging modern society into legal standards proclaimed by Napoleon.[6] It not only marked the formation of the civil law system and became the core and foundation of this system, but also started the legislation of legal branches. Since then, every civil code in the world has been more or less influenced by the *Napoleonic Code*. Many countries, including Austria, Netherlands, Germany, Switzerland, Greece, Turkey, Japan, Canada, Argentina, Brazil, Senegal, and Guinea, all followed suit to formulate their own codes of legal branches. Eventually, the basic characteristics of the code of the civil law system spread worldwide. According to Friedrich Engels, the *Napoleonic Code* had then become a reference for every new code of laws in different countries.[7] Several years after the formulation of the civil code, France had also formulated another four codes, i.e. the *Code of Civil Procedure*, the *Commercial Code*, the *Penal Code*, and the *Code of Criminal Procedure*, constituting the "six-code" legal system of France together with the *Constitution*. There was less possibility and necessity for the administrative law to be codified due to its own characteristics; however, the special status of administrati ve law in the whole legal system could not be replaced by any other statute on the books or laws. The division of these legal branches was related to the social relations they regulated; on the other hand, instead of being divided into political law, economic law, cultural law, religious law and education law in accordance with the social relations, because it was probably determined by the regulating methods, these laws were divided in another way. General regulation was stated in the *Constitution* to provide basic principles for the whole legal system. Its regulations were often realized through specific legal relations of the laws in other legal branches. Administrative law included subordinate regulation, targeting administrative state organs and their counterparts and regulating the subordinate relations between administrative state organs as well as the relations between administrative organs and their administrative counterparts. Criminal law consisted of criminal sanctions as regulations; although the regulating objects included all social relations, only if the social relations regulated by the laws were severely damaged and the parties concerned could not fix it, the criminal law would come into force. Civil and commercial laws were enacted via equal status-oriented regulating method. Procedural law was enforced through a regulating method different from that of substantive laws by which no substantive right could be obtained without appropriate procedure. Therefore, the social relations they regulated featured their own characteristics. This typical division disclosed the importance and purity of the five basic legal branches from the differences between the constitutional law and the law of different branches, civil law, and administrative law, the law confirmation rights (including constitutional law, administrative law, and civil law) and the law protection rights (criminal law), substantive law, and procedural law. It seemed that this kind of division could include all legal norms without any omission. Some jurists even commented that they were distinct, contrasting, and of an incompatible nature in a legal sense. They were organized in a scientific and logical structure, which was a clear presentation of legal regularity. In other words, although the legal institutions of various legal branches were different, there are still some basic and original elements (regulation and protection, they still shared common basic legal principles: adjustability and protectiveness, concentration and arbitrariness, substantive and procedural nature. All these characteristics were well-presented in the five major legal branches.[8] It was an incomparable structure of legal branch division and combination. It was perfect to address all social relations, and to include any changes of the social relations into the whole system seemingly. In fact, the classical discipline system of jurisprudence and Begriffsjurisprudenz (conceptual jurisprudence) in the late nineteenth century was also formed in this way.

As social relations have been more complicated since the twentieth century, the legal regulations and the relations between them become more complex. This complexity has resulted in many new issues in which national interests, social interests, and personal interests get interconnected; public power and private rights influence each other; litigation law and procedural law interact with each other; and international law and national law transform simultaneously. On the one hand, many new fields with the characteristics of different legal branches have appeared; on the other hand, the incompatibility of the original five legal branches is also influenced by their according counterparts. It gives rise to the privatization of public law, publicization of private law, and the emergence of mixed legal branches. It will be too simplified to classify various legal regulations with the dichotomy of public law and private law. The new social relations have resulted in the regulations which are not fully conformed to the original legal branch; these regulations are at the verge instead of the core of the original branch. Those regulations have led to inharmonic phenomenon within the legal branch and the number of such regulations has been climbing so that the original legal branch can no longer accommodate them. Eventually one or more legal documents for regulating the same social relations are formed. New branches are formed through the theorization by jurists. According to the original standard of the division of branch, it seems that confusion has resulted — a legal branch with several incompatible legal principles and legal regulating methods. In terms of practice, both jurists and legal practitioners are learning to view and solve problems from a new perspective. Instead of from the angle of certain legal branch or focusing on certain issues, they concentrate on the problems and address the problems to find out various regulations which may be constitutional, criminal, or administrative ones. In addition, they may even resort to non-legal regulations such as custom, morality, and etiquette. Consequently, new legal combinations have appeared; for example, some people propose taking interest as the standard to divide the legal system into national law, social law, family law, and autonomy law with reference to the *Constitution*.[9] Someone proposes to divide the legal system into basic rights law, freedom right law, social rights law, participation right law, and relief right law from the perspective of rights.[10] This kind of division of legal branches is a completely new idea. Although it may be questioned for its abandonment of legal tradition and culture, and for its confusion in the original division, it is still controversial for a reformation of the division of legal branches.

The penetration and influence among different legal branches can be found in many countries. In the 1930s, the realistic jurisprudence proposed that there was no clear boundary between the public law and the private law, as well as the private autonomy and the public power, based on the intensified state intervention in the period of Roosevelt's New Deal Period. Even the most typical private rights — private property rights and freedom of contract — are not completely private in a sense. They have to be confirmed and guaranteed by the state, and they are closely related to law enforcement. The so-called "division into public law and private law" and the "private autonomy" proposed by classic jurists are just theories. The so-called private law is only a form of public law.[11] Since World War II, realistic jurisprudence has been criticized for its deficiencies including the uncertainty and skepticism on law. However, their viewpoints about the division in terms of public law and private law have been widely adopted by later scholars. They believe that the boundaries between public law and private law as well as the field of private autonomy and the field of public power are not fixed and absolute but mobile. Moreover, some "middle fields" with the characteristics of both the public law and private law are taking shape. This eclectic viewpoint involves many legal fields such as the boundary of jurisdiction, the boundary between contractual behavior and non-contractual behavior, and the boundary between liability for breach of contracts and the liability for tort; even the boundary between life and death is not absolute but relative and mobile. The judgment of the Supreme Court of the United

States on abortion is one of the examples about these issues. The abortion during the first three months of pregnancy is protected by the privacy rights, belonging to the sphere of private law; the abortion during the last three months of pregnancy falls into the sphere of public rights; while the abortion during the middle three months is partly private rights and partly public rights.[12] These new changes in the Western society have shocked the jurisprudential circle. John Merryman probes into the reasons and phenomena of the privatization of public law, the publicization of private law, and the integration of the public and private laws, proposing that due to the enormous change of government, economy and society, the division of contemporary civil law system into public and private law is in crisis.[13] Roberta Unger advocated the connection between a welfare state and the decline of the rule of law. He believed that the gradual similarity of state and society and the gradual integration of public law and social law in post-liberal society erodes the universality, publicity, and substantiality of law and destroys the autonomy of legal order which leads to the disintegration of the rule of law.[14] Harold Berman explicitly pointed out the fundamental changes in the field of public law, private law, and social law. The concerted legal system in contemporary Western countries had been falling into disorder, and the legal tradition had been facing the risk of collapse.[15]

Public Law and Private Law in Contemporary China

The general division of the legal system into public law and private law

Public and private laws are the most common division of the legal system. Public law usually includes the constitution, administrative law, and criminal law; and private law includes the civil and commercial laws. For procedural laws, according to their attachment to different substantive laws, the criminal procedure law and the administrative procedure law are included in public law, while civil procedure law is classified as a part of private law.

There are various reasons why the constitution, the administrative law, and the criminal law are regarded as public law in the traditional sense.

- First, the subjects of these laws are all involved in the state organs that exercise state power, such as the different national institutions at different levels mentioned in the constitution such as the legislative, executive, and judicial authorities, the central government and local governments; the executive institutions that exercise administrative power in different areas mentioned in the administrative law; and public security organs, procuratorial organs and people's courts that exercise the investigation right, prosecution right, and jurisdiction mentioned in the criminal law.

- Second, since they are all with the feature of exercising state power, it is inevitable that the relationships these laws regulate are unequal, regarded as either a subordinate or a restrictive relationship. In other words, one party has to be obedient to the commands and arrangements of the other party, or to be subject to the supervision and constraint of the other party. It includes the relationship, regulated in the constitution, between the central organs and the local organs and that between legislative organ and executive, judicial, and prosecution organs at the same level; the relationship, regulated in the administrative law, between administrative organs at different levels and that between administrative organs and their administrative counterparts; the relation, regulated in the criminal law, between suspects and courts exercising jurisdiction on behalf of the state.
- Third, these laws protect social interests rather than private ones. For example, the constitution, as the national law, protects the country's overall interests; administrative organs also maintain the social security and national interests of relevant fields by means of the administrative law; and the criminal law has long been out of the scope of private revenge and it safeguards the national and social interests by imposing penalties on criminals.
- Fourth, the norms these laws contain are not arbitrary, but compulsory and imperative. In other words, as the subjects, state organs have no opportunity to make choices according to their own interests. Their behaviors have to be in accordance with the modes formulated by laws; otherwise, they will be regarded as overstepping or abusing their authority. In other words, "what is forbidden by the law means prohibition."

Although the constitution is abstract and directive, its regulation in state organs, on the aspects of nature, structure, functions, and relations, is not arbitrary, but compulsory. The nature of administrative law is the most imperative and compulsory towards both lower administrative organs and administrative counterparts. The nature of "inevitability of punishment" of the criminal law determines that the law should not be arbitrary at all. A large part of, especially the core part of China's *Constitution*, administrative law and criminal law acquire the above properties in terms of their subjects, relations, interests, and norms if these laws are evaluated by these standards.

Regarding private law, civil and commercial laws have completely different properties. First, the subject of the civil and commercial laws is an individual or legal entity rather than the country. Second, the relationships that the civil and commercial laws regulate possess the nature of equal rights rather than the nature of mutual subordination. For example, as stated in the *General Principles of the*

Civil Law, "The Civil Law of the People's Republic of China shall adjust property relationships and personal relationships between civil subjects with equal status, that is, between citizens, between legal persons and between citizens and legal persons." Although the state is also involved in civil relations as the subject of state-owned enterprises, it does not possess the nature of exercising state power in such cases. For another example, the *Property Law* provides that the Socialist market economy system shall be practiced by the state as well as that the equal legal status and development rights of all market subjects shall be protected. And the real right of the state, collective, individual or any other right holder shall be protected by law, and may not be damaged by any entity or individual. Thirdly, the civil and commercial laws are aimed at protecting the individual interests of citizens rather than national or social interests. The first article of the *General Principles of the Civil Law* explicitly provides that this law is formulated "for the purpose of protecting the lawful civil rights and interests of citizens and legal persons." Fourthly, norms of the civil and commercial laws are arbitrary rather than compulsory. The regulations of an arbitrary nature are widely applied in the *Contract Law* and the *Marriage Law*. For example, in a sales contract, the contracting parties can negotiate about the price and quality by themselves, and the market price or relevant provisions of the product quality law will be consulted only if the contracting parties do not reach an agreement and get involved in disputes. In addition, in divorce cases, the parties can discuss by themselves the problems about the rearing of their minor children and the division of property, and the principle of the greater interest of children as well as the principle of joint ownership of postnuptial properties will not be consulted unless the two parties fail to reach an agreement. Inviolability of private rights and freedom of contract have been regarded as the two major principles of the civil and commercial laws for a long time. This fully reflects that citizens and legal persons can possess, use, and dispose their own properties without any intervention from government, social organizations, and other individuals. This feature conforms to the principle, "what is not prohibited by the law means permission," namely the autonomy of private rights. There is no doubt that the distinction between public and private law is with its own positive significance. The widely accepted principle of public law — "what is forbidden by the law means prohibition" and that of private law — "what is not prohibited by the law means permission" have their own sphere of application, and to keep an appropriate distance between them is of great significance for demarcating the boundary of public rights, preventing the abuse of public rights in the field of private rights, maintaining the autonomy of private rights, and protecting private rights against the expansion of public rights, especially in current China where awareness about private rights is weak and the market economy and democracy are not yet well-established. The current practice of the division of the legal system into public and private law, to a large extent, is related to its inevitability and vitality, proving that "it originated from the needs of social life and reflects the regularity of legal regulation."[16]

However, in contemporary China, due to the strengthening of state intervention and the influence of civil society on the political realm, various legal branches have undergone considerable changes in three major aspects, namely publicization of private law, privatization of public law, and the emergence of mixed legal branches with the features of both public and private law.

Publicization of private law in China

The so-called "publicization of private law" means that those laws belonging to private law have been increasingly influenced by state intervention. In contemporary Western society, the core of private law, i.e. the principle of inviolability of private rights and freedom of contract formulated during the period of laissez-faire capitalism, is being challenged. The autonomy of private rights is not absolute, it cannot violate social and public interests and the legitimate rights of others. While in China, since the Socialist market economy is practiced by the state, the tendency of publicization of private law has its own characteristics. On the one hand, with the transition from planned economy to market economy, civil and commercial laws, characterized by guaranteeing equal status of subjects of the market economy and reflecting civil activities' principles of voluntariness, fairness, making compensation for equal value, undergo rapid development, totally changing the previous situation in which economic activities are regulated by executive orders in the planned economy. On the other hand, this kind of civil and commercial laws has a distinct Socialist flavor, for it emphasizes that civil activities should not violate national and social interests, infringe upon others' interests, or disrupt the order of the Socialist economy, and they should protect the disadvantaged groups, comply with public order and fair norms, and abide by state laws.

In Article 4, 6, and 7 of the *General Principles of the Civil Law* of the PRC, honesty and credibility, compliance with the law, respect for public virtue, no harm to social public interests, and no disruption of social economic order are regarded as the basic principles of civil activities, which become the essential premise of the autonomy of private rights.

In Article 7 of the *Property Law* of the PRC, the provision that "One shall, when acquiring or exercising a real right, comply with the law, respect social morals and not infringe upon the public interests or the lawful rights and interests of any other person" is regarded as the basic principle of the *Property Law*. There is also a great number of compulsory and restrictive provisions in different forms of the property right in other articles. For example, in Article 41, as for state ownership, it is stipulated that "As regards a realty or chattel that is exclusively owned by the state as prescribed by law, its ownership may not be acquired by any entity or individual." As regards owners' partitioned ownership of building areas, Article 71 formulated that "Any owner may not endanger the safety of the building or infringe upon the lawful rights and interests of any other owner when exercising his or its rights." Article 77 provides that "Any owner may not alter a residential house into a house used for business purposes with violation of any law, regulation or management stipulation." As far as neighboring relationships are concerned, it is regulated in Article 84 that "A neighboring right holder of realty shall, in accordance with the principles of facilitating production and livelihood, solidarity and mutual aid, as well as fairness and equity, handle the neighboring relationship in a correct manner." With respect to usufructuary right, Article 120 provides that "When exercising this right, a usufructuary right holder shall comply with the provisions on protecting, reasonably exploring and utilizing resources as provided for in the laws." As for right to the contracted management of land, it is stipulated in Article 128 that "The holder of the right to the contracted management of land has the right, in accordance with the provisions in the law on the contracting of rural land, to circulate his/her such right in forms such as subcontracting, interchanging, and transferring. The circulated term may not be more than the remnant term of the original contract. Any contracted land may not be used for non-agricultural constructions without approval."

In Article 6 and 7 of the *Contract Law* of the PRC, complying with the principle of good faith, abiding by the relevant laws and administrative regulations, observing social ethics, and not disrupting social and economic order or harming the public interests are regarded as an important prerequisite for the principle of freedom of contract. Article 52 provides that a contract is invalid in any of the following circumstances:

(i) One party induced conclusion of the contract through fraud or duress, thereby harming the interests of the state;

(ii) The parties colluded in bad faith, thereby harming the interests of the state, the collective or any third party;

(iii) The parties intended to conceal an illegal purpose under the guise of a legitimate transaction;

(iv) The contract harms public interests;

(v) The contract violates a mandatory provision of any law or administrative regulation.

Article 53 provides that the following exculpatory provisions in a contract are invalid:

(i) excluding one party's liability for personal injury caused to the other party;

(ii) excluding one party's liability for property loss caused to the other party by its intentional misconduct or gross negligence.

In Section 2 of Article 54, it is stipulated that "If a party induced the other party to enter into a contract against its true intention by fraud or duress, or by taking advantage of the other party's hardship, the aggrieved party is entitled to petition the People's Court or an arbitration institution for amendment or cancellation of the contract."

In Article 2 of the *Marriage Law* of the PRC, protecting the lawful rights and interests of women, children and old people and practicing family planning as well as freedom of marriage are regarded as the basic principles of the *Marriage Law*. Article 39 provides that "At the time of divorce, the disposition of the property in the joint possession of husband and wife is subject to agreement between the two parties; in cases where an agreement cannot be reached, the people's court shall make a judgment in consideration of the actual circumstance of the property and on the principle of caring for the rights and interests of the wife and the child or children."

Article 5 of the *Company Law* of the PRC takes the provision that "When undertaking business operations, a company shall comply with the laws and administrative regulations, social morality, and business morality. It shall act in good faith, subject itself to supervision of the government and the general public, and bear social responsibilities." The basic principles of the *Company Law* also include that a company should conduct its business autonomously, be responsible for its own profits and losses and accept limited liability. Besides, a series of compulsory and restrictive provisions concerning a company's business activities has also been made. For example, Article 17 provides that "A company shall protect the lawful rights and interests of its employees, conclude employment contracts with the employees, buy social insurances, strengthen labor protection so as to achieve workplace safety." Article 18 provides that "The employees of a company shall, in accordance with the Trade Union Law of the People's Republic of China, organize a labor union, which shall conduct union activities and safeguard the lawful rights and interests of the employees. The company shall provide necessary conditions for its labor union to conduct its activities. The labor union shall, on behalf of the employees, conclude the collective contract with the company with respect to the remuneration, working hours, welfare, insurance, operation safety and sanitation and other matters. According to the *Constitution* and other relevant laws, a company shall implement democratic management in the form of meeting the representatives of the employees or any other ways. To make a decision on restructuring or any important issue related to business operation, or to formulate any important regulation, a company shall solicit the opinions of its labor union, and shall solicit the opinions and proposals of the employees through the meeting of the representatives of the employees or in any other way." Article 19 provides that "An organization of the Chinese Communist Party shall, according to the Charter of the Chinese Communist Party, be established in the company to carry out activities of the Chinese Communist Party. And the company shall provide necessary conditions for the activities of the Chinese Communist Party." Article 20 provides that "The shareholders of a company shall comply with the laws, administrative regulations and articles of association, and shall exercise the shareholder's rights according to law. None of them may injure any of the interests of the company or of other shareholders by abusing the shareholder's rights, or injure the interests of any creditor of the company by abusing the independent status of legal person or the shareholder's limited liabilities." Article 21 provides that "Neither the holding shareholder, nor the actual controller, any of the directors, supervisors or senior managers of the company may injure the interests of the company by taking advantage of its connection relationship. Anyone who has caused any loss to the company due to violation of the preceding paragraph shall be subject to compensation." Article 22 provides that "The resolution of the shareholders' meeting, shareholders' assembly or board of directors of the company that has violated any law or administrative regulation shall be null and void."

Undoubtedly, the background of the publicization of private law in China is totally different from that in the West. In many Western countries, capitalism develops from the stage of free competition to the stage of monopoly, state monopoly in particular. Since the original private law is well-established and the principle of autonomy of private rights is universally accepted, state intervention is needed so as to deal with social injustice caused by the market. The publicization of private law in China occurs under two circumstances: One is in the transition from planned economy to market economy. The private law has just taken shape and is not well-established, thus the regulation of market relations and commodity relations, to a certain extent, is still effected by state intervention and the principle of equality between subjects of private rights is often challenged. The so-called publicization of private law simply indicates that the transition toward market economy is not complete and there are still many traces of planned economy. The other circumstance is related to the kind of "market failure," similar to what appears in many contemporary capitalist countries. This phenomenon does occur in some areas of China's market-oriented reform, coupled with corruption and power rent-seeking, the "invisible hand" needs to be assisted by the "visible hand" and be corrected through state intervention. It is noted that China's reform of the Socialist market economy is not one-dimensional. On the one hand, a market economy needs to be established; on the other hand, macroeconomic regulation and control needs to be strengthened. These two aspects need to be handled by different means. To the former, the market-oriented reform needs to be further promoted and administrative intervention should be reduced; to the latter, state intervention is needed so that the consequences brought by the autonomy of private rights that may endanger the interests of the society and other people can be prevented. Both of the cases are the facts, and the negation of either of them is just arbitrary.

Privatization of public law in China

The privatization of public law means that those laws in the sphere of public law have been gradually influenced by private law, and develop with the features of private law due to marketization and democratization.

The privatization of public law is most prominently reflected in the administrative law. As a kind of typical public law, the administrative law changes from being under control to autonomy, from command — obedience to consultation — participation, from rigid management to flexible guidance.[17]

(1) The public participation in administration

A traditional administrative act is unilateral, which means that an administrative subject can perform unilateral acts that may impact the rights and obligations of administrative counterparts without consulting them, listening to their views, or obtaining their consent. By contrast, the administrative laws of contemporary China, such as the *Administrative License Law* and the *Law on Administrative Penalty*, provide that when an administrative subject conducts an administrative act, he should fully consider views of administrative counterparts through certain means and accept their participation in it. Although the approval from administrative counterparts is not a necessary condition for an administrative act, the consultation with administrative counterparts is the general procedure of an administrative act. Regarding abstract administrative acts, namely acts for formulating normative administrative documents, both the *Law on Legislation* of the PRC and the *Ordinance concerning the Procedures for the Formulation of Administrative Regulations* make provisions on the procedure of public participation in the process of legislation. In addition, procedures of public participation for the acts of administrative decision and administrative handling are mentioned in the outline for the Implementation of the Program for Comprehensively Promoting "Administration by Law" by the State Council in 2004.

In virtue of public participation, the government gradually achieves its administrative goals through its interaction with non-governmental organizations. In fact, labor unions, youth organizations, women's organizations in China are playing an increasingly important role in the formulation and implementation of relevant laws. China's grassroots autonomous organizations, namely residents committees and villagers committees, are also a significant form of state administrative management. They are not only the fundamental unit of administrative management at the grassroots level in China, but also the basic unit of the autonomy of residents and villagers, fully indicating the unity of administrative management and the people's autonomy in the People's Republic of China.

(2) Macroeconomic regulation and control

In traditional administrative management, the government usually manages enterprises, public institutions, and social organizations on the basis of the operation of their internal affairs such as the production, supply, marketing, human resource, property and material of an enterprise, and the interventions of the government involved on every aspect. By contrast, current forms of administrative management in China have undergone tremendous changes. It is pointed out in the outline for the Implementation of the Program for Comprehensively Promoting "Administration by Law" that one of the goals of building a government ruled by law is to separate government functions from enterprise management and market operation. The fundamental functions of government are economic regulation, market supervision, social management, and public service. In Article 13 of the *Administrative License Law*, matters for which an administrative license may be established are listed; besides, matters for which administrative licenses are not required to be established are specifically provided, including:

(i) Those that can be decided by the citizens, legal person, or other institutions themselves;

(ii) Those that can be effectively regulated by the market competition mechanism;

(iii) Those that may be subject to the self-discipline management of the trade organizations or intermediary institutions;

(iv) The matters that can be solved by the administrative organs by means of supervision afterwards or through other administrative methods.

(3) Administrative guidance

Coerciveness is an important feature of the traditional administrative law.

However, the administration's coerciveness is weakening in the development of administrative law in modern times, and administrative guidance has been widely used in the implementation of specific administrative acts. Administrative organs achieve their expected goals and objectives more effectively with the help of flexible measures such as recommendation, advice, encouragement, inspiration, and guidance. In recent years, the development of administrative guidance in China has been greatly affected by the characteristic of "people's government" of administrative organs at all levels in China and the Communist Party of China's idea of "assuming power for the people." The *Constitution* in force in China provides that the government should offer guidance and aid for both the collective economy and the individual economy, as well as organize and encourage forest planting and protection. In addition, there are many other provisions on administrative guidance in the current *Constitution* by the use of various wordings such as "direct," "guide," "advocate," "help," "encourage," and "reward." From a legal perspective, administrative guidance is reflected in many provisions. Article 28 of the *Agriculture Law* of the PRC provides that "The State shall encourage and support the circulation of agricultural products in various forms." In this law, there are other provisions concerning agricultural administrative guidance by using wordings like "encouragement," "support," etc. For another example, both the *Regulations for the Implementation of the Law on Joint Ventures Using Chinese and Foreign Investment* and the *Regulations on Unemployment Insurance for Staff and Workers of State-Owned Enterprises* stipulate the function of administrative guidance of relevant administrative organs.[18] In local laws and regulations (including autonomous regulations and specific regulations), rules of ministries and commissions and local rules, there are also many provisions on administrative guidance, especially after the formulation of the *Administrative License Law* and the *Law on Administrative Penalty*. Legislation at this level can no longer implement the management only by the means such as administrative penalties and administrative license, so administrative guidance has gradually become an effective means.

(4) Administrative contract

Administrative orders are the main form in traditional administrative management; while, current governments are increasingly in partnership with administrative counterparts. Administrative contract refers to the unanimous agreement made by administrative organs and administrative counterparts after their negotiation in order to maintain and promote public interests and achieve the goal of administration. In administrative contacts, the administrative subject acts as the subject of administration rather than the civil legal person to make agreements about rights and obligations with administrative counterparts. The purposes of maintaining and promoting public interests are achieved in the forms of contracts. The administrative contracts adopted in China currently include the contract for the transfer of the right to the use of the state-owned land, the management contract for industrial enterprises owned by the whole people, the contract for compensation for public expropriation, the state research contract, the land contract in rural areas, the government procurement contract, the contract for public works, and the contract for family planning, etc. Therefore, it is obvious that administrative contracts play an important role in administrative management.

(5) Administrative reconciliation

Traditional ways to resolve administrative disputes include administrative penalty and administrative litigation, which means the disputes are settled through administrative or judicial means. In recent years, administrative reconciliation has emerged in the development of China's administrative laws to become a major alternative for the parties no matter if they resort to an administrative means or a judicial one. On January 16, 2008, the Supreme People's Court promulgated the *Rules on Some Issues Concerning the Withdrawal of an Administrative Suit*. Article 1 of this judicial interpretation clearly provides that "Where, after examination, the people's court considers that the alleged specific administrative action is illegal or improper, the people's court may suggest the defendant to change its specific administrative action before announcing a judgment or ruling." The rate of withdrawal of administrative suit by plaintiffs is as high as 30% in China, closely related to such means of administrative reconciliation as judges' mediation, suggestion, and defendants' promise.

In other areas of public law, the privatization of public law is manifested in different forms. In the *Criminal Law*, with the increasing attention to the rights of victims, the pattern of state monopoly in a high degree loosens and shows such a tendency of the privatization, such as the establishment of the system of criminal private prosecution, plea bargain,[19] criminal reconciliation,[20] and other non-penalty punishments.[21] In some countries, there are other systems and practices in the nature of private law such as measures of replacing criminal punishment with compensation, i.e. compensation for losses of the victim is used as an alternative measure to replace penalties, privatization of prisons and investigation rights, etc.

In the scope of the constitution, it has been controversial that if the constitution is just merely a public law. On the one hand, the constitution, as the national law, has the nature of a public law, stipulating the nature of the state, the state system, the regime, the various state organs, and the relations among the upper and lower levels of state organs. On the other hand, the provisions on citizens' fundamental rights and obligations in the constitution are apparently not consistent with the typical feature of public law, namely the inequality of its subjects. Moreover, a constitution in modern society usually advocates the principle of popular sovereignty. Since state organs and citizens' basic rights and obligations are two major elements of a constitution, it is obviously inappropriate to say that state organs have priority over the basic rights of citizens. Therefore, the view of the constitution as simply a public law is untenable. In the legal system, the constitution is not only the source of public law that includes administrative law and criminal law and private law that includes civil and commercial laws, but also the foundation of mixed law that includes economic law, social law, and environmental law. Therefore, it is one-sided to restrict the constitution to the scope of public law. In fact, all legal branches regard the constitution as their most important source and derive their legitimacy from the constitution. In this sense, the constitution is not a public law but a mother law of a country's legal system.

The privatization of public law in China also happens in a context different from that in the West. The privatization of public law in the West emerged after the establishment of the "administrative state" and "bureaucracy." It requires active participation of citizens and democratization so as to overcome occupational monopoly and elite politics. "Conciliatory" approach and means of private laws are also required to reflect that the government is gentle and humanistic except for its compulsory means so as to strengthen its administrative affinity. The privatization of administrative organs, including prisons and institutions of reeducation through labor, can also help reduce the huge financial burden. In contrast, the background of the occurrence of the privatization of public law in China is very different. Before the reform and opening up, although a huge administrative system has been established in China, its level of specialization, professionalization, and technicalization is not high. "Serving the people" is the objective of the people's government, and the motto of "from the people, to the people" remains the basic principle of China's administrative organs. The process of professionalization and specialization is accelerated after the reform and opening up. In this sense, the so-called privatization of public law may indicate that public laws and private laws still mutually affect each other. The separation between a civil society and a political state is still underdeveloped, and the process of professionalization has not been completely accomplished. However, it is undoubted that with the advance of professionalization, problems caused by "administrative state" and "bureaucracy" in the Western society indeed can be found in China. For example, some civil servants alienate themselves from the people and abuse their power for personal benefits, which is exactly the reason why President Hu Jintao has been repeatedly stressing the importance of "building the party for the people," "exercising state power for the people," and "enforcing the law for the people" in recent years. The strategies adopted for the above two issues are also different. As for the former, we need to further speed up the process of professionalization, enhance scientific administration, and improve the efficiency of administration; as for the latter, we need to make administration democratic and people-oriented, and prevent bureaucracy and elite politics. Both of these two issues can be found in China, thus the goal of the reform of administrative system in China is not simple. Law-based administration, scientific administration, and democratic administration are the overall goals of China's administrative reform.

Mixed laws in China

Mixed laws are mainly composed of the economic law, the labor and social security law, and the environmental and resources law. Mixed laws are also called social laws. Yet, the term "social laws" sometimes specifically refers to the labor and social security law, we use the term "mixed laws" in order to distinguish it from social laws in this sense. Jürgen Habermas proposed that the public factors of public interests and the factors of private laws of contracts are mixed together. It cannot be completely classified into neither the sphere of private laws nor the sphere of public laws. In other words, it is difficult to classify it into traditional legal branches of public law or private law, thus it is called "the third law field." (Some other people hold that these laws should be classified into the legal branch of administrative law or civil and commercial laws.) Habermas also pointed out that this field grew out of "the interaction between socialization of the nation and nationalization of the society in which the public factors of public interests and the factors of private laws of contracts are mixed together. It is neither a pure private sphere nor a real public sphere; for it cannot be completely classified into either the field of private laws or the field of public laws.[22]

Economic law, the labor and social security law, and the environmental and resource law emerge under a common social background. To a certain extent, they are all the inevitable products of the industrialization and socialization of capitalism since the nineteenth century. Economic law is mainly about the overall balance between various sectors of the economy and economic interests. Labor and social security law stress the overall balance and coordination between employers and employees, between economic and social development. Environment and resource law pays attention to the overall balance and coordination between economic and social development, and environment as well as resources. They all indicate that it is imperfect and unsuccessful to regulate the economic and social relations solely dependent on private laws; state intervention should be strengthened so as to maintain the sustainable economic and social development and ensure the overall interests of capitalism. Nevertheless, they do not simply rely on means of administrative law or degenerate into the "police state" where the mode of command — obedience or compulsory regulations — are adopted. Instead, they resort to a variety of civil, administrative, and criminal legal means, including means of socialization and marketization. There are also common principles in their adjustment, that is, they do not focus on individualism and autonomy of private rights which are stressed by private laws, but on society, paying attention to the overall balance between economic and social development especially the protection of vulnerable groups in the economic and social development, and potential unfavorable factors that may influence the overall interests of the society as well as the general conditions of economic and social development.

China is a Socialist country in which the people are the decision-makers and the proletariat is the leading class. So, economic law, social law, and environmental and resource laws are fundamentally different from those in the West. However, with China's transition from a planned economy to a market economy, its employment system of "lifelong secure jobs" is broken. Its welfare system with the problem of a lack of effective distribution, caused by the mode of "a unit as the whole society" disintegrates. The enterprises are under external competitive pressure brought by globalization. All these factors encourage the inclination regarding economic development, especially GDP growth, as the first priority, resulting in the sacrifices of employees' interests as well as environmental pollution. Under such a circumstance, the development of China's economic law, social law as well as environmental and resources law is of great urgency; state intervention is needed to protect workers with rights and interests. At the same time, it is also important to guarantee the basic living conditions of vulnerable groups and practice citizens' economic, social, and cultural rights, so as to create the basic favorable conditions for sustainable economic and social development.

Economic law, social law as well as environmental and resources laws are interconnected with civil and commercial laws as well as administrative law, yet there are obvious differences between them. Regulated by the civil law, social relations are treated as equal interactions between individuals, and the principle of party autonomy is implemented, aiming to balance the interests between the parties and ensure that civil interactions are in line with the true will of all parties. This kind of regulation is safe and efficient, positively preventing these interactions from violating others' interests, collective interests, and social public interests. In contrast, through the regulations by economic law, social law as well as environmental and resources law, economic and social relations are regarded as a part of the social interactions or that of the society as nature interactions. The regulation strives to make these interactions beneficial to the entire economic and social life through active means. Economic law, the social law as well as environmental and resources laws are also related to administrative law. Some scholars believe that economic law is actually the economic administrative law; social law and environmental and resources law are only a branch of economic law or administrative law and what they adjust are vertical economic and social relations. However, with the development of the modern economic law, social law as well as the environmental and resources law, they are not limited to the regulation of vertical relations, but also involved in the regulation of horizontal relations concerning economic contracts, labor contracts, social security contracts and environment contracts, etc. For example, existing contracts in current China, such as government procurement contracts, contracts of management under government franchise, contracts of the transfer of the possession of state-owned land use, contracts of the transfer of rural land, labor contracts, social security contracts, insurance contracts and environmental protection contracts, directly reflect the government's will and interact with economic, social, and cultural factors, which, in a sense, are a kind of means for the state or the government to implement economic and social management, to allocate public resources, to carry out industrial policies, and to offer public services.

Consequently, in contemporary society, "there are a variety of social relations which can no longer be categorized as private law or public law."[23] Almost each scope of law is a mixture of factors of public law and private law to varying degrees. If public law is regarded to be directed at state power, while private law is directed at individual rights, then the intertwining of state power and individual rights seems to indicate the complex structures of public law and private law. If public law is considered to be directed at public interests, while private law is directed at private interests, then the conflict and tension between public interests and private interest seems to indicate that public law and private law are inevitably combined. Such blending or integration originates from the diversification of national, social, and individual relations, from the gray areas of public and private spheres as well as the complication of public and private interests, from the complication of social life, social relations, and social structures, and from the complication of the means of social adjustment and the forms of legal regulation.

Substantive Law and Procedural Law in Contemporary China

Substantive law and procedural law are another traditional division of the legal system. Procedural law (or adjective law) is a term created by Jeremy Bentham. Different from substantive law, procedural law does not make specific provisions of individual rights and obligations, yet, it is used to claim, prove, or realize means to achieve the rights and obligations, or to ensure that violated rights can be remedied.[24] In China, much attention is paid on substantive law instead of procedural law. With the continuous advance in the rule of law in China, discussions on issues such as due process, procedural justice, and procedural autonomy are constantly deepened in China and consensus has been reached on several aspects. For example, "the fairness of a procedure means to exclude arbitrary factors to ensure that decisions are objective and correct."[25] Procedures not only acquire the nature of subordination which guarantees the realization of substantive law, but also have their own independent significance. Their substantive justice can be achieved through procedural justice, etc., so as to promote the theory and practice of the rule of law in China.

Thus, we should distinguish between substantive law and procedural law and recognize the prominent significance of procedural law in respect of achieving substantive rights. Meanwhile we should also observe the connection between the two and their mutual penetration since the boundary between them is sometimes ambiguous. In particular, if we fail to interpret procedural law only as litigation law in the narrow sense, the theoretical differentiation between substantive law and procedural law will only have relative significance after it is strictly tested by the practice, and the boundary between the two is not entirely obvious under many circumstances.

To begin with, the autonomy and independence of procedures have given the procedures in themselves substantive significance, yet the inadequacy of some procedures or violation of procedures may result in the failure or invalidity of acts. For example, due process of law of the United States is one regulation of substantive significance.[26] The *Bill of Rights* of the United States (the *First Amendment to the United States Constitution*) mainly resorts to procedural provisions to declare substantive rights. Article 41 of the *Administrative Penalty Law* of PRC provides that "If, before making a decision on administrative penalty, an administrative organ or its law-enforcing officer, fails to notify, as stipulated in Article 31 and 32 of this *Law*, the party of the facts about the violation, grounds and basis on which the administrative penalty is imposed, or refuses to heed the party's statement and self-defense, the decision on administrative penalty shall be invalid, except that the party relinquishes the right to make a statement or to defend himself." Section 2 of Article 3 provides that "Administrative penalty that is not imposed in accordance with law or in compliance with legal procedures shall be invalid."

Second, the same legal regulation can be defined differently from different perspectives. The *Civil Procedure Law* of the PRC stipulates that "Citizens of all nationalities shall have the right to use their native spoken and written languages in civil proceedings." (This provision can be found in both Section 1 of Article 11 of the *Civil Procedure Law* and Article 134 of the *Constitution*.) This can be regarded as a procedural right ensuring that citizens of the minorities can better safeguard their substantive rights; it can also be considered as a substantive right which is a basic human right concerning human dignity. Provisions concerning "jurisdiction" are also a case in point, for jurisdiction can be considered as both a part of procedural operation and substantive provisions about jurisdiction organs' authority division which is similar to the authority division among legislative, judicial, and administrative organs.

Third, identical regulations or principles may be simultaneously accepted by procedural law and substantive law. For example, both the *Constitution* and the procedure law stipulate the principle that judicial organs in China perform their duties and rights independently in accordance with the law and the principle that people's courts, people's procuratorates, and public security organs should take their own responsibilities according to their division of labor, coordinate with each other, and restrict each other in the resolution of criminal cases. Moreover, the same legal regulation is regarded to be in the sphere of substantive law in one country but in the sphere of procedural law in another country. Such a kind of difference is most obviously reflected in private international law, i.e. issues concerning "identification" in private international law. For example, the issue of limitation is regarded as a procedural issue in some countries but a substantive one in some other countries. Therefore, different identifications of the nature of this issue will lead to the application of different laws, for according to the general rules of private international laws, issues concerning substantive rights and obligations of the parties concerned shall resort to legal systems in which their legal relations are dependent, while procedural issues shall resort to lex fori. Thus, different identification of procedural and substantive issues will substantively affect the substantive rights and obligations of the parties concerned.[27] This is the reason why expanding the sphere of application of lex fori through the expansion of procedural law's interpretation becomes a legitimate skill usually used by courts so as to extend its jurisdiction. Thus, many scholars reckon that it is often difficult to clearly illustrate whether one issue should be identified as an issue of substantive law or an issue of procedural law.[28]

Fourth, many legal documents in real life often contain both substantive and procedural provisions. The combination of substantive and procedural factors is prominently reflected in the administrative law, which can be proved by the *Law on Administrative Penalty*, the *Administrative Supervision Law*, and the *Administrative License Law*, etc. For example, in the *Administrative License Law*, chapters such as "General Provisions," "The Establishment of an Administrative License," and "Legal Liabilities" are mainly composed by substantive provisions; while the chapter "Procedures for the Administrative License" is obviously made up of procedural provisions. For another example, the *Law on Administrative Penalty* is composed of chapters such as General Provisions, Types and Creation of Administrative Penalty, Organs Imposing Administrative Penalty, Jurisdiction and Application of Administrative Penalty, Decision on an Administrative Penalty (summary procedure, ordinary procedure, procedure of hearing), Enforcement of Administrative Penalty, Legal Liabilities, etc., which is also a combination of procedural provisions and administrative provisions. The *Administrative Supervision Law* is also an example which is composed of chapters such as General Provisions, Supervisory Organs and Supervisors, Functions and Duties of Supervisory Organs, Jurisdiction of Supervisory Organs, Procedure for Supervision, and Legal Liabilities.

In terms of criminal law and civil law, the *Criminal Procedure Law* and the *Civil Procedure Law* are respectively enacted. Although the two laws and their corresponding civil substantive law and substantive criminal law are not bound as inextricably as that of administrative law, they are also closely connected with each other. Especially in the sphere of criminal laws, the *Rome Statute of the International Criminal Court* is considered to be the model of the combination of substantive law and procedural law, in which fundamental penalty principles such as obligations erga omnes and international criminal responsibility of individuals are provided. Constitutive elements of crime such as crime of genocide, crime against humanity, war crime, are stipulated. It also includes the contents about organic law such as the establishment, composition, authority as well as rewards and punishments of a court. Procedural factors such as investigation, prosecution, trial and execution, as well as international cooperation and judicial assistance of criminal liabilities are also provided.[29] Moreover, an idea of "criminal justice integration" or "integrated criminal jurisprudence" has been proposed in both the international and domestic scopes of criminal law in recent years. A representative viewpoint is that criminal integration aims at achieving the optimal social benefits of criminal law and its connotation is the internal and external balance between criminal law and operation of criminal law."[30] The so-called "inside and outside of criminal law" includes both substantive criminal law and procedural criminal law. Some scholars have proposed a more creative idea that the so-called criminal justice integration should include substantive criminal law, criminal procedure law, criminal evidence law, criminal enforcement law, crime prevention law, and minor punishment law. The legal system of criminal law is an integrated structure of interrelated laws concerning prevention of crime, restraint on crime, prosecution of crime, and execution of penalties (or reform of criminals). This idea completely breaks the structure of the existing legal system in China, for it classifies not only the criminal law and the criminal procedure law, but also a variety of other laws into the system of criminal law, including the *Narcotics Control Law*, the *Prison Law*, the *Institution of Reeducation through Labor*, the *Public Security Administration Punishments Law* (administrative laws); the *Anti-Money Laundering Law* (economic law); and the *Law on the Prevention of Juvenile Delinquency* (social law). In fact, in respect of the division of legal branches, the idea of criminal justice integration law breaks the inclination of "pure scientism" which takes objects and methods of legal regulation as its standards, and focuses on prevention of crime, restraint on crime, prosecution of crime, and correction of criminals. Its emphasis has been shifted to the problems.

The basic characteristic of ancient legislations is no distinction between procedural law and substantive law in both China and the West. Although more emphasis is put upon substantive law (such as the *Book of Law* and other codes of various feudal dynasties) in China, while more importance is given to procedural law (such as the *Law of the Twelve Tables*) in the West. The separation of procedural law and substantive law occurred after the French Revolution in the nineteenth century. France enacted the first independent *Code of Civil Procedure* in the world in 1806 and promulgated the first independent *Code of Criminal Procedure* in 1808, since then the separation of procedural law and substantive law prevailed in the civil law system. However, to emphasize the importance that procedural law cannot be separated from substantive law in any case, and to stress the importance of procedural law that does not necessarily mean to take the form of separating procedural law and substantive law, Marx once strongly advocated the significance of procedural law for substantive law. He expressed that if the trial was nothing but an empty form, then such a trifling formality had no independent value. According to this viewpoint, Chinese law would become French law if it was forced into the French procedure, but substantive law had its own necessary, native form of trial. Court trial and the law were no more indifferent to each other than, for instance, the forms of plants were indifferent to the plants themselves, and the forms of animals to their flesh and blood. There must be the same motive animating the trial and the law, for the trial was only the form of life of the law, the manifestation of its inner life.[31] His thought clarifies the idea that procedural law and substantive law strike a balance and integrate with each other. The criminal law system should be established in accordance with "the same motive" mentioned here rather than a different spirit. Actually, ideas about the criminal law system can be found in the *Constitution* in China. For example, Article 26 of the *Constitution* provides that the National People's Congress exercises the functions and powers of enacting and amending basic statutes concerning criminal offences, civil affairs, the state organs, and other matters. The basic statutes concerning criminal offences and civil affairs mentioned here include not only criminal law and civil law that are substantive laws, but also the *Criminal Procedure Law* and the *Civil Procedure Law* that are procedural laws. To consider substantive law and procedural law as a whole will not only reflect a more systemic and effective theory, but will also avoid the inconsistency between laws caused by the different time of enactment and amendment of substantive laws, procedural laws, and other relevant laws in practice.

In fact, the idea of criminal justice integration can also be applied to the civil law, including civil substantive law (civil and commercial laws, economic law, social law), civil procedure law, civil enforcement law, civil evidence law, civil arbitration law, civil mediation law, etc. It shares the same advantage of aiming at the settlement of civil disputes and systematically handling a series of concerned laws at once. Undoubtedly, civil law is with its own characteristics, unlike the one-to-one relationship between substantive law and procedural law in criminal law. In civil law, the *Civil Procedural Law* is corresponding to not only the civil and commercial laws, but also to economic law and social law. Further exploration is needed due to its practical significance and characteristics. In the field of procedural law, in addition to civil, criminal, and administrative procedure law, there is also constitutional procedural law in many countries, such as the constitutional litigation through the constitutional court or constitutional council in the civil law system and the judicial review through the general courts in the common law system. In accordance with the provisions of the *Constitution* in China, the National People's Congress and its Standing Committee shall supervise the implementation of the *Constitution*, however, in case a constitutional dispute occurs, as for what procedures can be resorted to and whether or not there are problems concerning the integration of substantive law and procedural law in the implementation of the *Constitution*, we should further explore them.

With the same idea of structuring different kinds of law with the focus on the problems, some scholars in the field of Chinese procedural law propose to establish a judicial system as a whole to meet the requirements of judicial reform, including the *Law on the Organization of the People's Courts*, the *Organic Law of the People's Procuratorates*, the *Judges Law*, the *Public Procurators Law*, the *People's Police Law*, and the *Administrative Procedure Law* in both civil and criminal scopes. Besides, the scholars reckon that the judicial reform should also cover the non-procedural law, with the *Arbitration Law* and the *Mediation Law* included, as well as the *Evidence Law*, the *Execution Law*, the *Prison Law*, the *Lawyers Law*, and the *Notary Law*. According to the current division of legal branches, the *Law on the Organization of the People's Courts*, the *Organic Law of the People's Procuratorates*, the *Judges Law*, and the *Public Procurators Law* belong to the Constitution and the Related Laws; the *People's Police Law*, the *Prison Law*, the *Lawyers Law*, and the *Notary Law* belong to the branch of administrative law; the *Administrative Procedure Law* in both civil and criminal scopes, the *Arbitration Law*, and the *Mediation Law* belong to the branch of procedural and non-procedural laws. Some Chinese scholars who study the multi-diversified dispute resolution also bring forth the idea of focusing on the dispute resolution and mixing all kinds of litigious, non-litigious, legal, non-legal, civil, administrative, and judicial means together to settle various disputes. This idea has been adopted in China's judicial reform, forming a reformative idea — "grand mediation." It means organizing the civil mediation, the administrative mediation, and the judicial mediation to be interconnected with and complementary with each other. The contribution of this idea to the Socialist legal system with Chinese characteristics is that the legal system is regarded as something open and closely related to social life rather than closed and constant so that it can constantly conform to the demand from the social life and improve itself. The key to establishing a positive and interactive connection between law and society, legal norms and non-legal norms, government and people through dispute resolution mechanism does not lie in how the law stimulates on paper, or how it is divided, but in the practical solution to disputes.

The idea of regarding problems as the focus does not mean to deny the traditional division of the legal system, but attaches importance to the re-combination of existing normative legal documents for the purpose of problem-solving. The starting point of each idea is always the various kinds of current normative legal documents, according to the traditional way of division, those legal documents can be classified into the Constitution and the Related Laws, administrative law, criminal law, civil and commercial laws, economic law, social law, and procedural and non-procedural laws. Since convenience and practicability are always the top priority in codification of legal documents, and a legal document sometimes contains the norms of different legal branches, these factors lead to the controversy of the classification of the legal documents in terms of legal branch. The problem-centered approach can solve these problems caused by this kind of division. We can completely ignore the ascriptions of these documents in theory, and we can just think over their ascriptions focusing on the problem-solving process or the emphasis of problems as long as the existing problems can be solved. Such an idea may also cause instability to the structure of the legal system, because every problem has its own solution and laws can be classified in different ways according to different problems, thus leading to the lack of relative stability. So, how to combine the different ways of classification together and make best use of the advantages and bypass the disadvantages is still a problem that needs further exploration.

The Structural Analysis of the Socialist Legal System with Chinese Characteristics: The Legislation Quantity and the Degree of Systematization

The legislation quantity

At the first session of the 11th National People's Congress, Chairman Wu Bangguo announced that the Socialist legal system with Chinese characteristics, constituted seven legal branches and three levels of laws with the *Constitution* as its core and laws as its backbone, including administrative regulations, local ordinances, and other regulatory documents, that had basically taken shape.[32] By the end of 2009, there were a total of 232 current laws in effect formulated by the National People's Congress and its Standing Committee, among which 38 belonged to the Constitution and the Related Laws which accounted for 16.4%. The number of administrative laws was 80, accounting for 34.5%; the number of criminal law was 1, accounting for 0.4%; the number of civil and commercial laws were 33, accounting for 14.2%; the number of economic laws were 55, accounting for 23.7%; the number of social laws were 16, accounting for 6.9%; the number of procedural laws were 9, accounting for 3.9%.[33] In addition, there are more than 600 administrative regulations as well as 7,000 local regulations enacted by the State Council currently in effect. (See Table 1.3 and Fig. 1.4 for the classification and structure of China's current laws.)

Table 1.3 The classification of current laws in China (by 2009)

Classification	Number of law	Law
Constitution and the Related Laws	38	The Constitution, Organic Law of the National People's Congress, Organic Law of the State Council, Organic Law of the Local People's Congress and Local People's Governments, Organic Law of the People's Courts, Organic Law of the People's Procuratorates, Organic Law of the Urban Residents Committees, Organic Law of the Villagers Committees, Electoral Law of the National People's Congress and Local People's Congresses, Measures for Election of Deputies from the Chinese People's Liberation Army to the National People's Congress and Local People's Congresses at or Above the County Level, Provisions of the Standing Committee of the National People's Congress for the Direct Election of Deputies to People's Congress at or Below the County Level, Law on Deputies to the National People's Congress and Deputies to the Local People's Congresses, Judges Law, Public Procurators Law, Anti-Secession Law, Law on Regional National Autonomy, Basic Law of the Hong Kong Special Administrative Region, Basic Law of the Macao Special Administrative Region, Law on Garrisoning the Hong Kong Special Administrative Region, Law of the People's Republic of China on Garrisoning the Macao Special Administrative Region, Decision on the Establishment of Maritime Courts in Coastal Port Cities, Nationality Law, Regulations Concerning Diplomatic Privileges and Immunities, Regulations Concerning Consular Privileges and Immunities, Law on the Procedure of the Conclusion of Treaties, Law on the Territorial Sea and the Contiguous Zone, Law on the Exclusive Economic Zone and the Continental Shelf, Law on Immunity of the Property of Foreign Central Banks from Compulsory Judicial Measures, Rules of Procedure for the Standing Committee of the National People's Congress, Rules of Procedure for the National People's Congress, Supervision Law of Standing Committees of People's Congresses at Various Levels, Law on Legislation, Law on the National Emblem, Law on the National Flag, State Compensation Law, Martial Law, Law on Assemblies, Processions and Demonstrations, Decision on Conferring Military Medals on Retired Veteran Cadres of the People's Liberation Army
Administrative law	80	Administrative License Law, Administrative Reconsideration Law, Law on Administrative Penalty, Administrative Supervision Law, Emergency Response Law, Civil Servant Law, Law on Diplomatic Personnel Stationed Abroad, Public Security Administration

(Cont'd)

Classification	Number of law	Law
		Punishments Law, Decision Regarding the Question of Reeducation Through Labor, Supplementary Provisions for Rehabilitation Through Labor, Narcotics Control Law, Regulations on the Police Ranks of the People's Police, Household Registration Regulations, Law on Resident Identity Cards , Passport Law, Law on the Control of the Exit and Entry of Citizens, Law on Control of the Entry and Exit of Aliens, Customs Law, Regulations on the Customs Ranks, Road Traffic Safety Law, Environmental Protection Law, Law on Prevention and Control of Pollution from Environmental Noise, Law on the Prevention and Control of Atmospheric Pollution, Water Pollution Prevention and Control Law, Law on Prevention and Control of Radioactive Pollution, Marine Environment Protection Law, Island Protection Law, Law on Appraising of Environment Impacts, Law on the Prevention and Control of Environmental Pollution Caused by Solid Waste, Law on Desert Prevention and Transformation, Cleaner Production Promotion Law, Meteorology Law, Law on the Protection of Wildlife, Law on Prevention and Treatment of Infectious Diseases, Law on Maternal and Infant Health Care, Pharmaceutical Administration Law, Law on Practicing Doctors, Law on Blood Donation, Food Hygiene Law, Food Safety Law, Frontier Health and Quarantine Law, Law on Science and Technology Progress, Law on Promoting the Transformation of Scientific and Technological Achievements, Law on Promulgation of Science and Technology, Education Law, Teachers Law, Higher Education Law, Regulations on Academic Degrees, Compulsory Education Law, Non-state Education Promotion Law, Vocation Education Law, Law on the Standard Spoken and Written Chinese Language, Law on Physical Culture and Sports, Cultural Relics Protection Law, Construction Law, Law on Protecting Against and Mitigating Earthquake Disasters, Fire Protection Law, Law on Population and Family Planning, Notary Law, Prison Law, Archives Law, Surveying and Mapping Law, Urban and Rural Planning Law, Law on Urban Real Estate Administration, Law on the Protection of the Rights and Interests of Returned Overseas Chinese and the Family Members of Overseas Chinese, Interim Procedures on the Resettlement of the Sick and Elderly Cadres, Interim Provisions for Veteran Cadres to Leave Their Posts in Order to Rest, Law on National Defence, State Security Law, Law on Guarding State Secrets, Law on Control of

(Cont'd)

Classification	Number of law	Law
		Guns, Law on the Protection of Military Installations, Military Service Law, Law on Officers in Active Service, Reserve Officers Law, National Defense Education Law, Civil Air Defense Law, Regulations on the Military Ranks of Officers of the Chinese People's Liberation Army, Law on the People's Armed Police Force, People's Police Law
Criminal law	1	Criminal Law
Civil and commercial laws	33	General Principles of the Civil Law, Marriage Law, Law of Succession, Adoption Law, Property Law, Contract Law, Tort Law, Trademark Law, Patent Law, Copyright Law, Company Law, Law on Industrial Enterprises Owned by the Whole People, Law on Individual Proprietorship Enterprises, Partnership Enterprise Law, Law on Farmer Specialized Cooperatives, Law on Chinese-Foreign Contractual Joint Ventures, Law on Joint Ventures Using Chinese and Foreign Investment, Law on Foreign-Funded Enterprises, Anti-Unfair Competition Law, Law on the Protection of Consumer Rights and Interests, Enterprise Bankruptcy Law, Maritime Code, Law on Commercial Banks, Negotiable Instruments Law, Guarantee Law, Insurance Law, Trust Law, Auction Law, Securities Law, Bidding Law, Law on the Contracting of Rural Land, Law on Securities Investment Fund, Law on Electronic Signature
Economic law	55	Budget Law, Audit Law, Statistics Law, Price Law, Anti-Monopoly Law, Law on the People's Bank of China, Banking Supervision Law, Anti-Money Laundering Law, Individual Income Tax Law, Enterprise Income Tax Law, Law Concerning the Administration of Tax Collection, Decision Concerning the Application of Interim Regulations on Such Taxes as Value-added Tax, Consumption Tax and Business Tax to Enterprises with Foreign Investment and Foreign Enterprises, Law on the State-Owned Assets of Enterprises, Agriculture Law, Law on the Popularization of Agricultural Technology, Agricultural Product Quality Safety Law, Law on Promotion of Agricultural Mechanization, Seed Law, Fisheries Law, Animal Husbandry Law, Forestry Law, Grassland Law, Water Law, Water and Soil Conservation Law, Land Administration Law, Mineral Resources Law, Energy Conservation Law, Renewable Energy Law, Circular Economy Promotion Law, Electric Power Law, Coal Industry Law, Law on the Promotion of Small and Medium-sized Enterprises, Law on Township Enterprises, Highway Law, Railway Law, Civil Aviation

(Cont'd)

Classification	Number of law	Law
		Law, Maritime Traffic Safety Law, Law on Ports, Law on the Administration of Sea Areas, Foreign Trade Law, Law on Import and Export Commodity Inspection, Postal Law, Law on Tobacco Monopoly, Animal Epidemic Prevention Law, Law on the Entry and Exit Animal and Plant Quarantine, Product Quality Law, Metrology Law, Standardization Law, Accounting Law, Law on Certified Public Accountants, Advertising Law, Flood Control Law, Government Procurement Law, Regulations on Special Economic Zones in Guangdong Province, Law on the Protection of Taiwan Compatriots's Investment
Social law	16	Trade Union Law, Labor Law, Labor Contract Law, Employment Promotion Law, Provisional Regulations on Retirement and Resignation of Workers, Provisions for Home Leave for Workers and Staff, Law on the Protection of Disabled Persons, Law on the Protection of Minors, Law on the Protection of Rights and Interests of the Aged, Law on the Prevention of Juvenile Delinquency, Law on the Protection of Rights and Interests of Women, Mine Safety Law, Law on the Red Cross Society, Law on the Prevention and Control of Occupational Diseases, Work Safety Law, Law on Donations for Public Welfare
Procedural law	9	Criminal Procedure Law, Civil Procedure Law, Administrative Procedure Law, Arbitration Law, Extradition Law, Special Maritime Procedure Law, Decision on Exercising Criminal Jurisdiction over the Crimes Prescribed in the International Treaties to Which the People's Republic of China is a Party or has Acceded, Labor Dispute Mediation and Arbitration Law, Law on the Mediation and Arbitration of Rural Land Contract Disputes

The formation of a country's legal system, on the one hand, depends on the development level of legislation; on the other hand, depends on the systematic level of its legislation. Without a certain amount of laws formulated, the so-called formation of a country's legal system will be nothing but empty words. The problem of the division of legal system has existed for a long time. The division of civil law legal system into public law and private law can be traced back to Ancient Rome, and the division of the common law system can be traced back to the formation of the common law and equity, which was discussed as early as in the 1920s and the 1930s in the Soviet Union. The division of China's Socialist legal system has also undergone a 30-year development since the 1980s, especially the discussion of the

Fig. 1.4 The structure of current legal system in China (by 2009)

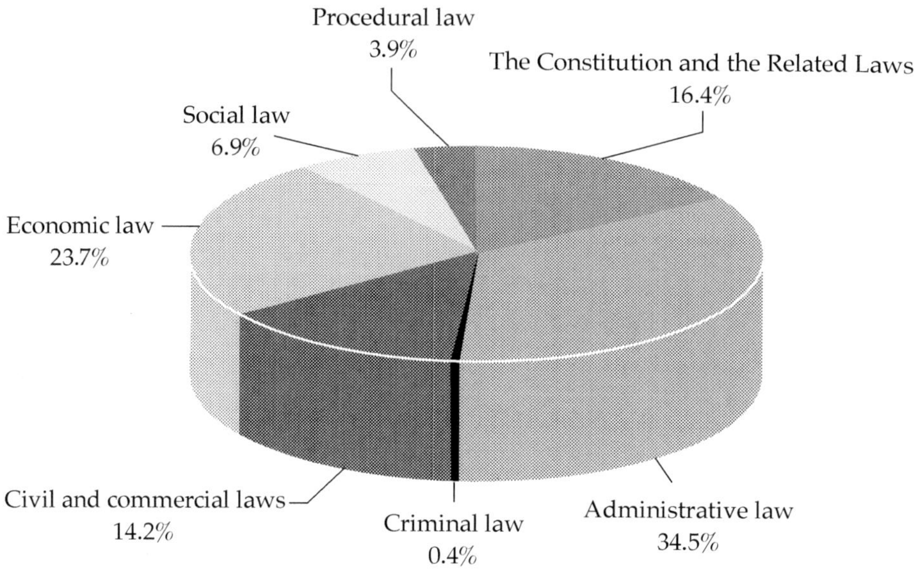

relationship between civil law and economic law. Compared with the past, the biggest difference in the present study of this problem is that Chinese legislation has made considerable achievements after years of unremitting efforts, which laid a solid legislative basis for the division of the legal system. The division of the legal system has been more than an academic topic, and become an issue concerned by various departments of legislation, judiciary, and law enforcement.[34] Various legal branches of contemporary China's legal system are listed as follows in the order of the number of laws in each legal branch: administrative law, economic law, the Constitution and the Related Laws, civil and commercial laws, social law, procedural law, and criminal law. Undoubtedly, the calculation of the number of laws in the legal branches is only with relative significance, for many laws often have the characteristics of several legal branches at the same time. For example, the *Trade Union Law* can be classified as both the Constitution and the Related Laws and social law. The *Organic Law of the State Council* and the *Organic Law of the Local People's Governments* can be classified as both the Constitution and the Related Laws and administrative law; the *Administrative Procedure Law* can be classified as both procedural law and administrative law. Those laws related to subjects of economic relations, all kinds of enterprise laws, company laws, and partnership laws can be classified as both civil and commercial laws and economic law, etc. Therefore, there is no meaning to compare the degree of development of different legal branches simply in terms of quantity.

The systematic level of legislation

The formation of the legal system depends on the systematic level of its laws. For any country, its legal system is not the random accumulation of various legal documents, there must be a rationale behind the laws, and the degree of codification is often one of the signs to measure the systematic level of a country's legal system.[35] Obviously, we cannot consider that the more laws a legal branch contains, the more developed it is, nor vice versa. In the development of legal system and legal branch, the increase of the number of laws is necessary at the beginning, for it is impossible to form a legal branch without a certain quantity. However, with the growth of the quantity, the laws have to be integrated with the ones formulated and to be codified if necessary. Eventually, the number of laws will decline. In China's legal system, the *Constitution* and the criminal law rank the highest in terms of the degree of codification, followed by procedural laws and civil and commercial laws, while administrative law, economic law, and social law are far from codification, or in other words, not suitable for codification.

Since the founding of New China, there have been four constitutions, respectively enacted in 1954, 1975, 1978, and 1982. The current constitution also has also undergone amendment four times, nevertheless, all of them are always conducted within a standardized constitutional framework. Therefore, there is only one constitution, and it is impossible for any specific constitution to coexist with the *Constitution*; yet, the Constitution and the Related Laws involve a number of normative documents, such as the *Organic Laws of State Organs*, the *Electoral Laws*, the *Judges Law*, the *Public Procurators Law*, the regional laws (special administrative region laws, the *Law on Regional National Autonomy*), the *Grassroots Autonomy Law*, the *Foreign Affairs Law*, the *Laws of Procedure for the NPC*, the *Law on Legislation*, the *Supervision Law of the NPC*, the *Laws on National Symbols* (national flag, national emblem, and national anthem), the *Anti-Secession law*, the *State Compensation Law*, the *Martial Law*, and the *Law on Assemblies, Processions and Demonstrations*. In accordance with the theory of the Soviet Union, the Constitution and the Related Laws was once known as the "National Law," which also includes constitutional documents in addition to the *Constitution*. The current title "the Constitution and the Related Laws" is not necessarily an appropriate name, because any law is related to the *Constitution*, and it is difficult to define its scope. Comparatively speaking, it is better to call it the branch of National Law as ever than the branch of the Constitution and the Related Laws. However, the problem does not mainly lie in the title, but rather in its scope. For example, whether the *Organic Law of the Villagers' Committees* and the *Organic Law of the Urban Residents Committee* belong to administrative law or the Constitution and the Related Laws; the *Laws on Garrisoning the Hong Kong Special Administrative Region and Macao Special Administrative Region* belong to military administrative law or the Constitution and the Related Laws. The *State Compensation Law*, the *Martial law*, and the *Law on Assemblies, Processions and Demonstrations* belong to administrative law or the Constitution and the Related Laws should be further considered. These normative documents may have double or even multiple properties. In spite of this, to a certain extent, it still reflects that the boundaries between the Constitution and the Related Laws and administrative law are ambiguous.

Administrative law is an extensive legal branch, involving a great number of normative legal documents, which can be divided into general administrative law and special administrative law. The general administrative law stipulates the basic principles, guidelines, and policies of state administration; the status, powers, and duties of state organs and their person-in-charge; the appointment and removal, assessment, rewards, and punishments of state personnel; regulations regarding the reform of administrative system, and the improvement of administrative organs' work efficiency, etc. The general administrative law can be further divided into administrative task law, administrative organic law, administrative effect law, and administrative supervision and relief law. These laws involve each area of administrative law and normalize administrative acts. The special administrative law refers to the laws that normalize various specialized administrative functional departments in respects of public security, civil affairs, national security, statistics, postal services, customs, personnel, defense, military, education, science and technology, culture, health, and other aspects of administration activities.

China's criminal law has experienced a tortuous development process. Since the enactment of the *Criminal Law* in 1979, the NPC Standing Committee has amended it for 25 times in the form of decisions and set accessory criminal norms in 107 non-criminal laws. In 1997, the *Criminal Law* in 1979 was completely revised on the basis of these separate laws and accessory laws; since then the revision of the *Criminal Law* more often took the form of *Amendment to the Criminal Law* (seven amendments were enacted) and *Interpretation of the Criminal Law* (nine interpretations were issued), which undoubtedly had positive significance to the standardization and stability of the criminal code, and also enabled the criminal law to become the branch with the highest degree of codification and systematization among various legal branches of China.

Civil law has completed the formulation of its major laws such as the *General Principles of the Civil Law*, the *Marriage Law*, the *Law of Succession*, the *Adoption Law*, the *Property Law*, the *Contract Law*, the *Tort Law*, the *Trademark Law*, the *Patent Law* and the *Copyright Law*, and what it lacks are only a general rules of civil law and the amendments to corresponding legislations as well as a civil code compiled on the basis of these. Nevertheless, there is still a large number of separate laws concerning civil and commercial cases, thus in the area of civil and commercial laws, it is difficult to form the situation where the degree of codification is as high as that in the scope of criminal law. According to the experience of other countries, owing to the basic role of the civil code in the entire legal system, its codification is often regarded as a sign of the formation of a country's legal system. In the French legal system, the role of the *Civil Code* even exceeded that of the *Constitution* in the nineteenth century — "Civil law is the genuine constitution." However, in modern times, in any country the constitution plays a supreme role in its legal system. Commercial law includes the *Company Law*, the *Negotiable Instruments Law*, the *Insurance Law*, the *Auction Law*, the *Securities Law*, the *Guaranty Law*, etc. If China follows the practice of combining civil law and commercial law, which is adopted by most countries around the world at present, these laws will remain out of the civil code as special laws of civil and commercial cases after the compilation of the civil code.

Economic law is a huge legal branch as well, in terms of its core law — the public economy administration law, it is similar to the classification of administrative law which can be divided into two parts, namely, the comprehensive function administration law and the industry administration law. The comprehensive function administration law contains the *Budget Law*, the *Audit Law*, the *Statistics Law*, the *Price Law*, the *Anti-Monopoly Law*, the *Bank Law*, the *Banking Supervision Law*, the *Anti-Money Laundering Law*, the *Tax Law*, the *Law Concerning the Administration of Tax Collection*, the *Product Quality Law*, the *Metrology Law*, the *Standardization Law*, the *Accounting Law*, the *Law on Certified Public Accountants*, etc. At the time when the public economy administration law, as the core of the economic law, is focused on the tax law, fiscal law, financial law and other means of macroeconomic regulation and control, the lack of state planning law (planning law) is indeed an inadequacy. The industry administration law includes the *Agriculture Law*, the *Law on the Popularization of Agricultural Technology*, the *Agricultural Product Quality Safety Law*, the *Law on Promotion of Agricultural Mechanization*, the *Seed Law*, the *Fisheries Law*, the *Animal Husbandry Law*, the *Highway Law*, the *Railway Law*, the *Civil Aviation Law*, the *Maritime Traffic Safety Law*, the *Law on Ports*, the *Law on the Administration of Sea Areas*, the *Foreign Trade Law*, the *Law on Import and Export Commodity Inspection*, the *Postal Law*, the *Law on Tobacco Monopoly*, the *Animal Epidemic Prevention Law*, the *Law on the Entry and Exit Animal and Plant Quarantine*, the *Advertising Law*, the *Flood Control Law*, and the *Government Procurement Law*, etc. In addition, economic law also includes the laws regulating all kinds of subjects of economic activities such as the *Company Law* and various kinds of enterprise law, as well as the laws regulating economic activities themselves such as the *Contract Law*, the *Competition Law*, the *Bankruptcy Law*, and the *Law on Protection of Consumer Rights and Interests*. All these laws are the same as civil and commercial laws except that this kind of laws as economic law has different emphasis and regulating means, and economic law attaches more importance to the overall economic benefits and comprehensive balance.

In other countries, the branches of administrative law and economic law are difficult to develop towards codification. On the contrary, the environmental and resources laws that range over the scopes of economic law and administrative law are more likely to develop towards codification, for China has formulated a great number of laws now such as the *Environmental Protection Law*, the *Law on Prevention and Control of Pollution from Environmental Noise*, the *Law on the Prevention and Control of Atmospheric Pollution*, the *Water Pollution Prevention and Control Law*, the *Law on Prevention and Control of Radioactive Pollution*, the *Marine Environment Protection Law*, the *Island Protection Law*, the *Law on Appraising of Environment Impacts*, the *Law on the Prevention and Control of Environmental Pollution by Solid Waste*, the *Law on Desert Prevention and Transformation*, the *Law on Promoting Clean Production*, the *Meteorology Law*, the *Law on the Protection of Wildlife*, the *Forest Law*, the *Grassland Law*, the *Water Law*, the *Water and Soil Conservation Law*, the *Land Administration Law*, the *Mineral Resources Law*, the *Energy Conservation Law*, and the *Renewable Energy Law*. These laws' regulating objects are relatively centralized and their connections between each other also show the systematization. Besides, the *Environmental Protection Law*, regarded as the basic law of the environmental and resources law, has been enacted for a long time. In 2005, the *Suggestions of the Central Committee of the Communist Party of China on the Formulation of the 11th Five-Year Plan for National Economic and Social Development* passed in the 5th Plenary Session of the 16th Central Committee of the Communist Party of China clearly put forward the policies of adopting a scientific viewpoint to direct China's overall economic and social development and building a resource-saving and environmentally-friendly society, preparing for accelerating environmental and resources legislation. In the same year, the State Council issued the *Decision on Implementing the Scientific Outlook on Development and Strengthening Environmental Protection*. In 2007, the State Council promulgated the *National Program on Climate Change*. In the 17th National Congress of the Communist Party of China, Hu Jintao reiterated and further elaborated the scientific content of the scientific outlook on development, and explicitly put forth the request and content of the establishment of ecological civilization. In addition, with regard to the perfection of the Socialist legal system with Chinese characteristics, the 17th Party Congress proposed new requirements for the establishment of the environmental legal system, that is, "to improve laws and policies that are beneficial to energy, resources, ecological, and environmental conservation, and speed up the formation of systems and mechanisms for sustainable development." This means that the environmental legal system in China has entered a crucial era of making further improvements so as to adapt to the new situation.

The number of laws in the scope of social law is small, and there are still inadequacies. Meanwhile, although some countries have formulated the social code, it can only make progress in the form of separate laws. The current social law in China mainly consists of two parts, namely, the labor law and the social security law. The former includes the *Labor Law*, the *Labor Contract Law*, the *Trade Union Law*, the *Employment Promotion Law*, the *Mine Safety Law*, the *Law on the Prevention and Control of Occupational Diseases*, the *Work Safety Law*, the *Provisional Regulations on Retirement and Resignation of Workers*, and the *Provisions for Home Leave for Workers and Staff*; while the latter contains the *Law on the Protection of Disabled Persons*, the *Law on the Protection of Minors*, the *Law on the Protection of Rights and Interests of the Aged*, the *Law on the Prevention of Juvenile Delinquency*, and the *Law on the Protection of Women's Rights and Interests*. Besides, it also involves the *Law on Donations for Public Welfare* and the *Law on Red Cross Society* which belong to the third category, i.e. law on social benefit and charity. Since the 1990s, the State Council has promulgated the *Decision on the Reform of the Old-Age Insurance System for Enterprise Employees* (1991), the *Provisions on Working Hours of Workers and Staff* (1991, 1995), the *Notice on the Establishment of the Minimum Living Security System for Urban Residents* (1997), the *Notice on Further Deepening the Reform of the Urban Housing System and Accelerating Housing Construction* (1998), the *Opinions on Issues Concerning Migrant Workers* (2006), the *Notice on the Establishment of the Rural Minimum Living Security System* (2007), the *Opinions on Solving the Housing Difficulty of Urban Low Income Families* (2007). The Central Committee of the CPC and State Council have issued the *Notice on Effectively Doing the Work of Basic Living Allowances and Reemployment for Employees Laid off from State-owned Enterprises* (1998), the *Opinions on Deepening the Reform of the Medical and Health Care System* (2009), etc. All these are the important measures for the reform of China's labor and social security system. Currently, the reform of the issues regarding China's labor and social security has entered a crucial stage, in which employment security, collective labor contracts, workers' democratic management, labor security, social insurance, social relief, social welfare, housing, medical care, education are all involved. Thus, the way to regulate and legalize these measures so as to make them a critical part of China's social law is still under further exploration and improvement.

Procedural law consists of both procedural and non-procedural laws, in which procedural law is an area with a rather high degree of codification, although the laws within it are very small both in quantity and proportion, so far three codes have been codified, namely, the *Criminal Procedure Law*, the *Civil Procedure Law*, and the *Administrative Procedure Law*. It seems that the revision of these three codes will assume the form similar to the amendments to criminal law rather than formulate some other separate laws. In addition, it also includes some separate procedural laws concerning foreign affairs. Constitutional procedural law mainly includes the problem of the constitutional review system. In China, the power of constitutional review is in the hands of the People's Congress instead of that of the people's court. Therefore, it is impossible to formulate a constitutional procedure law. At present, the constitutional review system in China is mainly composed of the *Constitution*, the *Law on Legislation*, and the *Law on the Supervision of Standing Committees of People's Congresses at Various Levels*. Non-procedural law includes arbitration law and mediation law: The former has been enacted and the latter is still in the drafting stage, which is limited to the fields of labor disputes and land contract in rural areas in the meantime. The 15th, the 16th, and the 17th Party Congresses all put forward the task of judicial reform. Accordingly, since 1999, with the advance in the judicial reform, the Supreme Court promulgated three policies of the "Five-Year Reform Program for the People's Courts," which play an important role in guiding China's judicial reform, especially the reform of procedural law.

The Constitution and the Related Laws

Legal system refers to an organic and unified whole constituted by all the current laws and regulations of a country in a systematic manner according to different legal branches.[1] The goal of the construction of China's legal system was to form a Socialist legal system with Chinese characteristics. It is generally acknowledged that the Socialist legal system with Chinese characteristics is a harmonious and unified whole constituted of seven legal branches and three levels of laws with the Constitution as its basis and laws as its backbone, including administrative regulations, local ordinances, autonomous regulations, separate regulations, and other normative documents. The 15th Party Congress proposed the overall goal and requirements of the Socialist legal system with Chinese characteristics which was expected to have formed by 2010. The process of achieving this goal can be divided into three stages: the "emergence" in the 9th National People's Congress; the "basic formation" in the 10th National People's Congress; and the "formation" in 2010.[2] On February 28, 2008, the State Council Information Office issued a white paper entitled "*The Construction of the Rule of Law in China*" which clearly stated: "The Socialist legal framework with Chinese characteristics, and with the Constitution as the core, has basically formed with the unremitting efforts over many years. The modern Chinese legal system is with complete branches, distinctive levels, a balanced and scientific structure, mainly consisting of seven legal branches and three levels. The seven legal branches are the Constitution and the Related Laws, civil and commercial laws, administrative law, economic law, social law, criminal law, and procedural and non-procedural laws. The three levels are: laws; administrative regulations; and local ordinances, autonomous regulations, and separate regulations. The NPC and its Standing Committee have enacted 229 laws currently in effect.[3] All the laws in effect cover seven branches; and they have made the most of each branch, including basic laws as the framework of the Socialist legal system with Chinese characteristics and the laws urgently demanded by reform, development, and stability. The State Council has also enacted nearly 600 administrative regulations currently in effect supplementary to the laws. Local people's congresses and their standing committees at various levels have enacted over 7,000 local regulations currently in effect; and the people's congresses of the national autonomous areas have enacted over 600 autonomous regulations and separate regulations currently in effect. The departments under the State Council, the people's governments of the provinces, the autonomous regions, the municipalities directly under the central government, and the larger cities have also enacted numerous rules. It indicates that China's Socialist legal system has been basically formed. In the construction and development of China's Socialist legal system, the Constitution, as the fundamental law of the state, plays a vital role. To achieve the formation and sustainability of the legal system, it is important to explore the relationship between the Constitution and other ordinary laws.

The Development and Changes of China's *Constitution* and Legal System

The origin of New China's Constitution can be traced back to the *Common Program of the Chinese People's Political Consultative Conference* (hereinafter referred as the *Common Program*) passed on September 29, 1949. After the success of the War of Liberation and on the eve of the founding of New China, the 1st Plenary Session of the Chinese People's Political Consultative Conference, with the participation of all sectors of society, was held on September 21, 1949 under the proposal by the Communist Party of China. The *Common Program* defined the state system, the social system as well as some important national policies and overall missions concerning other aspects. Since the revolutionary war had not ended, and without enough favorable factors, the *Common Program,* as the highest rule for all people to comply with, played a role of interim constitution in the early days of New China. Meanwhile, along with the imminent victory of the revolutionary war, the recalling work of the old legal system left by the Kuomintang was also progressing intensively. On February 22, 1949, Wang Ming, the director of the Central Working Committee on Law, drafted the *Instructions on Abrogating Kuomintang's Complete Literatures on Six Laws and Defining the Judicial Principle in Liberated Areas*. It was clearly stated that "Kuomintang's Complete Literatures on Six Laws has been abrogated and the judicial work of the people should be based on their new laws... Before people's new laws are promulgated in a systematic way, the policies of the Communist Party as well as all kinds of programs, laws, orders, regulations and decisions issued by the People's Government and the People's Liberation Army shall prevail." "The judiciary should be engaged in the legal construction, with the principles of contempt and criticism towards *Kuomintang's Complete Literatures on Six Laws* and all other reactionary laws and decrees as well as all anti-people laws and decrees of the capitalist countries such as Europe, the United States and Japan."[4] In this regard, Article 17 of the *Common Program* provided that "All laws, decrees and judicial systems of the Kuomintang reactionary government which oppress the people shall be abolished. Laws and decrees protecting the people shall be enacted and the people's judicial system shall be established," which, in fact, reiterated the basic stance of abolishing the old legal system and establishing a new one.

The *Common Program,* as an interim constitution of New China, was endowed with the function and role of the *Constitution*. It was irreplaceable for legislation, especially in the construction of New China's legal system. In the early days of New China, all the ordinary laws were formulated based on the *Common Program.* For example, Article 1 of the *Provisional Organic Regulations of the People's Courts of the People's Republic of China* announced on September 3, 1951 provided that "This Regulation is formulated in accordance with the Article 17 of the Common Program of the Chinese People's Political Consultative Conference." For another example, Article 1 of the *Electoral Law of the National People's Congress and Local People's Congresses of the People's Republic of China* passed on February 11, 1953 provided that "According to Article 12 of the Common Program of the Chinese People's Political Consultative Conference, the National People's Congress and local People's Congresses of the People's Republic of China are elected by people of all ethnic groups through universal suffrage." All these provisions fully indicate that the *Common Program*, as China's interim constitution, plays a role of "Mother Law" in the construction of a new legal system. Just as Professor Xu Chongde suggested, "the *Common Program* is obviously constitutional in nature. Although it is not a formal constitution, but only acts as an interim constitution, as a matter of fact it is an untitled *Constitution* as well as the initial interim constitution in the history of China."[5] Thus, in the construction of the legal system during the early years of New China, the *Common Program* in fact played a fundamental role of the legislative basis. The legal documents announced during this period are shown in Table 2.1.

Table 2.1 The legal documents announced during the period of the *Common Program*

Legal document	Date of promulgation
Resolution on the Capital, the Way of Numbering the Years, the Anthem and the Flag of the People's Republic of China	September 27, 1949
Organic Law of the Central People's Government of the People's Republic of China	September 27, 1949
General Principles of Organic Regulations for the Conferences of People's Representatives from Various Circles of Cities	December 2, 1949
General Principles of Organic Regulations for the Government Administration Council of the Central People's Government and Its Subordinate Organs	December 2, 1949
General Principles of Organic Regulations for the Conferences of People's Representatives from Various Circles of Provinces	December 2, 1949
General Principles of Organic Regulations for the Conferences of People's Representatives from Various Circles of Counties	December 2, 1949
Marriage Law of the People's Republic of China	April 13, 1950
Trade Union Law of the People's Republic of China	June 29, 1950

(Cont'd)

Legal document	Date of promulgation
Order on the National Emblem of the People's Republic of China Proclaimed by the Central People's Government	September 20, 1950
Provisional Organic Regulations of the Supreme People's Procuratorate of the Central People's Government	September 4, 1951
Provisional Organic Regulations of the People's Courts of the People's Republic of China	September 4, 1951
General Orga nic Principles of the Local People's Procuratorates at Various Levels	September 4, 1951
Provisional Regulations on the Appointment and Removal of State Organ Personnel by the Central People's Government	November 5, 1951

Although the *Common Program* determined the construction of China's legal system during the early years of New China, objectively speaking, it is after all just an interim constitutional document. With all the favorable factors ready, the formulation of a constitution conforming to the national conditions was included in the agenda.

From September 15 to 28, 1954, the 1st Session of the National People's Congress was held in Beijing. It unanimously passed the Constitution of the People's Republic of China, i.e. the 1954 *Constitution*, by secret ballot on September 20. The 1954 *Constitution* was the first Socialist constitution after the founding of New China with great historical significance. The 1954 *Constitution* had a very distinct positive effect on the construction of the legal system since its promulgation, on the basis of which many legal documents were able to be enacted, and thereby it laid a preliminary foundation for the construction of China's legal system. With the guidance of the 1954 *Constitution*, a number of legal documents meeting the needs of that time were adopted during this period (see Table 2.2).

Table 2.2 The legal documents announced during the period of the 1954 *Constitution*

Law	Date of promulgation
Organic Law of the State Council of the People's Republic of China	September 28, 1954
Organic Regulations of the Urban Neighborhood Offices	December 31, 1954
Organic Regulations of the Police Stations	December 31, 1954

(Cont'd)

Law	Date of promulgation
Regulations on Overseas Chinese's Application for the Use of State-owned Barren Hills and Wasteland	August 6, 1955
Regulations on the People's Republic of China on Administrative Penalties for Public Security	October 22, 1957
People's Police Regulations of the People's Republic of China	June 25, 1957
Regulations of the People's Republic of China on Household Registration	January 9, 1958
Frontier Health and Quarantine Regulations of the People's Republic of China	December 23, 1957
Regulations of the People's Republic of China on Agricultural Tax	June 3, 1958

The 1954 *Constitution* was a milestone of the basic framework of the legal system. After 1958, especially during the Cultural Revolution, China's constitutional system was severely damaged, and the construction of the legal system also came to a standstill. On January 17, 1975, the 1954 *Constitution* was amended at the 1st Session of the 4th National People's Congress, which led the development of the *Constitution* astray into an extremely leftist situation. The 1975 *Constitution*, as the product of the specific historical conditions in China, legalized and institutionalized many of the erroneous theories and practices in the Cultural Revolution and regarded them as the highest principles for state affairs. This constitution stipulated a large quantity of extremely leftist content, narrowing the basic rights and the range of freedom of citizens. In addition, the number of its articles and words also declined sharply, leaving merely 30 items and about 4,300 words. Moreover, it was written with numerous political mistakes and the illogical legal terms, in short, it was an imperfect constitution with serious shortcomings and errors.

On March 5, 1978, the 1st Session of the 5th National People's Congress made amendments to the 1975 *Constitution*. To a certain extent, those extremely leftist contents were revised, such as the abolition of the provisions of "all-round dictatorship," and a series of organic laws with fundamental meaning on the basis of the revised constitution were passed. These revisions had been favorable for the construction of the legal system in the period of reform and opening up. Some major legal documents adopted during the period of the 1978 *Constitution* are listed in Table 2.3.

Table 2.3 Major legal documents issued during the period of the 1978 *Constitution*

Law	Date of promulgation
Forest Law of the People's Republic of China (for Trial Implementation)	February 23, 1979
Regulations of the People's Republic of China on Arrest and Detention	February 23, 1979
Environmental Protection Law of the People's Republic of China (for Trial Implementation)	September 13, 1979
Law of the People's Republic of China on Joint Ventures Using Chinese and Foreign Investment	July 8, 1979
Criminal Procedure Law of the People's Republic of China	July 7, 1979
Criminal Law of the People's Republic of China	July 6, 1979
Organic Law of the People's Courts of the People's Republic of China	July 5, 1979
Organic Law of the People's Procuratorates of the People's Republic of China	July 5, 1979
Electoral Law of the National People's Congress and Local People's Congresses of the People's Republic of China	July 4, 1979
Organic Law of the Local People's Congresses and Local People's Governments of the People's Republic of China	July 4, 1979
Regulations of the People's Republic of China on Academic Degrees	February 12, 1980
Interim Regulations of the People's Republic of China on Lawyers	August 26, 1980
Income Tax Law of the People's Republic of China on Chinese-Foreign Equity Joint Ventures	September 10, 1980
Nationality Law of the People's Republic of China	September 10, 1980
Marriage Law of the People's Republic of China	September 10, 1980
Individual Income Tax Law of the People's Republic of China	September 10, 1980
Income Tax Law of the People's Republic of China for Foreign Enterprises	December 13, 1981
Economic Contract Law of the People's Republic of China	December 13, 1981
Cultural Relics Protection Law of the People's Republic of China	November 19, 1982
Food Hygiene Law of the People's Republic of China (for Trial Implementation)	November 19, 1982
Marine Environment Protection Law of the People's Republic of China	August 23, 1982
Trademark Law of the People's Republic of China	August 23, 1982

The 1978 *Constitution* had contributed to the construction of China's Socialist legal institution and legal system. The legal system in China had been basically formed even though the legislation at that time was not perfect, and with the social development, most of these laws were repeatedly amended or annulled. Undoubtedly, although the 1978 *Constitution* had made remarkable contributions in history, at that time, the country had just recovered from the Cultural Revolution, many distorted political theories as well as the sense of right or wrong had not been clarified or restored. The experience and lessons learned from the Cultural Revolution and the Socialist construction had not been able to be fully and fairly summarized yet.

These defects in the 1978 *Constitution* were not fundamentally revised until the enactment of the 1982 *Constitution*. On December 4, 1982, the *Constitution* of the People's Republic of China was approved at the 5th Plenary Session of the 5th National People's Congress. The 1982 *Constitution* is regarded as the best constitution since the founding of New China. It is also the basis and foundation of the construction of the socialist legal system which even at present is also being carried out on the basis of the 1982 *Constitution*.

Since the promulgation of the *Common Program* in 1949, New China's legal system has been shaped for more than 60 years. From the development experience of New China in the past 60 years, the function of the rule of law should be fully revealed in the social development so that a scientific and rational socialist legal system can be constructed. The authority of the *Constitution* should be maintained to realize its function at large in the process of constructing a legal system. The constitution is the groundwork of the national system. If it cannot play its supreme role as the fundamental law in a country, the foundation of the country will be unstable, resulting in a chain reaction that affects other aspects of the country. If a constitution cannot play its role as the paramount law to lead the overall situation in the construction and development of the legal system, then the legal system will lose its source of legitimacy and it will be difficult to guarantee its nature of goodness. Generally speaking, the development and changes of China's *Constitution* and its legal system have the following two distinct characteristics.

First, the development and changes of China's *Constitution* and its legal system are obviously affected by political factors. After the founding of New China, the development of China's political situations can be generally divided into three stages: The first stage is the period of the establishment and consolidation of the revolutionary regime from 1949 to1954; the second stage is the period of Socialist construction from 1954 to 1978; the third stage is the period of reform and opening up after 1978. In correspondence with these three historical periods of the development of political situations, the development of China's *Constitution* and legal system also has distinct characteristics of the times, and it would present different developmental characteristics in each stage, affecting the construction of the legal system in different periods.

Second, the development of China's *Constitution* and legal system has gradually shifted from a political and instrumental role to a social and value role. During the early years of New China, we were apt to treat the *Constitution* as "the general charter for governance of the country and good order of the nation," putting emphasis on its instrumental role in governing the state. Meanwhile, other branch laws and related legislations were also regarded as some kinds of tools and means of social control, which were colored by distinct pragmatism. After the promulgation of the 1982 *Constitution*, the academic circles started to pay attention to the norm and value of the constitution, enabling the *Constitution* to play its part in the regulation and distribution of state power as well as in the protection of citizens' basic rights. The Socialist legal system constructed on this basis also gradually adapted itself to the value transition of the constitution, began to focus on the social and normative role of law, and made more efforts to economic legislation and social legislation, as well as strengthened its function of protecting civil rights.

Role of the *Constitution* in the Construction and Development of China's Legal System

In the construction and development of China's legal system, the *Constitution*, as the basis of the distribution and operation of legislative power as well as the foundation of the construction and development of the legal system, was very fundamental. As stated in the white paper entitled "*The Construction of the Rule of Law in China*," "In the Socialist legal system with Chinese characteristics, the *Constitution* is in the core and dominant position. The present *Constitution*, on the basis of the 1954 *Constitution*, was passed at the 5th Session of the 5th NPC in 1982 after public discussion. The *Constitution*, as the fundamental law of the state, has supreme legal authority. All ethnic groups, all state organs, the armed forces, all political parties and public organizations, and all enterprises and public institutions in the country must take the *Constitution* as the basic standard of conduct, and they have the duty to uphold the dignity of the *Constitution* and ensure its implementation. To implement the basic principle of governing the country by law, the first priority goes to an all-round and practical implementation of the *Constitution*."

The *Constitution* as the basis for the distribution and operation of legislative power

The constraint of the Constitution on the legislative power of the state

In the dichotomy of the legal system between public law and private law, the constitution has the nature of a public law. If the constitution is regarded as a public law that controls state power, then its regulating object is the state public power. According to the Western classical theory of the separation of powers (trias politica), the state public power is divided into three parts: legislative, executive, and judicial powers. The legislative power is exercised by the parliament that is mainly responsible for the legislation work and fiscal budget of the state; the executive power is exercised by the government that is primarily responsible for the implementation of the legislation of parliamentary authorities; and judicial power is exercised by the court that is mainly responsible for the relief of the civil rights recognized in the legislation. Among these three powers, legislative power is the primary one, determining the content and scope of the other two powers. Thus, a highly effective regulation of the legislative power becomes the goal pursued by constitutionalism.

The constraint of China's *Constitution* on legislative power is mainly embodied in its distribution of the power of China's legislature, that is, the National People's Congress and its Standing Committee. Paragraph 3 of Article 62 of the *Constitution* provides that the legislative power of the NPC is "to enact and amend basic laws governing criminal offence, civil affairs, the state organs and other matters," indicating that the basic laws governing criminal offence, civil affairs, the state organs, and other matters should be enacted by the National People's Congress. The basic law, just as its name implies, is the law with overall significance regulating the national politics, economy, and social life. For example, the *Criminal Law* and the *Criminal Procedure Law* adopted at the 2nd Session of the 5th NPC in 1979 are basic criminal laws; the *General Principles of the Civil Law* passed at the 4th Session of the 6th NPC in 1986, the *Civil Procedure Law* formulated at the 4th Session of the Seventh NPC in 1991, the *Contract Law* enacted at the 2nd Session of the 9th NPC in 1999 and so on are basic civil laws. The *Organic Law of the Local People's Congresses and Local People's Governments*, the *Electoral Law of the National People's Congress and Local People's Congresses*, the *Organic Law of the People's Courts*, and the *Organic Law of the People's Procuratorates* adopted at the 2nd Session of the 5th NPC in 1979, as well as the *Organic Law of the National People's Congress* and the *Organic Law of the State Council* passed at the 5th Session of the 5th NPC in 1982 are the basic laws concerning state organs. In addition, the *Law on Regional National Autonomy*, the *Military Service Law*, the *Compulsory Education Law*, the *Law on Foreign-Funded Enterprises*, the *Law on Industrial Enterprises Owned by the Whole People*, the *Law on Chinese-Foreign Contractual Joint Ventures*, the *Administrative Procedure Law*, the *Law National Defense Law*, the *Basic Law of the Hong Kong Special Administrative Region*, the *Basic Law of the Macao Special Administrative Region* and so forth also belong to the basic law.

Article 67 of the *Constitution* provides the legislative power of the NPC Standing Committee: "(2) to enact and amend laws, with the exception of those which should be enacted by the National People's Congress; (3) to partially supplement and amend, when the National People's Congress is not in session, laws enacted by the National People's Congress provided that the basic principles of these laws are not contravened." In accordance with the provisions of the *Constitution*, both the NPC and the NPC Standing Committee exercise the national legislative power. Over the past 30 years since the reform and opening up, a majority of laws are enacted by the NPC Standing Committee, including a large number of laws in respect of the Socialist market economy and laws of other aspects. For example, in order to protect citizens' rights, improve the structure of state organs, and regulate the behavior of state institutions and their personnel, the NPC Standing Committee developed the *Law on Administrative Penalty*, the *Administrative Supervision Law*, the *Administrative Reconsideration Law*, the *State Compensation Law*, the *Judges Law*, the *Public Procurators Law*, and the *People's Police Law*, and amended the *Electoral Law* as well as the *Organic Law of the Local People's Congresses and Local People's Governments*. In order to promote the development of education, technology, and health, the *Education Law*, the *Higher Education Law*, the *Teachers Law*, the *Vocation Education Law*, the *Law on Scientific and Technological Progress*, the *Law on Promoting the Transformation of Scientific and Technological Achievements*, and the *Law on Practicing Doctors* are formulated. In order to carry out the sustainable development strategy, a lot of laws concerning environmental protection and rational exploitation and utilization of resources are enacted. The *Law on Officers in Active Service* and the *Civil Air Defense Law* are formulated so as to strengthen the national defense construction. Besides, according to the principle of "One Country, Two Systems," the laws on garrisoning the Hong Kong Special Administrative Region and the Macau Special Administrative Region are also enacted.

In addition to Article 62 and 67 of the *Constitution*, the *Constitution*'s distribution of legislative power also manifested itself in Article 58, providing that "The National People's Congress and its Standing Committee exercise the legislative power of the state," which indicates the National People's Congress and its Standing Committee, as the organs that exercise the legislative power of the state, which is clearly provided for in the *Constitution*, enjoy the legislative power. However, according to the provisions of the *Constitution*, the limits and levels of their legislative power are different. In Paragraph 3 of Article 62, the NPC's legislative power over basic laws is stipulated, while in Paragraph 3 of Article 67, the NPC Standing Committee's legislative power over non-basic laws is stipulated, and these two provisions constitute the model of the dualistic structure of legislative power in China's legislative system. Due to this model, the laws enacted by the legislature are forced to be divided into two levels: the basic law and the non-basic law. Some scholars have doubted this division and held that it caused the chaos in China's current legislative system.[6] Although we do not agree with this dualistic mode either, since the *Constitution* made such a provision, we shall respect it and uphold the supreme authority of the *Constitution*, and proceed from the text of the *Constitution* to seek a more reasonable way to interpret it based on the premise of recognizing and accepting the legitimacy of this dualistic mode in the text of the *Constitution*.

According to the *Constitution*, the legislative power of basic laws is subordinate to the NPC, and that of non-basic laws is subordinate to the NPC Standing Committee. In accordance with this logic, it can be deduced that those laws enacted by the NPC should be basic laws, and those by the NPC Standing Committee should be non-basic laws, but as a matter of fact that is not the case. Generally speaking, the basic law refers to the law enacted by the NPC that ranks second only to the *Constitution* but above the other laws and regulates the matters with great and overall significance in a certain field of national politics, economy, and social life. Among the laws enacted by the NPC, it is obvious that there are many of them do not belong to basic law, such as the *Law on Chinese-Foreign Equity Joint Ventures*, the *Law on Chinese-Foreign Contractual Joint Ventures*, the *Law on Foreign-Funded Enterprises*, the *Income Tax Law on Chinese-Foreign Equity Joint Ventures*, the *Income Tax Law for Foreign Enterprises*, and the *Income Tax Law for Enterprises with Foreign Investment and Foreign Enterprises*.[7] Moreover, in practice, there are also some basic laws, supposed to be enacted by the NPC, actually completed by the NPC Standing Committee. For example, in September 1979, the Commission of Legal Affairs of the NPC Standing Committee undertook to draw up the first Civil Procedure Law of the People's Republic of China, and in December 1981, the 4th Session of the 5th National People's Congress approved the *Civil Procedure Law of the People's Republic of China* (Draft) in principle. Authorized by the NPC, the NPC Standing Committee examined and adopted the *Civil Procedure Law of the People's Republic of China* (For Trial Implementation) at the 22nd Session in 1982, promulgated by Order No. 8 and implemented on a trial basis as on October 1, 1982. The *Civil Procedure Law* (For Trial Implementation) belongs to the category of basic law, which means the right of its formulation belongs to the NPC rather than the NPC Standing Committee that was authorized inappropriately. Similarly, both the *Organic Law of the Villagers Committees* and the *Organic Law of the Urban Residents Committees* belong to the organic law of grass-roots autonomy. However, the former was approved by the NPC in principle, while the latter was directly examined and adopted by the NPC Standing Committee.[8] Owing to the lack of a precise definition of "basic law," such cases repeatedly occur in practice, in which the legislative power of basic laws that is supposed to be exercised by the NPC is granted to the NPC Standing Committee. On the contrary, those non-basic laws that are supposed to be legislated by the NPC Standing Committee are approved by the NPC. Therefore, the regulation of legislative power by China's *Constitution* still needs further improvement and strengthening. It should be clarified that the legislative power of basic law exclusively pertains to the National People's Congress and that of non-basic law is endowed to the NPC Standing Committee, in which the status of the National People's Congress as the supreme legislature must be ensured.

The constraint of the Constitution on administrative legislation

The role of the *Constitution* in the distribution and operation of legislative power is not only shown in the regulation and constraint on the state legislative power that exclusively belongs to the parliament, but also in the control of administrative organs' administrative legislative power. The shift from "parliament-centered" to "government-centered of the structure of national power has enhanced the power of administrative organs. The administrative organs in modern society do not only exercise the administrative enforcement power in the traditional sense, but also exercise legislative and judicial powers to a certain extent. Their typical legislative powers involves the power of formulating administrative regulations, department regulations and regulations of local government, and their typical judicial power includes the power of administrative reconsideration and the power of administrative adjudication. The legislative power of administrative organ is playing an increasingly important role in social life, which causes a huge impact on the traditional parliamentary legislative system. Under this circumstance, it is particularly necessary to bring administrative organs' legislative power, especially their power of formulating regulations, under the control of the *Constitution*.

In China, administrative regulation is a generic term for all kinds of regulations concerning politics, economy, education, science and technology, culture, foreign affairs, etc. enacted by the State Council in accordance with the *Constitution* and laws as well as the specific provisions in the *Ordinance concerning the Procedures for the Formulation of Administrative Regulations*, for the purpose of leading and managing a variety of administrative work of the state. Paragraph 1 of Article 89 of the *Constitution* clearly provides that the State Council as the highest administrative organ of the state could "adopt administrative measures, enact administrative rules and regulations and issue decisions and orders in accordance with the Constitution and the law." Thereupon, formulating administrative rules and regulations is an important power of the State Council granted by the *Constitution* as well as a major means for the State Council to promote the reform and opening up so as to organize the economic construction and fulfill its function of state management.

Admittedly, the administrative rules and regulations are essential in the improvement and construction of China's legal system, meanwhile they also bring about some important issues to be studied, especially those in relation to the constitutional basic rights. If a basic right, which should be stipulated in the parliamentary law, fails to become a law due to the lack of legislation, but is just stipulated at the level of administrative regulations or even lower levels, will it have impacts on its authority and effectiveness? For example, Article 35 of the *Constitution* provides that "Citizens of the People's Republic of China enjoy freedom of speech, of the press, of assembly, of association, of procession and of demonstration." However, there is no law on association and the current norms concerning freedom of association are provided for in the *Regulation on Registration and Administration of Social Organizations* enacted in 1989 and amended in 1998 by the State Council. In this regard, some scholars have questioned that protecting the basic right by administrative regulations is lacking in constitutional basis, or in other words, such protection in itself is a kind of disrespect and violation towards constitutional basic rights. Then, handling this phenomenon has become a puzzle. This concerns the constitutionality of administrative regulations' constraint on basic rights. We can analyze it from both practical and theoretical levels. At a practical level, is it rational in practice that basic rights are stipulated by the State Council in the form of administrative regulations on the condition that there is no legal provision or strict authorization? At a theoretical level, is it in line with the values of constitutionalism that basic rights are stipulated by the State Council in the form of administrative regulation?

At a practical level, on the premise that the parliamentary legislation does not prescribe the basic rights, is it rational in practice in a certain sense that basic rights are stipulated by the State Council in the form of administrative regulations, at least providing a minimum legal ground and remedy for the guarantee of basic rights? Otherwise it may lead the basic rights to a standstill and vacancy owing to the lack of legislation. Therefore, from the perspective of the guarantee of basic rights and its practical necessity, the stipulation on basic rights by administrative regulations is of positive significance in the particular context. However, at a theoretical level, stipulating basic rights in the form of administrative regulation is not in line with the basic concepts of constitutionalism and lacks a constitutional foundation. Although administrative regulations can make up for the deficiencies of legal regulations and protect basic rights to a certain extent, from the perspective of the basic concepts of constitutionalism, stipulating basic rights in the form of administrative regulations is short of a value basis, which may be contrary to the principle of legal reservation in the *Constitution*. In classical constitutional theory, legal reservation means "the violation of citizens' basic rights must be in accordance with the law," whose regulating connotation only limits the "violation" of citizens' basic rights without containing other cases such as stipulation, protection, and restriction. However, with the development of constitutional theory, traditional theory of legal reservation has already abandoned the field of simple "violation," but expanded to the fields of restriction and protection. A theory like this in legal reservation theory is called "materiality theory," which was clearly proposed by the German Federal Constitutional Court in the "Bill of Sex Education Curriculum," generally stating that "any matter concerning human rights is surely within legislator's scope, nevertheless the legislator shall not casually authorize administrative organs to stipulate in the form of administrative order, and the major part involving human rights shall be reserved for the legislator." In this bill, the German Federal Constitutional Court believes that offering sex education curriculum to middle school students is a significant matter concerning people's educational right, which means it must be explicitly defined by law, and administrative organs shall not be authorized to adopt their own discretion.[9] In consideration of the constitutional significance of basic rights and with reference to Germany's "materiality theory," it is concluded that stipulating basic rights by administrative rights is not consistent with basic rights' value. Therefore, although the *Regulation on Registration and Administration of Social Organizations of the State Council* is of some rationality at a practical level, as regards such a significant matter about citizens' basic rights like freedom of association, if administrative organs are given free rein to stipulate and restrict it, then the basic concepts of constitutionalism as well as the value connotation of basic rights will be violated, and the principle that "the state respects and preserves human rights" as prescribed in Paragraph 3 of Article 33 of the *Constitution* also fails to be manifested, which will inevitably lose its constitutional foundation. Based on such sense, some scholars have advocated to formulate the Association Law and the Press Law as soon as possible, so as to change the unreasonable situation at present in which such constitutional basic rights as freedom of association and freedom of the press are stipulated in the form of administrative regulation.

The constraint of the Constitution on judicial interpretation

Apart from being manifested in the control of parliamentary legislative power and administrative legislative power, the role of the *Constitution* in the construction of the legal system was also reflected in the control of the judicial power, which mainly involves that of judicial interpretation. According to *Sea of Words* (*Cihai* 辭海), judicial interpretation is a kind of legal interpretation, and it is the explication made by the judiciary concerning the specific application of laws and regulations, belonging to official explanation. The *Resolution of the Standing Committee of the National People's Congress Providing an Improved Interpretation of the Law* adopted on June 10, 1981 provides that "Interpretation of questions involving the specific application of laws and decrees in court trials shall be provided by the Supreme People's Court. Interpretation of questions involving the specific application of laws and decrees in the procuratorial work of the procuratorates shall be provided by the Supreme People's Procuratorate." In the scope of judicial work, questions involving "the specific application of laws" mainly include the following situations:

- To interpret those questions difficult to understand and implement caused by the legal provisions that are not specific and clear enough;
- To provide interpretations when there are different understandings of the basis of handling some kind of cases due to changes in circumstances;
- To explain the way of understanding and implementing some legal provisions in terms of some certain kind of cases so as to establish a unified standard for the trial;
- To interpret how different judicial organs coordinate with each other in hearing cases according to the principle prescribed by the *Constitution*

Judicial interpretation is usually made in terms of the application of law for some certain case, which is only effective in this case and without universal binding force. In practice, however, the interpretation provided by the Supreme People's Court is usually binding the lower courts. Furthermore, as for the documents, and even the meeting minutes of the superior courts, the lower courts need to "study, comprehend, and implement" them in earnest.

Judicial interpretation in most cases is conducted within the content and spirit of law in the applicable process. It is the supporting measures of the legal system, and its contents and spirit cannot go contrary to the provisions of the law and the *Constitution*, otherwise, it is null and void. However, in practice, the judicial interpretations of the Supreme Court are vast in number and heterogeneous in content, causing the content of some judicial interpretations to go far beyond the stipulations of law, which in fact, become substitutes for laws, resulting in the ineffectiveness of law, and even causing that some judicial interpretations to depart from the basic principles and spirit of the *Constitution*. For example, *Interpretation of the Supreme People's Court of Some Issues concerning the Application of Law for the Trial of Cases on Compensation for Personal Injury* (Interpretation No. 20 [2003], hereinafter referred to as "*Interpretation*") provides that the compensation for disability and for death shall be calculated in light of the per capita disposable income of the urban residents or the per capita net income of the rural residents. In judicial practice, household register is the fundamental basis to differentiate between the urban and rural residents, thus the implementation of the Interpretation may easily lead to the inconsistency in respect of the compensation standard between the urban and rural residents.

With this *Interpretation*, we can establish an effective supervisory mechanism according to the *Law of the People's Republic of China on the Supervision of Standing Committees of People's Congresses at Various Levels* (hereinafter referred to as the "*Supervision Law*") implemented on January 1, 2007. Article 31 of the *Supervision Law* stipulates that "Any interpretation of the Supreme People's Court or the Supreme People's Procuratorate regarding the specific application of laws in the judicial and procuratorial work shall be reported to the Standing Committee of the National People's Congress for the record within 30 days upon promulgation."

In Article 32, it is stated that "Where the State Council, the Central Military Commission (CMC) or the standing committee of the people's congress of the province, autonomous region or municipality directly under the Central Government finds that any interpretation of the Supreme People's Court or the Supreme People's Procuratorate regarding the specific application of laws conflicts with the law, or the Supreme People's Court or the Supreme People's Procuratorate considers that any interpretation of the other party conflicts with the law, it can put forward a written request for examination to the Standing Committee of the National People's Congress, and the working body of the Standing Committee shall send it to the relevant special committee for examination and putting forward opinions. Where any state organ, social group, enterprise, public institution or citizen other than those prescribed in the preceding Paragraph finds that any interpretation of the Supreme People's Court or the Supreme People's Procuratorate regarding the specific application of laws conflicts with the law, it or he can put forward a written request for examination to the Standing Committee of the National People's Congress, and the working body of the Standing Committee shall study it, and when necessary, send it to the relevant special committee for examination and putting forward opinions."

Article 33 of the *Supervision Law* provides that "Where the Law Committee or any other special committee of the National People's Congress finds upon examination that any interpretation of the Supreme People's Court or the Supreme People's

Procuratorate regarding the specific application of laws conflicts with the law, however, the Supreme People's Court or the Supreme People's Procuratorate does not revise or abolish the said interpretation, it can put forward a bill requiring the Supreme People's Court or the Supreme People's Procuratorate to make revision or abolition, or put forward a bill that the Standing Committee of the National People's Congress makes a legal interpretation, and the directors' meeting decides to submit the legal interpretation to the Standing Committee for deliberation."

One of the major missions of the *Supervision Law* is to examine the legality and constitutionality of the judicial interpretations made by the Supreme People's Court since its emergence. In respect of the construction of China's legal system, the *Supervision Law*'s examination of judicial interpretation is one of the significant measures to improve the overall conformity of China's legal system.

The *Constitution* as the basis for the construction and development of the legal system

The Constitution as the basis of legislation and the source of effectiveness of the legal system

The *Constitution*'s legislative basis in the construction of the legal system is mainly reflected in the text of laws as "This Law is formulated in accordance with the Constitution." In addition to this, the *Constitution* also has the highest effectiveness in the construction of the legal system, showing that the *Constitution* is the source of the effectiveness of the whole legal system.

Legal system is an integrated organism composed of a variety of laws and regulations, with the *Constitution* at the dominant position and basic laws as the main framework.[10] In the formation process of the legal system, the *Constitution* acts on a legislative basis. The *Constitution* is the legislative basis of the legal system, which means that in the construction of the legal system, the formulation of the law must be based on the *Constitution*, and the source of legitimacy must be sought from it. In the process of formulating ordinary laws, this role can be found in the text of laws as "This Law is formulated in accordance with the Constitution."

From a theoretical perspective, such a relationship between the *Constitution* and the laws is compared to that of mother and children in constitutional theory, in which the *Constitution* is the "mother law" that can give birth to other "sub-laws." So, what does "mother law" mean? According to academic research, "mother law" is interpreted as follows in Chinese jurisprudential etymology:

(1) If the formulation of a country's law is based on a foreign law, then this foreign law as the source is called the mother law, and the law enacted on its basis is called sub-law;

(2) The law on the basis of which the state formulates decrees or ordinances, is called the mother law, and those decrees and ordinances enacted based on it are called sub-laws. Thus, etymologically speaking, "mother law" does not originally refer to the *Constitution*, but refers only to the "basis" for the enactment of laws, regulations and ordinances, which of course includes both the domestic "basis" and foreign "basis."[11]

From a practical perspective, all of China's laws and regulations must take the *Constitution* as the basis and cannot be in conflict with the *Constitution*, otherwise they are invalid. However, when a law takes the *Constitution* as its basis, the standard forms of expression are varied:

(1) Some laws did not expressly mention their constitutional basis in the first articles, such as the *Organic Law of the People's Courts*, the *Organic Law of the People's Procuratorates*, the *Auction Law*, the *Law on Commercial Banks*, and the *Negotiable Instruments Law*.

(2) It is stated in the first articles of some laws that "This Law is enacted pursuant to the relevant provisions of the Constitution of the People's Republic of China."

(3) The majority of laws clearly state in the first articles that "This Law is formulated in accordance with the Constitution." Of course, in terms of the specific expressions, some are stated as "pursuant to the Constitution of the People's Republic of China" and some others are written as "in accordance with the Constitution."

(4) Some laws prescribe their constitutional basis in the preambles, such as the *Basic Law of the Hong Kong Special Administrative Region* and the *Basic Law of the Macao Special Administrative Region*, stating that "In accordance with the Constitution of the People's Republic of China, the National People's Congress hereby enacts the basic law of the Hong Kong (Macao) Special Administrative Region of the People's Republic of China..."

(5) In some of the laws, it is stated in the "Objective" in Article 1 that "This Law is formulated in accordance with the Constitution."

Therefore, the expressions of laws' legislative basis are quite different; however, as for those laws without explicit stipulations like "in accordance with the Constitution," their constitutionality remains a worthwhile topic for further exploration.

Regardless of whether the wordings like "in accordance with the Constitution" are mentioned, all laws are actually enacted by the legislature in accordance with the *Constitution*, otherwise they are regarded as invalid. Then, why are the wordings not stated in every law? One possible explanation is that the legislators may not consider it a worthwhile topic to be researched. It is a basic principle of the Chinese *Constitution* that all laws and regulations must be consistent with the *Constitution*, therefore being "in accordance with the Constitution" is an undoubted consensus, a premise as well as a de facto status, without the need for a value judgment. In spite of this, whether or not such words are written in laws is by no means just a question of form, neither can it be judged only by the presumption of principle. From the perspective of the relationship between the *Constitution* and basic laws, legislators must establish a principle to standardize which laws should include the provision of "in accordance with the Constitution," or which legislative policies or techniques can be chosen by legislators at discretion. In light of the present laws formulated by the NPC and its Standing Committee, it is hard to find strict legislative rules or principles, and it needs further regulation at least in terms of legislative techniques. Besides, such expressions as "pursuant to" and "in accordance with," "in accordance with the Constitution," and "in accordance with the Constitution of the People's Republic of China" should be standardized. Although "pursuant to" and "in accordance with" have the same meaning and the legislature's use of these words is not intentional, they still may bring unnecessary misunderstanding to the public.

Law, which must take the *Constitution* as its basis, may have the following meanings at the normative level: First, it indicates that the *Constitution* has the supreme legal authority and is the basis for the law to play its effectiveness. Second, it shows the rank of effectiveness between "this law" and the *Constitution*, that is, the superior legislations rank above the lower legislations in respect of effectiveness, and the lower legislations cannot violate the superior legislations. Third, it indicates that "this law" is the embodiment of the provisions in the *Constitution*, and its value and effectiveness are derived from the *Constitution*. Undoubtedly, "in accordance with the Constitution" is just an expression in the normative sense rather than a fact in a practical sense. There could be a variety of situations. The first is that the law is really enacted "in accordance with the Constitution." The law is drafted in accordance with the *Constitution*, and the *Constitution* restricts its operation. Second, although "in accordance with the Constitution" is written in the law, in fact, it does not design its content based on the *Constitution*, and some parts are inconsistent with the *Constitution*. Third, that the expression "in accordance with the Constitution" only manifests itself in the design of the content, while in the specific operation process, there is no connection between the law and the *Constitution*.

To judge whether a law is formulated "in accordance with the Constitution," the idea, basic principles, and specific content of law should be considered to see if they are in line with the norms, principles, and spirit of the *Constitution*. It reflects the constitutionality in both a substantial sense and a formal sense. When making a specific judgment, it is necessary to distinguish between the *Constitution* in a substantial sense and that in a formal sense. In cases of taking the *Constitution* in a substantial sense as the criterion, the judge should take account of both the meanings inside the *Constitution* and the questions of value outside the *Constitution*; while in cases of taking the Constitution in a formal sense as the criterion, he can only make judgments based on the norms defined in the *Constitution*, and cannot expand the extension of the criterion. This criterion of a formal sense as a matter of fact is the mechanical application of the "theory of authorization standard," which does not really show the value of the *Constitution* as a superior law; while the criterion of a substantial sense is to judge the constitutionality of ordinary laws based on the spirit, principles, and specific provisions of the *Constitution*. In the current period of social transformation in China, a strict interpretation in a formal sense is essential, but such an interpretative activity must be consistent with the overall principles of interpretation, avoiding the conflicts between provisions. The relative effectiveness between the *Constitution* and laws should be judged by considering the following factors:

Firstly, it should be considered whether the legislative spirit of the ordinary law is consistent with that of the *Constitution*. The constitution is actually the law that protects human rights, thus the legislative spirit of the ordinary law should be consistent with such a spirit of protecting human rights of the *Constitution*, otherwise the law is meaningless, even though such expression as "This Law is formulated in accordance with the Constitution" is clearly written in its provisions. The spirit of protecting human rights is honored as the "core" of the *Constitution* that cannot be revised or abandoned, and on which the *Constitution* depends.[12]

Secondly, it should be considered whether the content of the ordinary law is in line with the basic principles of the *Constitution*. The basic principles of the *Constitution* are the embodiment of its spirit, reflecting its fundamental value pursuit. Many principles prescribed in China's *Constitution* such as that of popular sovereignty, of basic human rights, and of the rule of law have already been internalized into the elements of the construction of the rule of law and play a guiding role in its overall construction. So, when examining the constitutionality of ordinary laws, apart from reviewing whether the legislative spirit of the ordinary law violates the principle of protecting human rights, its content should also be considered to see if it is in conflict with the basic principles of the *Constitution*.

Finally, the provisions of the ordinary law should be studied to see if they conform to that of the *Constitution*. Both the spirit and principles of the *Constitution* are very abstract and principled and not easy to be grasped in the specific constitutional practice. Whereas, the constitutional provisions are more realistic and concrete, in the legislative process of ordinary laws, the specific provisions in the constitutional text should be paid the utmost respect to, for the authority and the value of the *Constitution* are mainly manifested in the respect and observance of its test. As a result, if there are provisions that obviously violate the stipulations in the constitutional text in ordinary laws, we must adhere to the supremacy of the *Constitution* and declare it unconstitutional and therefore void, regardless of whether it is a virtuous one or a malignant one.

The Constitution as the criterion for the rank of effectiveness in the legal system

The *Constitution*, as the foundation of the effectiveness is the criterion, for the rank of effectiveness in the legal system. In an integrated legal system, the ranks of effectiveness between different laws, regulations, and rules are inconsistent. We should always take the *Constitution* as the ultimate criterion for judging the rank of effectiveness in the legal system.

According to the principle that a law is considered null and void if it is unconstitutional, the constitution not only provides a legislative foundation and a basis for the legislation of ordinary laws, nor does it just define the scope and authority for the legislation of ordinary laws, but it offers a criterion of examination to the legislation of ordinary laws, warning legislators not to violate the *Constitution* as a superior law, otherwise those laws will be declared to be unconstitutional and therefore void. This truly reflects the value of the *Constitution* as a superior law and provides a theoretical basis for the correct handling of the relationship between the *Constitution* and laws in constitutional practice. For example, according to Professor Lin Laifan, "the *Constitution* exists to provide a normative basis for examining all sorts of legislations rather than to provide legislative basis for them. This indicates that the *Constitution* as the supreme legal norm does not only manifest itself as an 'authorized norm' with the 'reproductive function' of producing various subordinate laws implied in the concept of 'mother law'."[13] Some other scholars summarize the fundamental role of the *Constitution*'s effectiveness in the legal system as a principle that "ordinary laws cannot be in conflict with the *Constitution*" and consider this as the basic principle for dealing with the relationship between the *Constitution* and ordinary laws. Two issues are implied in this principle: First, ordinary laws can exist without a constitutional basis, as long as they do not clash with the *Constitution*. Second, ordinary laws cannot be inconsistent with the *Constitution*, reflecting the *Constitution*'s control on ordinary laws. This signifies the supreme role and authority of the *Constitution*.

In the application of the *Constitution*, the principle "unconstitutional and therefore void" is of great significance. First, establishing the principle of ordinary laws not which do not conflict with the *Constitution* can ease the pressure of the constitutional amendment brought by social changes. In light of this principle, laws can be divided into the ones formulated based on the *Constitution*, and the ones without a constitutional basis but cannot violate the *Constitution*. As the society in modern times is constantly developing, the law that regulates social relations is also in progress, especially when the modern society becomes increasingly complex and diversified, different kinds of law will emerge and the contents will be up to date constantly. In addition, the existence of the second type of ordinary laws has allowed room for flexibility between the *Constitution* and social development, so as to alleviate the conflict between the *Constitution* and social reality. Not all of the social relations must be reflected in the *Constitution*, and not all the ordinary laws must be formulated based on the *Constitution*. The *Constitution* is based on the reality or the existing objects, but remains conservative towards the future. As long as some kind of social relation has not emerged yet, it is not necessary to stipulate it in the *Constitution*. Second, the establishment of the constitutional review system is the requirement for setting up the principle of ordinary laws which are not in conflict with the *Constitution*, which implies the supremacy of the *Constitution*. Consequently, an authoritative specialized organ is inevitable to judge whether the ordinary law conflicts with the *Constitution*. Comparatively, it is much easier to judge those ordinary laws that have a constitutional basis, for the constitutional provisions have already contained the basic principles and spirit of the issue. While for those that do not have a constitutional basis, it is a highly professional work to judge whether they have violated the *Constitution* in substance. A specialized and authoritative constitutional review body is required to perform this function.[14] As a model showing the *Constitution*'s function of judging the rank of effectiveness, the *Law on Legislation* adopted by the National People's Congress in 2000 has made important provisions on the authority, procedures, legal interpretations, as well as the settlement mechanism of conflicts in China's legislation. It is an especially clear and specific basis for the rank of effectiveness in the legal system. Owing to its outstanding contributions to the rank in the legal system, the *Law on Legislation* is regarded as the simplified version of the structure of the *Constitution*, and its power is second only to the *Constitution*'s, but above all the other ordinary laws' in terms of the rank of effectiveness. Based on the *Law on Legislation*, the rank system of China's laws can be summarized as follows:

- The rank of effectiveness of the *Constitution*, laws, regulations, and rules
  (1) The *Constitution* has the supreme legal authority, and no laws, administrative regulations, local regulations, autonomous regulations, separate regulations, or rules may contradict it;
  (2) The effectiveness of laws is higher than that of administrative regulations, local regulations, and rules. The effectiveness of administrative regulations is higher than that of local regulations, and rules;
  (3) The effectiveness of local regulations is higher than that of the rules of the local governments at or below the corresponding level. The effectiveness of the rules formulated by the people's governments of the provinces or autonomous regions is higher than that of the rules formulated by the people's governments of the comparatively larger cities within the administrative areas of the provinces and autonomous regions.
- The rank of effectiveness of autonomous regulations, separate regulations, regulations of special economic zones and rules
  (1) Where in autonomous regulations or separate regulations provisions are formulated in accordance with law to make adaptations with regard to certain provisions of laws, administrative regulations or local regulations, the provisions of the autonomous regulations or separate regulations shall apply in the autonomous areas concerned;
  (2) Where regulations of special economic zones are formulated, upon authorization, to make adaptations with regard to certain provisions of laws, administrative regulations or local regulations, the provisions of the regulations of special economic zones shall apply in the special economic zones concerned;
  (3) The effectiveness of the rules of different departments is equal between the departments, and the effectiveness of the rules of departments and of the rules of local governments is equal between the departments and local governments. Their regulating range shall be confined to the limits of authority of corresponding subjects who formulate the rules.
- Rules for the conflicts between legal norms
  Where the conflicts occur between legal norms at the same rank or at unidentified ranks, the application of laws should be bound by the following rules:
  (1) If laws, administrative regulations, local regulations, autonomous regulations, separate regulations or rules are formulated by one and the same organ and if there is inconsistency between special provisions and general provisions, the special provisions shall prevail; if there is inconsistency

between the new provisions and the old provisions, the new provisions shall prevail;

(2) Where there is inconsistency between the new general provisions and the old special provisions in different laws governing one and the same matter and it is hard to decide which provisions shall prevail, a ruling shall be made by the Standing Committee of the National People's Congress;

(3) Where there is inconsistency between local regulations and rules, disposing rules are as follows:

Where there is inconsistency between the new general provisions and the old special provisions formulated by one and the same organ, the said organ shall make a ruling; where there is inconsistency between the provisions of local regulations and those of the rules of departments governing one and the same matter and it is hard to decide which provisions shall prevail, the State Council shall make a decision; if it considers that the provisions of the local regulations should be applied, it shall decide that the provisions of the local regulations be applied in the locality concerned; if it considers that the rules of departments should be applied, the case shall be submitted to the Standing Committee of the National People's Congress for a ruling; and where there is inconsistency between the provisions in the rules of different departments or between the provisions in the rules of the departments and those in the rules of local governments governing one and the same matter, the State Council shall make a ruling; where there is inconsistency between the regulations formulated upon authorization and the provisions of laws and it is hard to decide which shall prevail, the Standing Committee of the National People's Congress shall make a ruling.[15]

From the perspective of normativism, the rank of effectiveness prescribed in the *Law on Legislation* actually involves the relationship between the *Constitution* and ordinary laws. To be more specific, it involves the specific effects and roles of the *Constitution* played in the enactment and adoption of ordinary laws in their formulating mechanism. The *Constitution* acts as a legislative basis for the formulation of ordinary laws, and the legislation of ordinary laws must take the constitutional provisions as the basic principles and the constitutional authorization as basic limits of authority, which in theory is well known as the theory of "authorized norm." According to this theory, the *Constitution* in the positive law system is "in the character of ultimate authorization norm, it can be said all the legal norms exist directly or indirectly based on the authorization of the *Constitution*."[16] As an authorized norm, the key function of the *Constitution* is providing a kind of legal basis in an ultimate sense for the authorized ordinary legal norms, enabling them to have a constitutional or legal source of legitimacy. Although the *Constitution* as an authorized norm can provide the legal basis or foundation for the ordinary legal norms including civil law, criminal law, and procedural law, in the legislative practice, this function is also subject to various constraints, which in fact are a kind of restriction on the scope of the *Constitution*'s authorizing function. Such constraints are mainly reflected in two aspects: First, the *Constitution* can negatively determine what contents shall be definitely forsaken by the law, like the congress will not pass any law that restricts freedom of religion. Second, the *Constitution* can also actively stipulate some contents in future laws like are stated in the *Constitution* of the United States, "In all criminal prosecutions, the accused shall enjoy the right to…"[17] Such an authorizing function of the *Constitution* has been obviously shown in Article 8 of the *Law on Legislation*: "The following affairs shall only be governed by law: (1) affairs concerning State sovereignty; (2) formation, organization, and the functions and powers of the people's congresses, the people's governments, the people's courts and the people's procuratorates at all levels; (3) the system of regional national autonomy, the system of special administrative region, the system of self-government among people at the grassroots levels; (4) criminal offences and their punishment; (5) mandatory measures and penalties involving deprivation of citizens of their political rights or restriction of the freedom of their person; (6) requisition of non-State-owned property; (7) basic civil system; (8) basic economic system and basic systems of finance, taxation, customs, banking and foreign trade; (9) systems of litigation and arbitration; and (10) other affairs on which laws must be made by the National People's Congress or its Standing Committee." These provisions are actually restrictions on the authorizing function of the *Constitution*, limiting the scope of the *Constitution*'s legislation to the ordinary laws. It means that any legislation concerning the matters above shall be enacted only by the National People's Congress and its Standing Committee, rather than by the authority given to the administrative organs or local people's congresses and their standing committees.

The Constitution as the basis of ensuring the consistency of the legal system

China's legislative system is a multi-office one. Not only the National People's Congress has legislative power, the NPC Standing Committee, the State Council, the local people's congresses and their standing committees also enjoy legislative power at different levels. The increase in the number of legislative bodies is likely to cause the inconsistency within the legal system, and sometimes brings about the situations that provisions of different laws or laws at different levels are inconsistent or even contrary to each other. It will seriously undermine the consistency of the legal system as well as the existing legal order, leading to the conflicts between legal values. From a normative point of view, an effective review mechanism is required for ensuring the consistency of the legal system. In other words, it is to establish a constitutional supervision mechanism, or a constitutional review mechanism. The *Constitution* of China establishes the people's congress system as a fundamental political system, based on which, China has initially established the constitutional supervision system with Chinese characteristics. In the construction of the legal system, establishing and strengthening the constitutional supervision system are of important theoretical and practical significance. They are conducive to perform the *Constitution*'s function of regulating social life and establishing its role of the fundamental law in the state so as to stabilize the constitutional order and safeguard the consistency of the legal system with the *Constitution* at its core. They are also protecting the rights and freedoms of citizens so that the basic rights provided for in the *Constitution* can be realized.

The supreme legal authority of the *Constitution* is the basis for the establishment of the constitutional supervision system. As stated in the last paragraph of the preamble to the *Constitution*, "This Constitution, in legal form, affirms the achievements of the struggles of the Chinese people of all nationalities and defines the basic system and basic tasks of the state; it is the fundamental law of the state and has supreme legal authority." This prescription provides a standard legal basis for the establishment of the constitutional supervision system of China, as well as a foundation for its improvement.

The *Constitution* also establishes the basic principles for supervision. In Article 5, in addition to the basic goal "The People's Republic of China governs the country according to law and makes it a socialist country under rule of law," it is also written that "The State upholds the uniformity and dignity of the socialist legal system. No laws or administrative or local regulations may contravene the *Constitution*. All State organs, the armed forces, all political parties and public organizations and all enterprises and institutions must abide by the *Constitution* and other laws. All acts in violation of the *Constitution* or other laws must be investigated. No organization or individual is privileged to be beyond the *Constitution* or other laws." This prescription sets up the general principle for the National People's Congress and its Standing Committee to exercise their supervisory power.

First, according to Article 62 of the *Constitution*, the National People's Congress has the right to regulate the legislative acts of its Standing Committee, i.e. has the right to "alter or annul inappropriate decisions of the Standing Committee of the National People's Congress." The "inappropriate decisions" of the NPC Standing Committee of course include the unconstitutional laws and decisions. In the basic content of China's constitutional supervision system, the strict restraint of the

National People's Congress on the legislative acts of its Standing Committee is an important part and a form of activity, reflecting the basic characteristics of China's constitutional supervision system.

Second, the constitutional supervisory power exercised by the NPC Standing Committee is a regular, authoritative, and practical form of supervision. The 1954 *Constitution* and 1978 *Constitution* provides that "The National People's Congress supervises the enforcement of the Constitution," on the basis of which, Article 67 of the current *Constitution* provides that the Standing Committee of the National People's Congress also has the power to supervise the enforcement of the Constitution, its constitutional supervisory power mainly includes the power of constitutional review, of constitutional interpretation, and of legal interpretation.

Third, the deliberation activity of the special committees is a kind of preventive review, which can be carried out either before or after the promulgation of the normative documents. The special committees assist the National People's Congress and its Standing Committee in exercising the constitutional supervisory power, assuming a great deal of preparatory work. The Legislative Record and Review Office set up by the Commission of Legislative Affairs of the NPC Standing Committee will play an important role in the review of normative documents below the level of law. The current *Constitution* also provides that the National People's Congress and its Standing Committee may, when they deem it necessary, appoint special committees for specific questions.

Fourth, the local people's congresses and their standing committees bear the responsibility of supervising the implementation of the *Constitution* in the locality concerned. The local people's congresses at all levels take the form of altering or annulling inappropriate decisions of their own standing committees and the standing committees of the local people's congresses take the form of altering or annulling inappropriate decisions of the people's governments at the corresponding levels, in fact, to fulfill the responsibility of supervising the implementation of the *Constitution* in the locality concerned, which is an important component of the system of constitutional supervision.

In addition, regarding the political protection of the constitutional supervision, the *Constitution* stipulates the obligation of the ruling party to comply with the *Constitution*. Besides, the *Constitution* of the Communist Party of China also stipulates the principle that "The Party must conduct its activities within the framework of the Constitution and laws of the country," which requires the party organization and party members to play an exemplary role in observing the *Constitution*, so as to provide a stable political basis for the implementation of the *Constitution*.

In the provisions of the constitutional text, the current *Constitution* stipulates a relatively complete system of the supervision of normative documents: First, the National People's Congress has the power to alter or annul inappropriate decisions of the Standing Committee of the National People's Congress, including inappropriate laws. Second, the National People's Congress Standing Committee has the power to annul those administrative rules and regulations, decisions, or orders of the State Council that contravene the *Constitution* or the law, and to annul those local regulations or decisions of the organs of state power of provinces, autonomous regions, and municipalities directly under the Central Government that contravene the *Constitution*, the law, or the administrative rules and regulations. Third, the State Council has the power to alter or annul inappropriate orders, directives, and regulations issued by the ministries or commissions, and to alter or annul inappropriate decisions and orders issued by local organs of state administration at various levels. Fourth, local people's congresses at and above the county level have the power to alter or annul inappropriate decisions of their own standing committees. Fifth, the standing committee of a local people's congress at or above the county level has the power to annul inappropriate decisions and orders of the people's government at the corresponding level, and to annul inappropriate resolutions of the people's congress at the next lower level. Sixth, local people's governments at and above the county level have the power to alter or annul inappropriate decisions of their subordinate departments and of the people's governments at lower levels. The National People's Congress and its Standing Committee supervise all the unconstitutional acts, and the state organs at a higher level can supervise the corresponding state organs at a lower level. The above-mentioned system of the supervision of normative documents is an important part of the constitutional supervision system in China, which can be considered as a significant development of the supervisory system for the highest organ of state power carried out by China's current *Constitution*.

The *Law on Legislation* makes a relatively detailed stipulation on the supervision and review system for normative legal documents, becoming the initiating procedure for China's constitutional supervision system.

(1) Object of supervision and review

According to Article 90 of the *Law on Legislation*, the administrative regulations, local regulations, autonomous regulations or separate regulations are the objects of the supervision and review carried out by the NPC Standing Committee in accordance with the *Constitution*.

(2) Initiating subject

When the State Council, the Central Military Commission, the Supreme

People's Court, the Supreme People's Procuratorate, and the standing committees of the people's congresses of the provinces, autonomous regions and municipalities directly under the Central Government consider that above-mentioned normative documents contradict the *Constitution* or laws, they may submit written requests for examination to the Standing Committee of the National People's Congress. The working offices of the Standing Committee shall refer the requests to the relevant special committees for examination and suggestions. When state organs other than these subjects, public organizations, enterprises and institutions, or citizens consider that administrative regulations, local regulations, autonomous regulations or separate regulations contradict the *Constitution* or laws, they may submit written suggestions for examination to the Standing Committee of the National People's Congress, and the working offices of the Standing Committee shall study the suggestions and shall, when necessary, refer them to the relevant special committees for examination and suggestions.

(3) Review procedure

When a special committee of the National People's Congress considers that administrative regulations, local regulations, autonomous regulations or separate regulations contradict the *Constitution* or laws after examination, it may submit written suggestions to the organ that has formulated the regulations for examination; or the Law Committee and other relevant special committees may convene a joint meeting for examination and request the said organ to attend the meeting and give an explanation, and then after examination submit to the organ written comments and suggestions. The organ that has formulated the regulations shall, within two months, study and put forth suggestions as to whether to revise the regulations, and shall give feedback to the Law Committee and other relevant special committees of the National People's Congress. If, after examination, the Law Committee and other relevant special committees of the National People's Congress consider that administrative regulations, local regulations, autonomous regulations, or separate regulations contradict the *Constitution* or laws and the organ that has formulated such regulations refuses to make revisions, they may submit written comments and suggestions on the basis of their examination and propose a motion for annulment of the regulations to the Council of Chairmen, which shall decide whether to submit the motion to a meeting of the Standing Committee for examination and decision.

In the specific implementation of the constitutional supervision system, the establishment of a standard record and review system in China has provided an effective guarantee for the consistency of the legal system. According to Article 100 of the *Constitution*, "The people's congresses of provinces and municipalities directly under the Central Government and their standing committees may adopt local regulations, which must not contravene the *Constitution* and the law and administrative rules and regulations, and they shall report such local regulations to the Standing Committee of the National People's Congress for the record." In Article 116, it provides that "the regulations on the exercise of autonomy and other separate regulations of autonomous regions shall be submitted to the Standing Committee of the National People's Congress for approval before they go into effect. Those of autonomous prefectures and counties shall be submitted to the standing committee of the people's congresses of provinces or autonomous regions for approval before they go into effect, and they shall be reported to the Standing Committee of the National People's Congress for the record." The system of record and review or approval is conducive for the constitutional supervisory organs to find and solve the constitutional problem in a timely manner. In order to further regulate the system of record and review for the relevant legislations, the State Council has promulgated the *Ordinance concerning the Procedures for the Formulation of Administrative Regulations* (2001), the *Ordinance concerning the Procedures for the Formulation of Rules* (2001), and the *Ordinance on the Archivist Filing of Regulations and Government Rules* (2001) that make special provisions for the record and review of administrative regulations and rules since the adoption of the *Law on Legislation* in 2000. For example, the *Ordinance concerning the Procedures for the Formulation of Government Rules* specifies the review procedures of the rules recording organs, and gives the specific subjects the power of suggestion for legal review. Its Article 35 provides that when the state organs, public organizations, enterprises and public institutions or citizens consider that any rule contradicts any law or administrative regulation they may submit to the Standing Committee of the NPC written suggestions for examination, and the legislative affairs organ of the State Council shall study and deal with it. On October 16, 2000, the 34th Chairmen's Meeting of the Standing Committee of the 9th National People's Congress adopted the *Working Procedures for the Record and Review of Administrative Regulations, Local Regulations, Autonomous Regulations, Separate Regulations and Regulations of the Special Economic Zones* (hereinafter referred as Working Procedures for the Record and Review of Regulations). On December 16, 2005, the 40th Chairmen's Meeting of the Standing Committee of the 10th National People's Congress amended it and adopted the *Working Procedures for the Record and Review of Judicial Interpretations*. The amendment to the *Working Procedures for the Record and Review of Regulations* stipulates that when citizens consider that any regulation contradicts the *Constitution* or any law and submit to the Standing Committee of the NPC written suggestions for review, the Commission of Legislative shall be responsible for receiving, registering, and studying the suggestions; and shall, when necessary, refer them to the relevant special committees for review upon the approval of the secretary general. According to the "*Report on the Work of the Standing Committee of the National People's Congress*" delivered by Chairman Wu Bangguo in 2009, in 2008, a total of 475 normative documents were received and filed, and 86 suggestions from ordinary individuals and organizations concerning review work were handled. The continuous development and improvement of the record and review system is beneficial to safeguarding the authority of the *Constitution* and laws, and ensuring the consistency of the Socialist legal system.

Regarding the provisions in the *Constitution*, the *Law on Legislation* and other laws, the NPC and its Standing Committee adopt different forms of the constitutional review, being able to not only conduct the preventive review beforehand, but are also able to carry out the constitutional review afterwards; not only conduct abstract principled review under the condition that no actual case occurs, but also carry out the review after the state organ found a normative legal document may contravene the *Constitution* when exercising its power, and then report to the relevant department.

The specific role of the *Constitution* in constructing and developing the legal system — political legislation as an example

Legislation can be divided into different types according to the content, basically including economic legislation, political legislation, cultural legislation, and social legislation, among which political legislation generally refers to the laws, regulations, rules, and other legislative documents related to the state's political system. Although political legislation has not been developed into a very mature and stable concept, generally speaking, it should at least include, but not be limited to legislation of a special administrative region, legislation of national autonomous areas, military legislation, organic legislation, electoral legislation. Since political legislation is often related to the most fundamental and most important issue in national affairs, it must strictly conform to the constitutional provisions, maintain the constitutional system, and preserve the constitutional order (see Fig. 2.1 for the framework of the Constitution and the Related Laws).

Fig. 2.1 Framework of the Constitution and the Related Laws

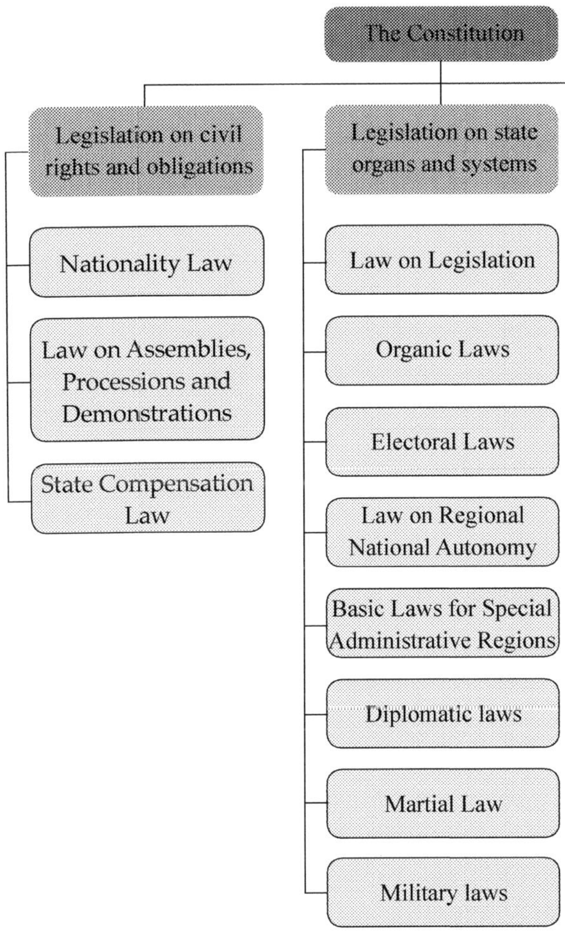

The Constitution and the legislation of special administrative region

The *Constitution* is the only legal basis for the formulation of the Basic Laws of the Special Administrative Regions

Professor Xiao Weiyun believes that the legislation of the Basic Laws of the Special Administrative Regions is in accordance with legal basis, policy basis, and practical basis.[18] The policy basis of the Basic Laws stems from the famous principle "One Country, Two Systems" proposed by Deng Xiaoping in June 1984. Then the Chinese Central Government signed the Joint Declarations with the British Government and the Portuguese Government in 1984 and 1987, respectively. Article 31 of the current *Constitution* also reflects the policy of "One Country, Two Systems." The Basic Laws are formulated in accordance with the historical and actual situations of Hong Kong and Macau, and with the Constitution of the PRC as the legal basis.

Regarding the legal basis of the Basic Law, there are two kinds of viewpoints in academia: One is the "theory of dual bases," holding that the Basic Laws are formulated on the basis of the Sino-British Joint Declaration, Sino-Portuguese Joint Declaration, and the *Constitution*. The other is the "theory of sole basis," considering Article 31 and Paragraph 3 of Article 62 of the Constitution as the basis. As claimed by the "theory of dual bases," the two "Joint Declarations" are the international treaties signed between the two governments, regarded as international laws. According to the principle that international law dominates domestic law, the Joint Declarations are higher than the Basic Laws, thus the Joint Declarations should be the legislative basis of the Basic Laws. As maintained by the "theory of sole basis," the Basic Laws are formulated based on the principle of "One Country, Two Systems", and the Article 31 and Paragraph 13 of Article 62 of the *Constitution* are exactly the constitutionalization of the principle, which are also specially authorized items. Therefore. Article 31 and Paragraph 3 of Article 62 of the Constitution are the sole legislative bases of the Basic Laws.[19] The two "Joint Declarations" are regarded as in the scope of the international treaty, with the obligations that the two governments are committed to fulfill. In China, the obligations provided by treaties can usually be applicable directly only through the transformation to domestic law. The issues on the formulation of basic laws and the source of effectiveness are all under the control of domestic law, which is the *Constitution*. The Basic Laws are formulated on the basis of the Constitution, supported by the provisions of the Basic Laws themselves. It is stated in the second paragraph of the Preamble to the Basic Law of the Hong Kong Special Administrative Region that "Upholding national unity and territorial integrity, maintaining the prosperity and stability of Hong Kong, and taking account of its history and realities, the People's Republic of China has decided that upon China's resumption of the exercise of sovereignty over Hong Kong, a Hong Kong Special Administrative Region will be established in accordance with the provisions of Article 31 of the Constitution of the People's Republic of China, and that under the principle of 'One Country, Two Systems,' the Socialist system and policies will not be practiced in Hong Kong. The basic policies of the People's Republic of China regarding Hong Kong have been elaborated by the Chinese Government in the Sino-British Joint Declaration." The third paragraph provides that "In accordance with the Constitution of the People's Republic of China, the National People's Congress hereby enacts the *Basic Law of the Hong Kong Special Administrative Region of the People's Republic of China*, prescribing the systems to be practiced in the Hong

Kong Special Administrative Region, in order to ensure the implementation of the basic policies of the People's Republic of China regarding Hong Kong." In the above paragraphs, the second paragraph of the Preamble specifies the basis for establishing the Special Administrative Region, namely practical basis, legal basis, and policy basis. The third paragraph of the Preamble states clearly that the enactment of the Basic Law is based on the *Constitution*. The same provisions also appear in the second and the third paragraph of the Preamble to the *Basic Law of the Macao Special Administrative Region*. Moreover, as stated in the *Decision of the National People's Congress on the Basic Law of the Hong Kong Special Administrative Region of the People's Republic of China* adopted at the 3rd Session of the 7th National People's Congress on April 4, 1990 and the *Decision of the National People's Congress on the Basic Law of the Macao Special Administrative Region of the People's Republic of China* adopted at the 1st Session of the 8th National People's Congress on March 31, 1993, "The Basic Law of the Hong Kong (Macao) Special Administrative Region is constitutional as it is enacted in accordance with the Constitution of the People's Republic of China and in the light of the specific conditions of Hong Kong (Macao)."

In addition, according to Article 11 of the *Basic Law of the Hong Kong Special Administrative Region* and the *Basic Law of the Macao Special Administrative Region*, it is clear that the enactment of the Basic Laws is on the basis of the Article 31 of the current *Constitution*, which provides that "The state may establish special administrative regions when necessary. The systems to be instituted in special administrative regions shall be prescribed by law enacted by the National People's Congress in the light of specific conditions." Besides, Article 62 of the *Constitution* is also a key basis for enacting the Basic Laws — "The National People's Congress exercises the following functions and powers…(13) to decide on the establishment of special administrative regions and the systems to be instituted there." It can be deduced from the above two articles that the state has the power to establish special administrative regions, whose systems are different from the existing provinces, municipalities, autonomous regions, or special economic zones. The establishment of special administrative regions and the systems to be instituted can only be determined by the law, and only the National People's Congress can establish special administrative regions and stipulate their systems, while the Standing Committee of the National People's Congress does not have this power.

Therefore, the only legal basis for the formulation of the two Basic Laws is the current *Constitution*. "Article 31 of the *Constitution* is the constitutional provision in respect of the principle of 'One Country, Two Systems,' and the Basic Law is the reification and legalization of the principle of 'One Country, Two Systems' which is provided by the *Constitution*, so the content of the Basic Law is constitutional as it is formulated in accordance with the *Constitution*."[20]

The *Constitution* has the supreme legal authority in the Special Administrative Regions

The Basic Laws are enacted in accordance with the *Constitution* and the legal status of the Basic Laws are lower than that of the *Constitution*, therefore the *Constitution* has the supreme legal authority in the Special Administrative Regions. Some scholars argue that the Basic Laws are special laws of the *Constitution*. This viewpoint is debatable, because the relation of application priority between ordinary law and special law can only be found among different laws at the same level of authority. If the Basic Laws are considered as special laws of the *Constitution*, it is implied that the Basic Laws are of the same legal status as of the *Constitution*, then the Basic Laws can be applied in special administrative regions while ignoring the *Constitution*. The current *Constitution* provides that China shall adopt the Socialist system. As stated in Article 5 of both the Basic Laws, "The Socialist system and policies shall not be practiced in the Hong Kong (Macao) Special Administrative Region, and the previous capitalist system and way of life shall remain unchanged for 50 years." Some people argue that this content may lead to conflicts. It is necessary to clarify the scope of authority and mode of application of the *Constitution*. Undoubtedly, the Special Administrative Regions are subject to the restriction of the *Constitution* of the state, but the *Constitution* allows the existence of the provisions with certain alterations. The *Constitution* has two modes of application in the Special Administrative Regions: One is general application, that is, the *Constitution* has the supreme legal authority in the Special Administrative Regions on the whole, the Basic Laws are subordinate to the *Constitution*, and the legislatures of the Special Administrative Regions cannot stipulate matters that have been provided in the *Constitution*. China is a united unitary state with only the *Constitution* generally applicable. Thus the Special Administrative Regions shall surely abide by the *Constitution*. The other is the application of specific provisions. Some provisions in the *Constitution* have direct binding effect on the Special Administrative Regions. For instance, the items concerning state organs and state sovereignty are applicable to special administrative regions based on the unitary system and unity of the state; while some items related to the economic, cultural, and social systems of the state shall not apply to special administrative regions according to the special provisions of the Basic Laws on the social system. Besides, those items about civil rights in the *Constitution* are applicable together with those in the Basic Laws, that is, Chinese citizens in special administrative regions enjoy the rights and fulfill the obligations provided in both the Basic Law and the *Constitution* at the same time.

Since the legislative, executive, and judicial organs of the Special Administrative Regions are subject to the restriction of the Constitution, whether the judicial organs of the Special Administrative Regions can directly refer to the constitutional provisions as the basis for judgment remains a question. In this regard, there is not relevant prescription in both the *Constitution* and the Basic Laws. In our opinion, the judicial organs of the Special Administrative Regions can quote the constitutional provisions to support the reason for its judgment, but cannot review whether the laws and regulations of the Special Administrative Region are contrary to the *Constitution*, because in accordance with the provisions of the *Constitution* and the *Law on Legislation*, only NPC and its Standing Committee have the power to interpret the *Constitution*.

Maintaining the stability of the order of the Basic Laws in accordance with the *Constitution*

The Basic Laws, since the implementation in Hong Kong and Macau Special Administrative Regions, have maintained the local political, economic, cultural, and social development and have maintained the stability of the Basic Laws. In the Hong Kong Special Administrative Region, the NPC Standing Committee resolved the conflicts which existed in the implementation process of the Basic Law through the four interpretations. The NPC's Interpretations are all made in the certain stage of development of Hong Kong and involve the principled questions in the political system of Hong Kong, playing an important role for Hong Kong's constitutional order and social development. According to Article 158 of the *Basic Law of the Hong Kong Special Administrative Region*, "The power of interpretation of this Law shall be vested in the Standing Committee of the National People's Congress," in which the NPC Standing Committee is declared to be the organ for the interpretations of the Basic Law, but this is not its only legal source. The *Basic Law of the Hong Kong Special Administrative Region* is a national law enacted in accordance with the *Constitution*, and its interpretation mechanism is established based on and subject to the constitutional system. Therefore, the normative system of the legal source of the Basic Law's interpretation mechanism should also include the relevant provisions in the *Constitution*, the *Law on Legislation*, the *Organic Law of the National People's Congress*, the *Rules of Procedure for the Standing Committee of the National People's Congress*, the *Organic Law of the State Council*, and other relevant laws.[21] In fact, it is the unified and multilevel legal normative system and with the *Constitution* as its supreme authority that constitutes the normative basis for the NPC's Interpretations.

The Constitution and the legislation of regional national autonomy

The establishment and development of the system of regional national autonomy

The system of regional national autonomy is a basic political system prescribed by China's *Constitution*. On September 29, 1949, the sixth chapter entitled "Policy towards Nationalities" was included in the *Common Program of the Chinese People's Political Consultative Conference* adopted by the 1st Plenary Session of the Chinese People's Political Consultative Conference. There are four items, in which Article 51 stipulates that "Regional autonomy shall be exercised in areas where national minorities are concentrated and various kinds of autonomous organizations of the different nationalities shall be set up according to the size of the respective populations and regions. In places where different nationalities live together and in the autonomous areas of the national minorities, the different nationalities shall each have an appropriate number of representatives in the local organs of political power." After the founding of New China, the Chinese Government issued the *Outline of the People's Republic of China for Implementing Regional National Autonomy* in 1952, provided for the establishment of the national autonomous areas, the composition of organs of self-government, the autonomous right of organs of self-government, and other important issues.

In the 1st National People's Congress held in 1954, the system of regional national autonomy was included in the *Constitution* of New China, and the 1954 Constitution also clearly stipulated the establishment of autonomous townships. According to Liu Shaoqi's statement in the *Report on the Draft Constitution of the People's Republic of China*: "even in the area where nationalities are concentrated and there is only one township, though it is impossible and unnecessary to establish organs of self-government to exercise the above autonomous powers, the nationality township should still be established, so as to adapt to the special circumstances of concentrated nationalities." Although the nationality township does not belong to national autonomous areas, it is an important element of the system of regional national autonomy. The 1975 *Constitution* retained the section of "The Organs of Self-Government of National Autonomous Areas" in the chapter of "The Structure of the State," but its provisions are rather brief, and those contents about setting up public security forces, formulating autonomous regulations and separate regulations, employing the spoken and written language commonly used in the locality in performing duties, as well as the provisions concerning nationality township have been cancelled. However, this constitution clearly stipulates that the organs of self-government of national autonomous areas are the

People's Congress and the Revolutionary Committee. The 1978 *Constitution* also specifically provides for the organs of self-government of national autonomous areas, which is in general similar to the provisions of the 1975 *Constitution*, but with some stipulations that the organs of self-government have the power to formulate autonomous regulations and separate regulations and to employ the spoken and written language commonly used in the locality while performing their duties. The Paragraph 3 of Article 4 of the current *Constitution* provides that "Regional autonomy is practiced in areas where people of national minorities live in concentrated communities; in these areas organs of self-government are established to exercise the power of autonomy. All national autonomous areas are integral parts of the People's Republic of China." It resumes the stipulation that the People's Congress in national autonomous areas has the power to formulate autonomous regulations and separate regulations, and improve the prescriptions concerning the organs of self-government of national autonomous areas. Clearly prescribed in its Chapter 3 "The Structure of the State," Section 6 "The Organs of Self-Government of National Autonomous Areas," including 11 items in total, provides an adequate constitutional basis for the establishment and development of the system of regional national autonomy in China.

On May 31, 1984, the *Law of the People's Republic of China on Regional National Autonomy* was adopted at the 2nd Session of the 6th National People's Congress, and on February 28, 2001, it was amended at the 20th Session of the 9th National People's Congress. In accordance with its provisions, by the end of 2008, China had established 155 national autonomous areas, including five autonomous regions, 30 autonomous prefectures, and 120 autonomous counties (banners). According to the data shown in the 5th National Population Census, conducted in 2000, among the 55 national minorities, 44 had their own autonomous areas. The population of national minorities following regional autonomy accounted for 71% of the total population of the national minorities, and the area where such regional autonomy was practiced accounted for 64% of the entire territory of China.[22]

According to Article 30 of the current *Constitution*, the nationality township is a kind of administrative division of China, but does not belong to national autonomous areas. Thus, the Chinese Government promulgated the *Regulation on the Administration of Nationality Township* on September 15, 1993, so as to guarantee the implementation of the system of the nationality township. This *Regulation* also stipulates that the people's governments of provinces, autonomous regions, and municipalities directly under the Central Government have jurisdiction over nationality townships to formulate measures for implementation in accordance with this *Regulation*. According to the statistics, by the end of 2008, China had established 1,100 nationality townships in areas equivalent to townships where national minorities are concentrated in.[23]

The legislative power of national autonomous areas

In accordance with the relevant provisions of the *Constitution,* the national autonomous areas enjoy a certain degree of legislative power and can implement laws and administrative regulations with certain alterations. At present, China has established a legislative system of national autonomous areas with the *Constitution* as its guideline and the *Law on Regional National Autonomy* as its core. The *Law on Regional National Autonomy,* as a basic law enacted on the basis of the *Constitution,* is not only the embodiment of the basic principles and spirit of the *Constitution,* but also the reification of the relevant provisions in the *Constitution.* As stated in the Preface, "The Law of the People's Republic of China on Regional National Autonomy is the basic law for the implementation of the system of regional national autonomy prescribed in the Constitution." Article 1 provides that "The Law of the People's Republic of China on Regional National Autonomy is formulated in accordance with the Constitution of the People's Republic of China." The *Law on Regional National Autonomy,* as the basic law for the implementation of the system of regional national autonomy prescribed in the *Constitution,* standardizes the relationship between the central government and national autonomous areas as well as the relationship between various nationalities in national autonomous areas. Its legal effectiveness is not confined to national autonomous areas, but has a nationwide binding effect. Moreover, the legislation of national autonomous areas based on the *Constitution* and the *Law on Regional National Autonomy* not only embodies the basic principles and spirit of the *Constitution,* but also further reifies the relevant provisions in the *Constitution* and the *Law on Regional National Autonomy.*

According to the provisions of the *Constitution* and the relevant laws, the autonomous areas have more autonomous legislative power. Article 116 of the *Constitution* stipulates that "The people's congresses of national autonomous areas have the power to enact regulations on the exercise of autonomy and other separate regulations in light of the political, economic and cultural characteristics of the nationality or nationalities in the areas concerned." The *Law on Regional National Autonomy* also has the same provision in Article 19. As stated in Article 20: "If a resolution, decision, order or instruction of a state organ at a higher level does not suit the conditions in a national autonomous area, the organ of self-government of the area may either implement it with certain alterations or cease implementing it after reporting to and receiving the approval of the state organ at a higher level." It is also stated in Article 33 that "In accordance with the principles set by the state and in the light of local conditions, the organs of self-government of national autonomous areas may work out supplementary provisions and concrete procedures with regard to the standards of expenditure, the sizes of the staff and the quotas of work for their respective areas." In addition, the *Law on Legislation* further provides that "Where certain provisions of the laws and administrative regulations are concerned, adaptation on the basis of the characteristics of the local nationality (nationalities) may be made in autonomous regulations and separate regulations...Where in autonomous regulations or separate regulations provisions are formulated in accordance with law to make adaptations with regard to certain provisions of laws, administrative regulations or local regulations, the provisions of the autonomous regulations or separate regulations shall apply in the autonomous areas concerned."

From the above information, the legislative power of national autonomous areas features the following four aspects:

(1) The power of the formulation of autonomous regulation

The social relations that autonomous regulation adjusts are of overall importance, and there can be only one autonomous regulation in each national autonomous area. The first autonomous regulation of national autonomous area in China is the "Autonomous Regulation of Yanbian Korean Autonomous Prefecture" enacted by Yanbian Korean Autonomous Prefecture, Jilin Province, in 1985. Nevertheless, there are still 22 national autonomous areas not having promulgated and implemented their autonomous regulations as yet, especially in the five major autonomous regions in China.

(2) The power of the formulation of separate regulations

Separate regulation refers to the autonomous norm with regard to a particular or local problem or specific matters formulated by national autonomous areas in accordance with the law, covering a wide range of content. Among the legislations of national autonomous areas, separate regulations account for the largest proportion.

(3) The power of the formulation of adaptive regulations

In China's current laws, there are 13 laws including the *Criminal Law* having made specific or similar provisions concerning authorization. According to the provisions of Paragraph 1 of Article 66 of the *Law on Legislation*, the range of adaptations in the legislation of national autonomous areas can be summarized as follows: First, the law clearly provides that the adaptations can be made by the national autonomous areas; second, although the law does not provide that the adaptations can be made by the national autonomous areas, the adaptations are really necessary in light of the characteristics of the local nationalities and practical situations in the locality concerned. A comprehensive survey of the adapted regulations in national autonomous areas shows that there are a relatively large number of adaptive regulations of the *Civil Law*, the largest quantity of adaptive regulations of the *Marriage Law*, quite a few adaptive regulations of the *Electoral Law*, and a relatively small number of adaptive regulations of the *Criminal Law*.[24]

(4) The power of the formulation of supplementary regulations

At present, there are not many supplementary regulations formulated by the national autonomous areas and the contents are mainly focused on the aspects such as marriage, election, inheritance, education, family planning, and land management of which most are supplementary regulations for the *Marriage Law*. According to the statistics, by the end of 2008, the national autonomous areas had formulated 637 autonomous regulations and separate regulations, as well as adaptive or supplementary regulations to relevant laws.[25]

The legislation of national autonomous areas is an important component of the legislative system of China. Therefore, the legislation of national autonomous areas should stay consistent with the *Constitution*, considering it as the highest norm, and maintain the supreme authority of the *Constitution*, which is required not only by the supremacy of the *Constitution*, but also by the standard of the Socialist legal system. The maintaining of the supreme authority of the *Constitution* in autonomous areas is manifested in the following three aspects:

Its supreme authority is reflected in the source of the legislative power of national autonomous areas. In China's legislative system, legislation of national autonomous areas is one of the local legislations, and the local legislative power is granted by the *Constitution* and law, thus its scope should be subject to the provisions of the *Constitution* and law and in a subordinate position. However, in the system of local legislative power, the legislative power of national autonomous areas has different characteristics. As for the limits to the ordinary local legislative power, the *Law on Legislation* proposes conditions in the form of enumeration; while for the limits to the legislative power of national autonomous areas, the *Law on Legislation* only defines in its Article 66 in a restrictive manner: "Where certain provisions of the laws and administrative regulations are concerned, adaptation on the basis of the characteristics of the local nationality (nationalities) may be made in autonomous regulations and separate regulations, but such adaptation may not contradict the basic principles of the laws and administrative regulations; where the provisions of the *Constitution* and the *Law on Regional National Autonomy* as well as the provisions in other laws and administrative regulations specially formulated to govern the national autonomous areas are concerned, no adaptation may be made." So, the legislative power of national autonomous areas is of independence to a certain degree.

In addition, it is also reflected in the principles in the exercise of national autonomous areas' legislative power. The first is the principle of complying with the *Constitution*, that is, the *Constitution* has the highest effectiveness, and the legislation of national autonomous areas must abide by the *Constitution*, the *Law on Regional National Autonomy*, and the *Law on Legislation*. In addition, the adaptive and supplementary regulations shall be formulated upon the authorization of the *Constitution*, the *Law on Regional National Autonomy*, the *Law on Legislation*, and other laws, and must not conflict with the law. The second is the principle of considering the practical situation in national autonomous areas, that is, the actual conditions in national autonomous areas should be taken into account, and the political, economic, and cultural characteristics in the autonomous areas should be based on. The third is the principle of consistency, the legislative effectiveness of autonomous areas is unitary, indicating that it can only be valid in the autonomous areas concerned and must not contravene the *Constitution* and other authorized laws.

Last but not least, it is reflected in the legislative procedures in the autonomous areas. In addition to the general local legislative procedures such as drafting, enactment, consideration, adoption, revision, and repeal, the legislation of national autonomous areas should be implemented with specific procedures of filing and approval, which is clearly provided for in Article 116 of the *Constitution*, Article 66 and Paragraph 3 of Article 89 of the *Law on Legislation*. The legislation of national autonomous areas must be implemented along with the procedure of submitting for approval, that is, the autonomous regulations are still not effective after being adopted by the legislative organ in the national autonomous areas, and they shall be submitted to the legislative organs in authority at the next higher level for approval before being effective.

The Constitution and military legislation

China's current *Constitution* prescribes in the Preamble that all the armed forces must take the *Constitution* as the basic standard of conduct, and they have the duty to uphold the dignity of the Constitution and ensure its implementation. A whole section is specially drafted to stipulate the composition and responsibilities of the Central Military Commission, which reflects the *Constitution*'s supreme authority upon military organs and military acts. The provision of "directing the armed forces according to law" was for the first time written into the *Law on National*

Defense promulgated by the National People's Congress in 1997. The 16th National Congress of the CPC held in November 2002 clarified that it was necessary "to improve the system of military rules and regulations so as to raise the level of directing the armed forces according to law." The principle of "directing the armed forces according to law" is the specific embodiment of the concept of "governing the country according to law" in the fields of national defense and army building. Governing the country according to law should mean to first of all govern the country according to the *Constitution*, thus meaning to direct the armed forces according to law must mean to direct the armed forces according to the *Constitution*. The military legislative act must abide by the *Constitution*, maintain its dignity, and take it as the fundamental principle, so as to develop the specific military legal system within the constitutional framework.

The *Law on Legislation* adopted and implemented in 2000 made clear provisions with regard to the procedures of formulating military legislation, rank of effectiveness, scope of application, and other major issues in Article 93, which provided the legal basis for facilitating military legislation. In fact, the provisions in the *Law of Legislation* have experienced substantial changes. In the *Law on Legislation* (Draft), the provision concerning military legislation was originally in Paragraph 3 of Article 2 and it stated: "The enactment, amendment and nullification of military regulations shall be prescribed by the Central Military Commission." Later, on the suggestion of some deputies and the Bureau of Legislative Affairs of the Central Military Commission, the Law Committee of the 9th National People's Congress proposed to move this content into the Supplementary Provisions as Article 93 and it was revised into four paragraphs: "The Central Military Commission shall, in accordance with the Constitution and laws, formulate military regulations...The General Departments, the various services and arms and the military commands of the Central Military Commission may, in accordance with the laws and the military regulations, decisions and orders of the Commission, formulate military rules within the limits of their power...Military regulations and military rules shall be implemented within the armed forces...Measures for formulating, revising and nullifying military regulations and military rules shall be formulated by the Central Military Commission in accordance with the principles laid down in this Law."[26] The guiding position of the *Constitution* and laws in the military legislation is highlighted in the revision of the *Law on Legislation*, and military regulations are enacted on the basis of the *Constitution* and laws, with the *Constitution* as the primary basis. The military rules must be enacted based on a clear limit of authority and shall not exceed the authority of laws.

In fact, before the adoption of the *Law of Legislation*, China's military legislative practice had already begun. On May 31, 1984, the 2nd Session of the 6th National People's Congress passed the *Military Service Law*, which was the first military law after the promulgation and implementation of the current *Constitution*. Since then, a series of military laws such as the *Law on Officers in Active Service*, the *Law on the Protection of Military Installations*, the *Civil Air Defense Law*, the *Law on National Defense*, the *Law on Garrisoning Hong Kong Special Administrative Region*, the *Law on Garrisoning the Macao Special Administrative Region*, the *National Defense Education Law*, have been promulgated and implemented, basically constructing the legal system of China's military legislation. According to the catalog issued by the Ministry of National Defense of the People's Republic of China, up to now, there have been 18 military laws currently in effect (see Table 2.4), among which, except six laws without their legislative basis clearly stated in their General Provisions or in the first articles, all the other laws make clear that their legislative bases are the *Constitution* or laws enacted based on the *Constitution*. This shows that military laws are the specific provisions of the military clauses in the *Constitution*, as well as the legalization and reification of the *Constitution* in national defense and military fields, which embodies the principle of the supremacy of the *Constitution* and reflects the universal validity of the *Constitution* as well as its highest effectiveness in the military field.

Table 2.4 The 18 sets of military laws currently in effect (up to March 3, 2010)

Law	Legislative organ	Legislative basis	Time of publication and implementation
Military Service Law of the People's Republic of China	The 2nd Session of the 6th NPC	The Constitution	Published on May 31, 1984 and implemented on October 1, 1984
Regulations on the Military Banks of Officers of the Chinese People's Liberation Army	Passed at the 2nd Session of the Standing Committee of the 7th NPC, and amended at the 7th Session of the Standing Committee of the 8th NPC	The Constitution and the Military Service Law	Published and implemented on July 1, 1988, amended and implemented on May 12, 1994
Law of the People's Republic of China on Officers in Active Service	The 3rd Session of the Standing Committee of the 7th NPC	—	Published on September 5, 1988 and implemented on January 1, 1989

(Cont'd)

Law	Legislative organ	Legislative basis	Time of publication and implementation
Law of the People's Republic of China on Guarding State Secrets	The 3rd Session of the Standing Committee of the 7th NPC, and amended at the Standing Committee of the 7th NPC	——	Published on September 5, 1988 and implemented on May 1, 1989
Law of the People's Republic of China on the Protection of Military Installations	The 12th Session of the Standing Committee of the 7th NPC	The Constitution	Published on February 23, 1990 and implemented on August 1, 1990
Law of the People's Republic of China on the Territorial Sea and the Contiguous Zone	The 24th Session of the Standing Committee of the 7th NPC	——	Published and implemented on February 25, 1992
Reserve Officers Law of the People's Republic of China	The 13th Session of the Standing Committee of the 8th NPC	The Constitution and the Military Service Law	Published on May 10, 1995 and implemented on January 1, 1996
Martial Law of the People's Republic of China	The 18th Session of the Standing Committee of the 8th NPC	The Constitution	Published and implemented on March 1, 1996
Civil Air Defense Law of the People's Republic of China	The 22nd Session of the Standing Committee of the 8th NPC	——	Published on October 29, 1996 and implemented on January 1, 1997
Law of the People's Republic of China on National Defense	The 5th Session of the 8th NPC	The Constitution	Published and implemented on March 14, 1997
Law of the People's Republic of China on Garrisoning the Hong Kong Special Administrative Region	The 23rd Session of the Standing Committee of the 8th NPC	The Constitution and the Basic Law of the Hong Kong Special Administrative Region	Published on December 30, 1996 and implemented on July 1, 1997
Law of the People's Republic of China on Garrisoning the Macao Special Administrative Region	The 10th Session of the Standing Committee of the 9th NPC	The Constitution and the Basic Law of the Macao Special Administrative Region	Published on June 28, 1999 and implemented on December 20, 1999

(Cont'd)

Law	Legislative organ	Legislative basis	Time of publication and implementation
National Defense Education Law of the People's Republic of China	The 21st Session of the Standing Committee of the 9th NPC	The Law on National Defense and the Education Law	Promulgated and implemented on April 28, 2001
Decision of the Standing Committee of the National People's Congress on Setting up the National Defense Education Day of the Whole People	The 23rd Session of the Standing Committee of the 9th NPC	The Law on National Defense Education	Promulgated and implemented on August 31, 2001
Anti-Secession Law	The 3rd Session of the 10th NPC	The Constitution	Promulgated and implemented on March 14, 2005
Law of the People's Republic of China on the People's Armed Police Force	The 10th Session of the Standing Committee of the 11th NPC	—	Promulgated and implemented on August 27, 2009
Island Protection Law of the People's Republic of China	The 12th Session of the Standing Committee of the 11th NPC	—	Promulgated on December 26, 2009 and implemented on March 1, 2010
National Defense Mobilization Law of the People's Republic of China	The 13th Session of the Standing Committee of the 11th NPC	The Constitution	Promulgated on February 26, 2010 and implemented on July 1, 2010

Source: Website of the Ministry of National Defense of the People's Republic of China, March 3, 2010, http://www.mod.gov.cn/policy/jsfl.htm.

In addition to military laws, military legislation also includes a large number of military regulations and rules. Before the publication of the *Law on Legislation* in 2000, the Central Military Commission had promulgated and implemented the *Provisional Regulations on the Legislative Procedure of Chinese People's Liberation Army* in 1990 and promulgated the *Rules of the Filing of Military Regulations and Military Administrative Rules* in 1993, providing the regulatory basis and institutional guarantee for a scientific and procedurally valid military legislation. After the enforcement of the *Law on Legislation* in 2000, further specification was needed for the legislative subjects, limits of power, and other aspects of military regulations and rules. Under such circumstances, in 2003, the Central Military Commission made amendments to the *Provisional Regulations on the Legislative Procedure of Chinese People's Liberation Army* and promulgated the *Rules of Military Regulations and Military Rules*, further specifying the subjects, limits of power, procedure of military legislation and making much detailed division of the power that the military regulations shall be formulated by the Central Military Commission and the military rules shall be formulated by the general departments, the various services and arms and the military commands. It is clearly stated in Article 1 of the rule that its legislative basis is the "relevant stipulations in the Constitution, the Law on Legislation and the Law on National Defense." Article 4 provides that "the enactment, amendment and repeal of military regulations and military rules shall be on the basis of the Constitution and laws, abide by the legislative principles prescribed in the Legislation Law, satisfy the requirements of statutory limits of power, procedure and regulation of legislative style, and safeguard the unity and dignity of the socialist legal system."

In the white paper on China's National Defense in 2006, it was pointed out that, during the period of the 10th Five-Year Plan, the Standing Committee of the NPC, the State Council and the CMC, exercising their prescribed functions and powers, formulated and revised 99 military laws and regulations. The general departments, military commands, and various services and arms formulated and revised nearly 900 sets of military rules. According to the statistics provided by the Legal Affairs Bureau of the Central Military Commission, by March 2008, the State Council and the Central Military Commission jointly formulated 94 sets of military administrative regulations, the Central Military Commission formulated 215 sets of military regulations, and the general departments, the various services and arms, the military commands and people's armed police force formulated more than 3,000 military rules, which cover almost all fields and aspects of national defense and army building, providing a legal guarantee for strictly directing the armed forces according to law.[27] China has basically realized the goal of establishing laws and regulations on the major parts of the national defense and army building, forming the multilevel system, guided by the military provisions of the *Constitution* and headed by the *Law on National Defense*, ranging from military laws, military regulations and military administrative regulations, military rules and military administrative rules to local military regulations and rules, and preliminarily established the legal system of military laws with Chinese characteristics.

The Constitution and organic legislation

Organic law refers to the law that specially stipulates the principles of the organization and the operation of certain types of state organs. In the broad sense, organic law includes those laws on organs and on officials; while organic law in the narrow sense does not include those on officials. According to this classification, laws on the management of personnel in the organizations such as the *Civil Servant Law*, the *Judges Law*, and the *Public Procurators Law* fall into the scope of organic law in the broad sense. The *Constitution* is closely related to organic law: On the one hand, the *Constitution* is the basis of organic law. The *Constitution* is the legislative basis of organic law, which is fully manifested in Chapter 3 "The Structure of the State" of the *Constitution*. The spirit of the *Constitution* is the guidance for the value of the organic legislation, and principles such as popular sovereignty, democratic centralism, and the rule of law provided for in the *Constitution*, which are directly and clearly reflected in organic law. On the other hand, organic law is the reification and institutionalization of the principles in the *Constitution*. Without the well-established content and rational structure of organ law, the *Constitution* will become less effective due to the lack of guidelines for its enforcement. In both China and other countries, the constitutional stipulations on state organs are principled and macro, while various organ laws are needed for carrying out the specific establishment of institutions and mode of operation, thereupon the development of organic laws can contribute to the implementation of the *Constitution*. If the subjects regulated by the *Constitution* are regarded as the state as a whole, then the subjects regulated by organic laws are some specific parts of the state.

In accordance with the provisions of the *Constitution*, the system of organic law in China can be divided into two major categories. The first is the organic laws on state organs, including organs of state power, administrative organs, judicial organs, and procuratorial organs, such as the *Organic Law of the National People's Congress*, the *Organic Law of the State Council*, the *Organic Law of the People's Courts*, the *Organic Law of the People's Procuratorates*, the *Organic Law of the Local People's Congresses and Local People's Governments* as well as the Basic Laws of the two special administrative regions. The second is the organic laws on organs of self-government, including two types, namely regional national autonomy and self-government of people at the grassroots level. The legal expression of the former is the *Law on Regional National Autonomy*, and that of the latter are the *Organic Law of the Urban Residents Committees* and the *Organic Law of the Urban Residents Committees*.

Organic law is the legal source of the legitimacy of the daily activities of state organs. In 1954, after the promulgation of the first *Constitution* of New China, some laws were immediately deliberated and passed at the 1st Session of the 1st National People's Congress, including the *Organic Law of the National People's Congress*, the *Organic Law of the State Council*, the *Organic Law of the People's Courts*, the *Organic Law of the People's Procuratorates*, the *Organic Law of the Local People's Congresses and Local People's Governments*, which are the institutional basis for the operation of state organs during the early years of New China. However, during the Cultural Revolution, the order of the work of state organs was seriously damaged. Their functions were even replaced by some organs without any legal basis, and the system of organic law came to a standstill. After the Cultural Revolution, on July 1, 1979, the 2nd Session of the 5th National People's Congress made amendments to the Constitution, among which contents concerning the system of organic law mainly included: Local people's congresses at and above the county level establish standing committees; local revolutionary committees at various levels are changed into local people's governments at various levels; deputies to people's congress at the county level are elected directly by constituencies; the superior-subordinate relationship in the people's procuratorates is changed from supervision into leadership. According to the amended Constitution, this Session re-adopted the *Organic Law of the Local People's Congresses and Local People's Governments*, the *Organic Law of the People's Courts*, and the *Organic Law of the People's Procuratorates*, so as to provide the constitutional and legal guarantee for the political stability, economic development, and social progress.

The development of organic laws reflects the development and improvement of China's democratic political system. On November 14, 1984, the 8th Session of the Standing Committee of the 6th NPC passed the *Decision on the Establishment of Maritime Courts in Coastal Port Cities*, supplementing and perfecting the organic system of the courts. On April 4, 1989, the 2nd Session of the 7th NPC passed the Rules of Procedure for the National People's Congress, offering a more detailed and specific legal basis to the operation of the NPC's daily work. The *Rules of Procedure of the Standing Committee of the National People's Congress* passed in 1987 and amended in 2009 further regulates the procedure of the Standing Committee and improves its efficiency. The *Law on the Supervision of Standing Committees of People's Congresses at Various Levels* implemented on January 1, 2007 specifies the procedure of the exercise of the power of supervision by the standing committees of people's congresses at various levels, further improving the system of the people's congresses. Organic laws are related to the degree of the development of democracy, and they are the concrete and step-by-step implementation of the constitutional provisions. For example, Article 111 of the current *Constitution* provides that "the resident committees and villager committees established among urban and rural residents on the basis of their place of residence are mass organizations of self-management at the grassroots level." However, after a long period of deliberation and preparation, the *Organic Law of the Urban Residents Committees* was not promulgated and enforced until 1989. The *Organic Law of the Villagers Committees* has been implemented on a trial basis since June 1, 1988, but until 1998 it was promulgated and enforced as a formal law after 10 years of exploration and practice.

The Constitution and electoral legislation

The electoral system is an important political system provided for in the *Constitution*. The current *Constitution* stipulates that the state organs of the People's Republic of China follow the principle of democratic centralism, which is the guiding principle for electoral legislation. The electoral system prescribed in the *Constitution* is reflected in the following three aspects:

(1) The election of members of the People's Congresses

Article 3 of the *Constitution* provides that the National People's Congress and the local people's congresses at various levels are constituted through democratic elections. They are responsible to the people and subject to their supervision. According to Article 3, Article 34, Article 59, Article 60, Article 65, Article 76, Article 77, Article 97, Article 102, Article 103, and Article 113 of the *Constitution*, in the election of the people's congresses, the National People's Congress and the local people's congresses at various levels are elected, deputies to the people's congresses at various levels are elected, members of the standing committee of local people's congresses at various levels are elected, and deputies to the people's congresses are subject to supervision and recall by the units which elected them

(2) The election of state organs

Article 62 and Article 63 of the *Constitution* stipulate that the National People's Congress has the power to elect and remove from office the President, Vice-President of the People's Republic of China, the Chairman of the Central Military Commission, the President of the Supreme People's Court and the Procurator-General of the Supreme People's Procuratorate. Article 101 prescribes the situation in which local people's congresses elect state organs at their respective levels

(3) The election of autonomous organizations

According to Article 111, the residents committees and villagers committees are elected by the residents.

The election of members of people's congresses is the most important aspect of the electoral system, as well as an important milestone in the development of the system of people's congresses in China. On the basis of the *Decision of the Council of the Central People's Government on the Convening of the National People's Congress and Local People's Congresses* adopted at the 20th Meeting of the Commission of the Central Government on January 13, 1953, China promulgated the *Electoral Law of the National People's Congress and Local People's Congresses at Various Levels of the People's Republic of China* on March 1, 1953, providing the basic legal foundation and institutional guarantee for the convening of the 1st National People's Congress in 1954 and offering organizational preparation to the promulgation of the 1954 *Constitution*. This electoral law stipulates that the NPC and local people's congresses at various levels are constituted through popular elections; prescribes the electoral procedures, electoral modes, and affairs of election among minority nationalities in various regions; establishes the system of democratic election in China; and reflects the developmental progression of the institutionalization of China's democratic politics. Undoubtedly, there are also some shortcomings in this law. For example, subjects' right to vote are limited, that is, on the basis that the popular election is provided, it excludes those people including landlords whose class property has not been changed, counter-revolutionaries deprived of political rights according to law, other persons deprived of political rights according to law and persons mentally ill from enjoying the right to vote and to be elected. In this regard, Deng Xiaoping pointed out that, "the nature of electoral law is the emphasis on actual democracy...those specific issues related to elections will be left to be resolved when provincial and municipal people's governments formulate detailed regulations on the implementation of elections so that different specific situations can be taken into consideration...this is the practical and feasible way to fully guarantee the people's democratic rights in the current environment."[28]

On July 1, 1979, the *Electoral Law of the National People's Congress and Local People's Congresses at Various Levels of the People's Republic of China* was passed at the 2nd Session of the 5th National People's Congress. This was the second electoral law in China which is also still currently effective. Compared with the *Electoral Law* of 1953, substantial amendments have been made to this law, which are mainly reflected in the following circumstances:

- The range of subjects of the right of election is expanded and others abolished.
- The limitation of the right of election of landlords and counter-revolutionaries deprived of political rights is abolished, stipulating that persons without the right of election are only confined to criminal offenders deprived of political rights.
- The scope of direct elections is expanded, from people's congresses at the grassroots level to people's congresses at the national level.
- The mode of voting is changed, from a secret ballot and a show of hands in grassroots elections to secret ballots exclusively.
- Non-competitive election is changed into competitive election, and the degree of the difference is prescribed.

- The number of deputies to local people's congresses at various levels is decided by provincial standing committees of people's congresses instead of fixed provision to independent decision.
- The electoral districts were divided according to residential area while they are now currently divided according to production unit, public institution, work unit, and residential areas area.
- The procedures of nominating candidates for deputies is further improved, prescribing that each minority shall have deputies to participate in the National People's Congress and candidates can be pre-selected. All political parties and people's organizations and constituents can make full use of various forms to promote their own candidates for deputies.
- The conditions of success in the elections of deputies are improved, changing from success in the elections of deputies on condition that the candidate gets more than half of the vote from constituents who are present to success in the elections of deputies on condition that the candidate gets more than half of the vote from all constituents in the electoral district or all representatives of the institution holding the election.

In China's electoral system, the equality of the right to vote is of the greatest concern, which is mainly reflected in the issue of "equal number for equal representation" of rural and urban areas. The *Electoral Law* of 1953 and that of 1979 stipulate that, the population that each rural deputy represents is eight times as much as the population represented by each urban deputy in the election of NPC deputies, namely 8:1, while the ratio of the population that a rural deputy represents to the population that an urban deputy represents in the election of deputies of people's congresses at the level of provinces and autonomous regions and that at the level of autonomous prefectures, counties, and autonomous counties are 5:1 and 4:1 respectively. In other words, in the election of NPC deputies, each rural constituent enjoys one-eighth of the right to vote of their urban counterpart; and in the election of deputies of people's congresses at the provincial and country levels, each rural constituent enjoys respectively one-fifth and one-fourth of the right to vote of their urban counterpart.

After several amendments, the *Electoral Law* of 1979 gradually narrows the ratio of the population represented by each rural deputy to that represented by each urban deputy. In the *Amendment* of 1982, the number of deputies to the people's congress at the county level is changed from 4:1 to the range of 4:1 to 1:1. The *Amendment* of 1986 maintains the ratio prescribed in the *Amendment* of 1982. In the *Amendment* of 1995, the ratios of the people's congresses at the provincial and national levels are changed from 5:1 and 8:1 to both 4:1, the ratio of the people's congress at the county level is maintained as 4:1 unchanged. The *Amendment* of 2004 maintains the ratio prescribed in the *Amendment* in 1995.

In accordance with Article 33 and Article 34 of the *Constitution*, all citizens of the People's Republic of China are equal before the law, have the right to vote, and stand for election except persons deprived of political rights according to law. Equal enjoyment of the right to vote and stand for election is the constitutional right of Chinese citizens; and the amendment of the *Electoral Law* shall conform to this constitutional requirement. As shown by the amendments of the *Electoral Law* of 1979, reducing the ratio of urban deputies to rural deputies and achieving full equality in respect of the right to vote are the orientation of the amendment of the *Electoral Law*. On December 23, 2009, at the 12th Session of the Standing Committee of the 11th National People's Congress, the *Amendment to the Electoral Law* (Draft) was deliberated for the second time. In this *Draft*, the stipulation that the populations represented by urban and rural deputies of people's congresses are different is abolished, achieving the development from "one deputy for one vote" to "one vote for one representation," which was a landmark in the development of the electoral system in China. The *Draft* also stipulates that "The deputies shall be broadly representative, and there should be an appropriate number of grassroots deputies...secret ballot booths shall be set up for election," which fully reflects the progress of the democratic system in China. The amendments to the *Electoral Law* realize the constitutional principle that "all citizens are equal before the law" and represent the achievement of the equality of individuals, areas, and nationalities in law.

Regarding the election of members of people's congresses, the currently effective legal documents also include the *Measures for Election of Deputies from the Chinese People's Liberation Army to the National People's Congress and Local People's Congresses at or above the County Level* enacted in 1981, the *Provisions of the Standing Committee of the National People's Congress for the Direct Election of Deputies to People's Congress at or Below the County Level* enacted in 1983, the *Law on Deputies to the National People's Congress and Deputies to Local People's Congresses* enacted in 1992, as well as specific regulations concerning the election of NPC deputies in the Hong Kong Special Administrative Region and the Macao Special Administrative Region made by the NPC. As for the election of organizations of self-government, the *Organic Law of the Urban Residents Committees* enacted in 1989 and the *Organic Law of the Villagers Committees* enacted in 1998 both have made relevant provisions. In the future, the enactment of the law on self-government for villagers and the law on self-government for urban residents is the basic orientation of further improving the electoral system and developing organizations of self-government at the grassroots level.

Prospect of the *Constitution* in the Construction and Development of the Legal System

In the construction and development of the legal system in China, the *Constitution* is significant and it is the foundation of the country's legal system. In the foreign countries, their constitutions also play a very important role of value guidance in the construction and development of their legal systems. Therefore, in the East and West, strengthening the *Constitution*'s core role of value guidance in the construction and development of the legal system would continue to be the top priority

Fundamental role of the *Constitution* in the construction and development of the legal system in China

In China's legal system, the *Constitution* is the highest law with the supreme legal authority. Therefore, strengthening the *Constitution*'s core role of value guidance in the construction of the legal system is the underlying trend of the development of China's legal system.

The strengthening of the Constitution as the legislative basis

In the construction of the legal system in China, it is important to strengthen the *Constitution*'s role as the legislative basis, ensuring that the exercise of legislative power is fully under the constraints of the *Constitution*. The reason why the *Constitution*'s strict control over legislative power is emphasized lies in the controlling nature of the *Constitution*. As far as the nature of the *Constitution* is concerned, it must be emphasized that the nature of the *Constitution* is a concept of control. Therefore, provisions of the *Constitution* as well as the subjects that the *Constitution* regulates should also be elucidated closely in light of the nature of the *Constitution* rather than deviating from the nature of the Constitution which may lead to the loss of the *Constitution*'s effectiveness. Thus, modern constitutionalism is mainly about "ensuring that everyone in society can live in a social condition that is consistent with his human dignity and human rights. Moreover, since history has proven that the abuse of political power is a common cause of the violation of human rights, constitutionalism advocates setting limits or constraints on political power. Constitutionalism is not anarchism, for it recognizes the legitimacy of national, governmental, and political power, thus the *Constitution* first of all grants power to the government, and then restricts this power and regulates the exercise of it."[29] In terms of form, the *Constitution* is just a book. Moreover, for those countries of non-constitutionalism, the *Constitution* is just an unessential paper; while for countries of constitutionalism, the *Constitution* is definitely not just a piece of paper, it represents profound values, under the guidance of which the *Constitution* is the criterion of conduct as well as the foundation of legitimacy of the exercise of state power. Any power can only be exercised with its value origin identified in the *Constitution*; otherwise, it is unconstitutional. According to the concept of constitutionalism, any unconstitutional exercise of power will be inevitably null and void. In constitutionalists' view, human beings are evil in nature and everyone has a potential tendency to abuse power, government officials are no exception. Therefore, in order to correct and avoid political abuses, a legal text at a higher level is needed to limit their power, and this legal text is exactly the *Constitution*. Under the protection of the *Constitution*, people will no longer be afraid of the arbitrariness and brutality of state organs; even if there are unconstitutional acts and violations of rights, specialized organs that safeguard the *Constitution* will give timely relief to those whose rights are infringed.

In the current society where social interests are diversified, state legislation has become interest-oriented and localized. Thus, in order to prevent state legislation from becoming an "experimental field of interests" of some state departments, it is necessary to make legislation more democratic and scientific, and the most fundamental way is to strengthen the *Constitution*'s control over the legislation and intensify the *Constitution*'s role as the basis of state legislation.

The strengthening of the normative and leading role of the Constitution

As the fundamental law of China, the *Constitution* plays a critical leading role in stipulating the form and content of national laws. All legislations in China have to take the *Constitution* as a normative basis and comply with it in respect of the legislations on both civil and public aspects. In terms of form, the theory that "the *Constitution* is the fundamental law" is derived from the classification of law between "fundamental law and ordinary law." Among various classifications of law, the division into fundamental law and ordinary law is a very common one. The so-called division of the law into fundamental law and ordinary law means to classify laws in accordance with their different statuses, effectiveness, content, enacting subjects, and procedures. Generally speaking, such kind of classification is only applicable in countries with written constitutions. In these countries, their fundamental law is the constitution that enjoys the supreme legal status and legal effectiveness. The constitution's content, enacting subject, enacting procedure, and amending procedure are all different from that of ordinary law and have higher and stricter procedural requirements; while the ordinary law refers to the laws except for the constitution. Its legal status and legal authority is lower than that of the constitution, its enacting subject and enacting procedure differs from that of the *Constitution*, and its content generally involves the adjustment of a certain type of social relations, such as civil law, criminal law, commercial law, procedural law, administrative law, etc.[30] Therefore, through the classification of the law, the entire legal system is divided into two categories: fundamental law and ordinary law. Since the requirements of the fundamental law are relatively high, the constitution is usually the only legislation in line with the standard of fundamental law in a country's legal system. Thus, the constitution has become the representative of the fundamental law. This view brings a converse result that as soon as people mention the *Constitution*, its property of fundamental law immediately comes to mind. Then, the view that "the constitution is the fundamental law" and the view that "the fundamental law is the constitution" influence each other and eventually become a conventional or self-evident legal phenomenon rooted in people's legal consciousness.

As a legal form, constitution is generally a generic term for the legislations that have the legal status of fundamental law in a country's legal system, with the constitutional origin as its external form and constitutional stipulations as its substance. In this sense, its connotation mainly refers to the fundamental law corresponding to the ordinary law.[31] From the perspective of constitutional stipulations, the Constitution's fundamental nature stems from the fundamental nature of constitutional stipulations. The fundamental nature of constitutional stipulations is mainly reflected in the following aspects:

- Fundamental nature is the inherent nature of constitutional stipulations, and its external manifestation is the supremacy of constitutional stipulations, namely, the supreme legal effectiveness of constitutional stipulations.
- The fundamental nature of constitutional stipulations lies in the fact that what constitutional stipulations regulate are the basic system and basic principles for all aspects of state affairs. They are the ultimate foundation and origin of various state affairs and specific systems and possess the nature of fundamental creativity.[32]

The constitution provides for the most fundamental issues of a country's social relations in a very wide range and is fundamental, macroscopic, and comprehensive in respect of its content in comparison with the law. In general, the constitution provides for the state nature, social systems, economic systems, cultural systems, structural form of state political power, citizens' basic rights and obligations, organizational and action principles of state construction, and the national symbols of a country.[33] The ordinary law only stipulates specific information which is directly related to this law, for example, civil law only lays down regulations on civil relations between subjects with equal status, and administrative law only stipulates information about the exercise of administrative power. The content of these ordinary laws is significantly different from that of the constitution, and this kind of difference in content is the fundamental key to distinguish the constitution from other ordinary laws. As for the reason why the constitution is titled the fundamental law, the primary basis lies in the fundamental nature of the content it stipulates — fundamental system and fundamental tasks of the state. Accordingly, "it becomes the legislative basis for other laws, becomes law of the law, and obtains the status as the state fundamental law."[34]

The strengthening of the Constitution's role of value guidance

As a regulatory pattern, the law reflects its inherent values just like other regulations do. The inherent values of the *Constitution* are restricting powers and protecting human rights. Since the *Constitution* is the legislative basis and dominant regulating force of the legal system, ordinary laws should also reflect the values of restricting power and protecting human rights. In a sense, the values of restricting power and protecting human rights should be the only value pursuit of the entire legal system. It is only in this way that we can ensure the goodness of ordinary legislation and guarantee the legitimacy of the construction of the rule of law. According to constitutionalism, the *Constitution* is used to protect human rights, which is a consensus in the academic circle. Classic statements such as "the *Constitution* is the Bible for protecting human rights" and "the *Constitution* is a piece of paper filled with human rights" have been widely accepted. The constitution's protection of human rights is mainly reflected in its provisions on fundamental rights, which are the key to distinguish the *Constitution* from other ordinary laws in terms of the guarantee of human rights. In accordance with the basic concept of modern constitutions, the *Constitution* is the guarantee of human rights and civil rights as well as the general rule for the protection of human rights. Human rights are the ultimate value target of the *Constitution* and the profound legitimacy foundation and the ultimate value pursuit of modern political rule as well. The history of constitution and the system of protection of human rights indicates that the *Constitution* and human rights are complementary to each other. One of the important tasks of constitutional culture and the construction of the constitutional system is to establish the values of modern human rights, to rebuild the humanistic spirit of the *Constitution*, and to improve the *Constitution*'s mechanism of protecting human rights and restricting state power, so as to achieve the ultimate objective of building a constitutional government country.[35] Consequently, the protection of human rights has become an important criterion for judging whether a country has a constitution and whether it is a constitutional government country. In respect of values, the term constitution is inseparable from the fundamental principles of traditional constitutionalism such as protection of human rights.

In constitutional practice, the constitutional protection is mainly embodied in the constitutional supervision or the constitutional review system. In China, an important part of the constitutional review is to inspect the constitutionality of ordinary legislation as the reification of the *Constitution*, namely the goodness of the law. Only if a law embodies the concept of restraint on power and protection of rights, can it have constitutionality. Otherwise, if a law is aimed at depriving and restricting citizens' rights, then even though this law is passed by the state legislature through proper legislative procedures, it will become invalid on account of its violation of the *Constitution*. Therefore, to enable the *Constitution* to fully play its role of fundamental law in the construction of the rule of law and achieve its goal of protection of rights and restraint on power, it is essential to strengthen the *Constitution*'s role of value guidance in the legal system.

Underlying trend of the role of the *Constitution* in the construction and development of legal system

To guarantee its legitimacy and consistency, the legal system should be based on the constitution. With the development of the legal system, the constitutions of different countries are engaged in the following trends.

The strengthening of the fundamental role of the Constitution in the construction and development of legal system

Undoubtedly, a constitution plays an important fundamental role in the formation of state legal system in both countries implementing common law system characterized by case law or in countries implementing civil law system characterized by statute law. In the twenty-first century, with the shift from legislative power to administrative power as the core of the state power, administrative legislation also becomes an important part of the control of constitutional values. Both parliament legislation and legislation of administrative organs should be on the basis of the *Constitution* and uphold values defined by the *Constitution*, so as to represent and strengthen the fundamental role of the *Constitution* played in the construction of the legal system.

The strengthening of the Constitution's role in the scientification and systematization of legal system

State legislation is a systematic project in which relations between various branch laws should be made consistent so that the legal system can become an organic unity rather than conflicting with each other. Based on the *Constitution*, different isolated branch laws form an organic unity. In the construction of the legal system, constitutional values are the core of the entire legal system; those countries with a well-established rule of law all plan their state legislation with constitutional values as the core, making their legal systems a scientific, systematic unity with the consistency of constitutional values. In this sense, roles of the *Constitution* in the construction and development of the legal system are prominently represented by a coordinating role. The *Constitution* regulates the development of the legal system through the consistency of the *Constitution* so as to ensure the scientification and systematization of state legislation.

The importance of the constitutional review system in the construction and development of the legal system

From the experience of the development of the legal systems of countries around the world, the *Constitution* has to be regarded as the core set of values in the development of a legal system. Without the guidance of constitutional values, the legislation made by legislative organs is likely to become bad laws that violate human rights. Therefore, in the construction and development of the legal system, we must follow the guidance of constitutional values and put state legislation under the control of the *Constitution*.[36] The fundamental purpose of all kinds of constitutional review is to maintain the constitutionality of state legislation and ensure that the construction and development of the legal system do not violate the value system established by the *Constitution*.

The guiding role of the Constitution in guaranteeing the legitimacy and consistency of legal system

The constitutional value requires the law to take protection of human rights as its value goal. The pursuit of value in human rights provides the law with the foundation of legitimacy. This inherent pursuit of justice is not the product of legislators' deliberate pursuit, but the inevitable product of state legislation under the influence of constitutionalism. Enacting a constitution with the supreme legal authority other than ordinary laws aims to declare that it not only enjoys various fundamental rights, but also has the value function of controlling state power, especially legislative power. Then, in the exercise of legislative power, the *Constitution* would be the first value basis to be followed. Through the control of constitutional value, state legislation will have to be carried out in the value system promoted by the *Constitution*. Laws enacted by the legislature also have to be in line with the *Constitution*'s value pursuit, and through the control of the legitimacy of the state legislative power, the goodness of the state legal system's order will be realized.

Strengthening the *Constitution*'s Status as the Foundation in the Construction and Development of China's Legal System

In the future construction of a Socialist country under the rule of law in China, the *Constitution*'s status as the foundation of the legal system should not be weakened; instead it should be further strengthened. In future legislative activities, both public laws concerned with state power and private laws concerned with individual subjects with equal status need to be focused on strengthening the *Constitution*'s status as the foundation in the construction and development of the legal system.

A comprehensive understanding of relations between the *Constitution* and the law in legal system

China's legal system is established on the basis of ordinary laws with the *Constitution* as the core. A comprehensive understanding of relations between the *Constitution* and other ordinary laws is beneficial for us to properly grasp the logic and scientific nature of the legal system, and to guarantee the consistency of it, which is of important theoretical and practical significance.

Logical relations between the Constitution and the law

Regarding the relations between the *Constitution* and the law, the ontological meaning of the term "law" is one of the issues to be clarified. Only if the normative meaning of the term "law" is clearly defined, will it be possible to explore the logical relations between the law and the *Constitution*; otherwise, if the connotation and denotation of the term are not clearly defined, it is impossible to define and position the *Constitution*. Although "law" is a very common concept, yet, "much acquaintance does not mean great insight," in the jurisprudential study in China, the terms "rule" and "law" are usually not distinguished; and in the law, "law in the broad sense" and "law in the narrow sense" are also not differentiated consciously, all of which cause confusions in the use of the term "law" in the construction of China's legal system. To solve this issue, two questions need to be addressed: One is the relations between the *Constitution* and the law in respect of ontological meaning involved in the issue on the differentiation between rule and law, and the other is the relationship between the *Constitution* and the law in the respect of normative meaning involved in the issue on law in the broad sense and law in the narrow sense.

(1) Relations between the *Constitution* and the law in respect of ontological meaning

In terms of ontological meaning, there are two views on relations between rule and law in the jurisprudential circles. One is the monism of rule and law, supporting that rule is equal to law which is the sum of regulations formulated or recognized by the state and rely on coercive power of the state to guarantee their implementation, and there is no so-called natural law, civil law, common law and so on except for constitutional law. The other is the dualism of rule and law, holding that rule and law are two concepts at different levels, the rule is the prototype of the law and the law is a reflection of the law. Before the first law is enacted, rules exist in our social lives and guide our behaviors in a covert form, and rules at this time are generally represented by mental rules, playing their roles imperceptibly on the basis of people's common beliefs and consensus values. Based on these mental rules, rules are formulated or recognized by the organs of state power, turning into regulations with clear manifestation, and thus become laws. Therefore, rule and law are closely related with each other. The dualism of rule and law is more in line with the modern idea of rule of good law, which is regarded as common views in the jurisprudential circles.

When relations between the *Constitution* and the law are explored, logical relations between the *Constitution* and the law according to the dualism of rule and law should be first of all studied at the level of ontology. According to the dualism of rule and law, as a specific regulatory pattern, the *Constitution* should be subordinate to the law in terms of the category; in other words, the *Constitution* is included in the scope of the law, and the *Constitution* is only a regulatory branch or an important component of the law. Actually, the law in the context of the dualism of rule and law is the law in the broadest sense; all positive law or the sum of all normative documents can be included in the scope of the law, and thus the *Constitution* is of course an intrinsic component of the law.

(2) Relations between the *Constitution* and the law in terms of normative meaning

When examining the relations between the *Constitution* and the law in terms of norms, normative meaning of the law remains the top priority to be addressed. In terms of normative meaning, law has two implications: general law and special law. General law refers to all normative documents formulated by state organs which are entitled to draw up normative legal documents. In other words, general law is a series of normative documents formulated and promulgated by specified state organs according to specific procedures to be complied with. According to different state organs that enact laws, general law emerges in the following specific forms: laws enacted by the NPC, administrative regulations formulated by the State Council, rules formulated by the ministries and commissions of the State Council, local regulations, autonomous regulations and separate regulations formulated by local people's congresses, and rules of local governments formulated by local governments. The so-called special law is the kind of law in a strict sense, only referring to normative legal documents formulated by the National People's Congress and its Standing Committee. Therefore, special law refers to the regulations passed by the NPC and its Standing Committee. The National People's Congress holds a meeting annually, and the Standing Committee of the NPC generally holds a meeting every two months; one of their main tasks is legislation, and laws they enact belong to the scope of special law mentioned here.

After differentiating between general law and special law, there is a question which needs to be solved: Is the *Constitution* to be included in the scope of general law? It is generally reckoned that the *Constitution* falls into the scope of general law. According to the division of China's legal branches, the *Constitution* is an independent legal branch. Therefore, in terms of branch laws, the *Constitution* belongs to general law. Firstly, as a normative pattern, the *Constitution* possesses the common properties of the law, for example, it is universal, normative, and under constraint of material conditions. Secondly, in terms of legal authority, the *Constitution* also has the characteristics of ordinary laws. All normative documents have a common feature, namely they have binding force, which means they can regulate and guide people in the society, and people are subject to legal sanctions or punishments if they violate these norms. One has to bear legal responsibilities if he violates ordinary laws, and one has to take constitutional responsibilities if he violates the *Constitution* so these two are the same in principle. However, if the law is regarded as "general law," then the exploration of relations between the *Constitution* and the law will be meaningless, for in this situation, the *Constitution* in itself is an important component of the law, thus it is impossible to make a comparison without separating itself from the law. Therefore, the logical relations between the *Constitution* and the law mentioned here mainly refer to the relations between the *Constitution* and special law, namely the relations between the *Constitution* and the legislation of legislative organs.

Value relations between the Constitution and the law

The formation and perfection of the legal system is the premise of the construction of the rule of law. A well-established legal institution can only be formed on the basis of a complete legal system. The mission of the construction of the rule of law is regulating public rights, guaranteeing private rights, and eventually achieving the ultimate value of the protection of human rights. Based on the mission of the rule of law in respect of value, the legal system should also reflect the spirit of human rights, take the protection of human rights as its mission, and is aimed at regulating public rights and guaranteeing private rights. The *Constitution*, as the supreme law of the state, adjusts the normative relations between state power and civil rights, and the value of the *Constitution* is mainly reflected in restricting state power and guaranteeing civil rights, on the basis of which the fundamental value of the legal system and constitutional value are identical with each other in terms of basic ideas. In the formation and improvement of the legal system, the *Constitution* is regarded as the core value and the protection of human rights as the fundamental mission, so as to combine the formation and improvement of the legal system with the realization of constitutional value, and to eventually form a legal system with the *Constitution* at the dominant position, in which the fundamental value of the *Constitution* can be reflected.

As the supreme embodiment of modern legal systems, the *Constitution* is not only a kind of institutional norm, but also a value concept. The *Constitution* is not a brief overview and summary of social phenomena, but embodies its framers' emotions and value orientation. Therefore, the most distinctive feature of the *Constitution* is its nature of value or justice. Other laws may become "bad laws" due to legislative techniques; however, the *Constitution* should not become a bad law anyway, for other bad laws can be amended through constitutional review, but if the *Constitution* becomes "depraved", what can amend the *Constitution*? Therefore, a basic idea of modern constitutionalism is that the rule of legislation is "the rule of law," of which the most important is "the rule of the *Constitution*." The value of the *Constitution* is mainly reflected as its nature of justice, "justice as constitutional value refers to the *Constitution*'s properties such as equality, fairness, and legitimacy."[37]

From the perspective of practice, the justice of the *Constitution* is mainly reflected in the actual functions of the *Constitution*. In the historical background of the formation of modern constitutions, the main purpose of constitutions is to regulate the exercise of state power and prevent citizens' basic rights from being infringed by state power. As for relations between the restraint of state power and the protection of citizens' rights, the former is the means while the latter is the aim; the restraint of state power will result in the protection of citizens' rights, which, however, does not mean that the restraint of state power is less important than the protection of citizens' rights in respect of the status. On the contrary, the restraint of state power is the premise and foundation of the protection of citizens' rights. Without the restraint, the state power will become the prime enemy of citizens' rights. Therefore, in terms of functions of the *Constitution*, the urgency of the restraint of state power takes priority over the ultimacy of the protection of citizen's rights. Constitutional restrictions on state power are mainly reflected in: Firstly, the existence of the *Constitution* in itself indicates that state power is restricted by the law and it is not without any boundary; secondly, the *Constitution* recognizes the principle of popular sovereignty as well as the principle of basic human rights, in which citizens' rights are believed to be the source of state power, and state organs exercise their power for the purpose of safeguarding the overall interests of the state and protecting citizens' rights; thirdly, the *Constitution* limits the scope of governmental authority and defines the boundary of authority between governments and citizens; fourthly, the *Constitution* provides the separation of responsibilities and functions between state organs and distributes state power among different state organs so as to impose constraints on and maintain a balance between each other and prevent state power being concentrated in some organs.[38]

The *Constitution* represents an idea of power-control; the primary function of the *Constitution* or the most essential attribute of it is to restrict the state power's infringement of citizens' rights. In other words, it is to ultimately achieve the purpose of controlling state power by restricting procedures and foundations for the exercise of state power. According to classical social contract theory, state power derives from the alienation of citizens' rights and with the consideration of providing services to citizens' rights. Otherwise, once state power degenerates into a threat to citizens' rights, people have the right to cancel the contract and withdraw their alienated rights. Based on this classical social contract theory, thinkers at the period of the Enlightenment give a classic description of relations between state power and citizens' rights provided for in the *Constitution*:

- In constitutional provisions, it is explicitly declared that citizens' rights and freedom are an extremely important basic element of the *Constitution*; a fixed pattern that a volume or a chapter of the *Constitution* is specially used to stipulate citizens' rights has taken shape in modern constitutions.

Regulations on state power are formed. As for state power, only those powers clearly enumerated in constitutional provisions can be exercised, vice versa.

- Methods of ceasing or correcting the abuse of power or wrongful exercise of power and protection of citizens' rights are clarified. Since state power possesses an intrinsic property of infringing citizens' rights, to clearly stipulate legal consequences of the abuse of power and legal remedy for infringed rights in constitutional provisions becomes a major task of the *Constitution*. Then, the *Constitution* will provide legal relief such as constitutional review or constitutional litigation for imposing sanctions on unconstitutional behaviors, the abuse of power, the infringement of rights in order to achieve the ultimate purpose of protecting human rights.

Normative relations between the Constitution and the law

Due to the commonness between basic values of the legal system and constitutional values, the formation and improvement of the legal system has to take the *Constitution* as its value basis and reflect the value pursuit of the *Constitution*. The *Constitution* is the legislative basis of ordinary laws, while ordinary laws are specific manifestations of the *Constitution*.

The *Constitution* is the legislative basis of ordinary laws

The *Constitution* is not to play its regulatory role in its specified range of adjustment, but to provide a legislative basis, legislative principle, and legislative foundation for other ordinary legal norms. As the "mother" of all legislation, the *Constitution* does not play its role only at the time of targeting at some specific legal norms or some specific legal matters; its role is mainly reflected in restricting and guiding various ordinary legal norms as its sub-laws — It can offer a legislative basis to other ordinary legal norms, enabling them to find their theoretical origins and proofs of rationality in the *Constitution*. It can provide other ordinary legal norms with a legislative principle, enabling them to have rules to follow in legislation. It can also prevent other ordinary legal norms from being declared to be unconstitutional or invalid due to the violation of basic spirits and principles of the *Constitution*. The *Constitution* provides a legislative foundation for ordinary legal norms, enabling them to have the legitimate basis and constitutional legitimacy for their enactment. Although specific systems of constitutional review and constitutional litigation are not expressly provided for in China's *Constitution*, a similar system is clearly defined in it, that is, the system of constitutional interpretation. In accordance with Article 67 of the *Constitution*, the Standing Committee of the National People's

Congress exercises the power of constitutional interpretation. Since the Standing Committee of the NPC is a permanent organ of the National People's Congress, it can be naturally inferred in logic that the National People's Congress is also endowed with the power of constitutional interpretation. Therefore, when people question the constitutionality of the legislation work on some specific legal issue, they can seek interpretation from the NPC and its Standing Committee. If the NPC and its Standing Committee hold that the legislation of ordinary laws is not against the basic principles and spirit of the *Constitution*, this is the constitutional interpretation made by the supreme organ of state power that enjoys the power of constitutional interpretation, which has the highest authority. If the NPC and its Standing Committee hold that the legislation of ordinary laws is indeed contrary to the basic principles and spirit of the *Constitution*, they can make unconstitutional interpretation and declare that the legislation is invalid or terminate its legislative acts. Whether the power of constitutional interpretation is exercised by the National People's Congress or the Standing Committee of the NPC depends on the nature of specific legislation.

Ordinary laws are specific manifestations of the *Constitution*

Theoretically speaking, as the supreme law, the *Constitution* in itself is the supreme norm and other ordinary laws can only abide by it rather than violating it, otherwise they will be declared to be null and void due to the violation of the *Constitution*. However, once the *Constitution* is regarded as the "mother law," the *Constitution*'s effectiveness of directly regulating, or function of directly adjusting, is greatly weakened, yet, its basic function is changing from adjusting relations between state powers into providing the legislative basis for other ordinary laws. Relations between the *Constitution* and ordinary laws also change accordingly: The *Constitution* becomes the "supervisor" of ordinary laws rather than their "procreator." The *Constitution* no longer directly adjusts specific social relations and legal issues, and when there are related issues, corresponding ordinary laws will resolve them. Therefore, as for the relations between the *Constitution* and ordinary laws, "the *Constitution* usually only stipulates legislative principles of a state, and its function only lies in providing the legislative basis for the legislature in their daily legislative activities. Moreover, since the *Constitution* can only stipulate legislative principles, it cannot replace ordinary laws with the judicial applicability just like that of ordinary laws."[39] In accordance with the basic theory of constitutionalism, relations between the *Constitution* and the law should be reflected in the following two aspects:

- The *Constitution* constitutes the legislative basis of other laws.
  In fact, other laws are not required to take specific provisions of the *Constitution* as their basis, but to ask other laws to represent principles and the spirit of the *Constitution*.
- The *Constitution* has the supreme legal authority and other laws shall not contravene the *Constitution*.
  The *Constitution* is the legislative basis of other laws which indicates the *Constitution*'s constraint on other laws beforehand; while the legal authority of the *Constitution* is higher than that of other laws indicates the *Constitution*'s constraint on other laws afterwards, and this needs to be protected by establishing the system of constitutional review.

The Constitution and the Related Laws

When dividing China's legal branches, it is necessary to pay attention to the relations between the *Constitution* and branch laws: Is the *Constitution* a component of China's branch laws or the supreme law beyond the branch laws? In legislative practice, in light of the needs of the legislation work, the Standing Committee of the NPC divides China's legal system into seven legal branches, namely, "the Constitution and the Related Laws, civil and commercial laws, administrative law, economic law, social law, criminal law, and procedural and non-procedural laws." Such kind of division results in many problems.

First, strictly speaking, the term "Constitution-Related Laws" is not very scientific, for as the mother law, the *Constitution* is the legislative basis for the other six legal branches, then all legislations are directly or indirectly related to the *Constitution*. However, naming the law like the *Electoral Law* as an example of the "Constitution-Related Laws" cannot reflect its essential characteristics as a branch law. And the use of the title "constitutional laws" is also not very appropriate, for from the perspective of the historical development of legal systems, "constitutional laws" is a term mainly used by countries implementing a common law system. In these countries where the system of unwritten constitution is carried out, the content of their constitutions is reflected in laws enacted by the Parliament, and these legal documents with the constitutional significance are often called "constitutional law." For example, the constitutional law of the U.K. includes *The Great Charter of the Liberties of England* (1215), *The Petition of Right* (1628), *Habeas corpus Act* (1679), *Bill of Rights* (1689), *Act of Settlement* (1707), etc.

Second, according to the theory of the division of China's branch laws, there are generally two principles in the division: the scope of legal relations adjusted by the legal branch concerned and the adjusting methods of the legal branch concerned.

For example, what the civil law adjusts is the legal relations between subjects with equal status and what the administrative law adjusts is "the regulation of administrative relations and the system of legal norms controlling administrative power."[40] However, the constitutional relations that the *Constitution* adjusts covers the entire scope of legal relations of the state, the scope of adjustment of civil and commercial laws, criminal law, administrative law, and economic law is subject to the constraints of the constitutional relations. Therefore, in terms of the logic, the scope of legal relations adjusted by the *Constitution* is larger than that of branch laws such as civil and commercial laws, criminal law, and administrative law. If the *Constitution* is regarded as one of the seven legal branches, it is actually equated with other legal branches and becomes a common branch of the entire legal system just like other legal branches, and there will be no significant difference between the *Constitution* and other legal branches, which potentially lowers the legal status of the *Constitution* and is not conducive to maintaining the supreme legal status of the *Constitution*.

Third, the safeguarding methods for constitutional relations are different from that of other legal branches. The examination of unconstitutional normative documents and behaviors of infringing citizens' basic rights is generally conducted through constitutional review. If the *Constitution* is regarded as one of the seven legal branches, constitutional review will face an institutional dilemma in which examination and judgment cannot be made, due to the equal regulatory effectiveness of various branches. Therefore, there are some factors that do not match well in China's legal system brought by the concepts of the "Constitution-Related Laws" and "constitutional law." To improve the current situation, defining "the name of the law," that is, changing the "Constitution-Related Laws" into "______________ basic laws," would help differentiate it from other ordinary laws.

The reasonable division of legislative power of the National People's Congress and its Standing Committee on the basis of the *Constitution*

In accordance with Article 58 of the *Constitution*, the National People's Congress and its Standing Committee have legislative power of the state. Paragraph 3 of Article 62 of the *Constitution* prescribes the NPC's legislative power over basic laws, while Paragraph 3 of Article 67 prescribes the legislative power of the Standing Committee of the NPC over non-basic laws. These two provisions constitute the model of the dualistic structure of legislative power in China's legislative system, dividing laws passed by the legislature into two levels: the basic law and non-basic law, which bring about two questions in practice. First, how to understand the constitutional status of the NPC and its Standing Committee? To be more specific, how to determine when the legislation of the two conflicts with each other? Second, how to understand the division between basic laws and non-basic laws?

Upholding the positioning of the NPC and its Committee in the Constitution

In accordance with the *Constitution* in China, both the NPC and its Standing Committee are entitled to exercise legislative power. Then, how to divide the power of the two, in particular, how to deal with the situation in which the legislation of the two is inconsistent or even conflicts with each other, becoming a problem must be addressed in the construction of the legal system. This problem is obviously reflected in the application of the new *Lawyers Law* and the *Criminal Procedure Law*.

On October 28, 2007, at the 30th Session of the Standing Committee of the 10th NPC, the new *Lawyers Law* was amended and adopted and it was enforced on June 1, 2008. Different from the amendments of laws in the past, there is much dispute over the amendment of the *Lawyers Law* at the very beginning. One of the foci is the linkage between the new *Lawyers Law* and the *Criminal Procedure Law*, especially when some provisions of the two laws are inconsistent with each other, how to resolve the conflict between them? How to choose the applicable regulating basis? In this regard, there has not been a consensus in the jurisprudential circles, while there are three viewpoints:

In light of the principle that "the *Criminal Procedure Law* takes priority" holds that laws enacted by the legislative organs can be divided into the two categories according to the text of China's *Constitution*, namely "basic laws" and "non-basic laws," and the NPC enacts basic laws, while the Standing Committee of the NPC enacts other laws except for basic laws. In terms of the status, the NPC is the supreme organ of state power, while the Standing Committee of the NPC is only the permanent organ of the NPC and it is subordinate to the NPC, which implies a logic that the legal effectiveness of basic laws enacted by the NPC is actually higher than that of non-basic laws enacted by the Standing Committee of the NPC. The *Criminal Procedure Law* is a basic law enacted by the NPC, while the *Lawyers Law* is a non-basic law enacted by the Standing Committee of the NPC, since basic laws are higher than non-basic laws in status, when there is a conflict in effectiveness between the two, "the principle that the superior law has priority over the lower law" should be followed and thus the *Criminal Procedure Law* shall prevail. Those who support this viewpoint are mainly some constitutional scholars and experts of substantive departments.[41]

The viewpoint that "the new *Lawyers Law* takes priority" supports China's *Constitution* prescribes that both the NPC and the Standing Committee of the NPC exercise the legislative power of the state. Both the *Criminal Procedure Law* enacted by the NPC and the new *Lawyers Law* amended by the Standing Committee of the NPC are actually laws enacted by the supreme legislative organ, having the same legal status and legal effectiveness. In accordance with the provisions of the *Law on Legislation*, among the laws enacted by the same organ, new laws have priority over old laws.[42] Supporters of this viewpoint mainly include some experts and lawyers in the circle of the *Criminal Procedure Law* and the circle of legal practitioners.[43]

The view that "it should be adjudicated by the Standing Committee of the NPC" holds that when there are conflicts between laws, and the laws in force fail to provide specific solutions to these conflicts, then in line with stipulations and spirits of the *Law on Legislation*, the Standing Committee of the NPC can be asked to adjudicate. If the enforcement of laws is affected by disputes caused by the inconsistency between provisions of the *Lawyers Law* and the *Criminal Procedure Law* and their applications cannot be determined, the Standing Committee of the NPC can be asked to give authoritative instructions.[44]

The view that "the *Criminal Procedure Law* takes priority" and the view that "the new *Lawyers Law* takes priority" differentiate from each other mainly in whether the difference in constitutional status between the NPC and the Standing Committee of the NPC is recognized, and whether the resulting difference in the rank of effectiveness between basic laws and non-basic laws is recognized. They are related to the relations between the NPC and the Standing Committee of the NPC, i.e. Are the NPC and the Standing Committee of the NPC regarded as the same organ or two different organs?

In this regard, the view that "the *Criminal Procedure Law* takes priority" upholds the viewpoint of "two different organs," supporting that the two are different legislative organs. Although there are relations of overlap and repetition between them in terms of legislative effectiveness, the Standing Committee of the NPC is the permanent organ of the NPC, with its own legislative power and legislative procedure. Since the NPC and the Standing Committee of the NPC are two different legislative organs, the basic laws enacted by the NPC and the non-basic laws enacted by the Standing Committee of the NPC have different characteristics and manifestations in terms of legal effectiveness.

In view of the provisions of China's *Constitution* and the *Law on Legislation* as well as the basic principles of constitutionalism, the claim that the NPC and the Standing Committee of the NPC is the same legislative organ is unconvincing. The reasons are as follows:

First, their constitutional foundations are different. The system of people's congresses is China's fundamental political system; the NPC and its Standing Committee together constitute the representative institutions of China. Although the two have similarities in respect of functions, they are totally different from each other in respect of the basis and structure of their constitutional foundations, which are mainly reflected in the determination and representativeness of representatives of the NPC and members of the Standing Committee of the NPC. Representatives of the NPC are indirectly elected by the people to manage state affairs on behalf of people of various ranks and occupations, thus they have broad representativeness. In contrast, the Standing Committee of the NPC consists of the Chairman, several Vice Chairmen, the Secretary-General and several members. The number of members of the Standing Committee of the NPC is not specified, the specific number of members of one session is usually determined according to the measures for election and decision on appointments of the first conference of that NPC. As for the determination of members of the Standing Committee of the NPC, first of all the presidium of the first conference of each NPC submits nominations, then different delegations consult with each other, after that, an official list of candidates will be determined by the presidium in line with majority opinion, finally, the members will be elected in a plenary session. Before the 6th National People's Congress, a non-competitive election is conducted to determine members of the Standing Committee of the NPC. Since the 1st meeting of the 7th NPC, members of the Standing Committee of the NPC are determined through competitive election, while the Chairman, Vice Chairmen, and the Secretary-General are also selected through non-competitive election. The proportion of the difference is not specified in laws and it is generally determined according to measures of election taken by meetings of the NPC. From the determination of members of the Standing Committee of the NPC, it can be found that although they are also selected from representatives by the NPC, the ways of determination of the two are obviously different.

Different ways of determination lead to different public representativeness of the NPC and the Standing Committee of the NPC. The 11 national people's congresses held in China show that the number of representatives of each National People's Congress is over 3,000, while the number of members of the Standing Committee of each NPC is very limited, ranging from 70 to 200. Compared with the democratic way of determination of NPC representatives and their broad representativeness, the democracy and representativeness of members of the Standing Committee of the NPC are relatively insufficient, which results in different constitutional foundations of the NPC and the Standing Committee of the NPC. "People exercise state power in the National People's Congress and local people's congresses." Although both the NPC and the Standing Committee of the NPC represent public opinion, they are different from each other in respect of manifestations and degrees of representation. The NPC directly represents the public opinion, while its Standing Committee indirectly represents the public inclination; they obviously have different manifestations and foundations in reflecting democratic values and opinions of the sovereignty. The differences in constitutional foundations at the same time determine their differences in constitutional status: The Standing Committee of the NPC is the permanent organ consisting of less than 200 people elected from all the representatives. Compared with the NPC, which is the supreme organ of state power, it can only be regarded as "the second highest organ of state power" rather than "the organ of state power with higher rank."[45] Consequently, due to the broader public will representativeness of the NPC, we have to truly place the NPC in an unshakable position of the supreme organ of state power.

Second, their constitutional statuses are different. In the time when the 1954 *Constitution* was being enacted, the framers attached great importance to the positioning of the supreme organ of state power in the *Constitution*. The draft constitution proposed by the CPC Central Committee once envisaged that the National People's Congress shall have a President and Vice Presidents and the Standing Committee of the National People's Congress is positioned as "a routine body of the supreme organ of state power;" later, it is changed into "a permanent body of the National People's Congress" and has been adopted continuously until the present Constitution. Article 22 of the *Constitution Draft* (first draft) once stipulated that "The supreme organ of state power of the People's Republic of China is the National People's Congress." In the discussion at the joint meeting of conveners of the constitution draft seminar, it has been suggested to modify this stipulation into "The National People's Congress of the People's Republic of China is the supreme organ of state power." From the process of enacting and amending these related provisions, it can be found that both the framers and participants in the discussion are very concerned about the status of the National People's Congress in the constitutional system, trying to clarify the boundary in respect of the functions between the NPC and the NPC Standing Committee in the *Constitution* and institutionally preventing the possible situation that the NPC Standing Committee infringes upon the authority of the NPC.

The *Draft Constitution* of 1982 once stipulated that the people exercise state power in the National People's Congress and the local people's congresses at various levels. The NPC is the supreme organ of state power. In this draft, the Standing Committee of the NPC is not regarded as the supreme organ of state power in China, nor is it prescribed as an independent organ. The reason why the Standing Committee of the NPC is later established as a permanent organ of the NPC lies in some practical considerations. In this regard, Peng Zhen gave detailed explanations in his "*Report on the Draft Constitution of the People's Republic of China*" delivered at the 5th Session of the 5th National People's Congress on November 26,

1982. Since there are a great number of representatives of the NPC, it is inconvenient to frequently carry out the work and exercise their powers, it has been assumed to reduce the number of representatives. However, China is large both in size and in population, with more than 50 nationalities and more than 2,000 counties, therefore, it is necessary for all classes, all ranks, all nationalities, all areas, all sectors, and all political parties to have an appropriate quantity of their own representatives in the NPC, so the number of representatives cannot be reduced. Accordingly, the draft stipulates that some functions and powers previously owned by the NPC will be exercised by the Standing Committee of the NPC so as to expand the functions and powers of the Standing Committee, to strengthen its organization, and to play its role as the supreme organ of state power in a better way. The members of the Standing Committee of the NPC in fact can be called Standing Representatives; they are serving on behalf of various sectors. Their quantity is appropriate, and it is relatively convenient for them to hold meetings frequently. The expansion of functions and powers of the Standing Committee of the NPC is mainly manifested as the expansion of legislative power. The 1954 *Constitution* provides that the NPC is the only legislative organ, and the Standing Committee of the NPC can only formulate ordinances. Later, although the functions and powers of the Standing Committee of the NPC are expanded a little, they are still limited to the enactment of separate regulations with a certain legal nature. Until the 1982 *Constitution*, the Standing Committee of the NPC was entitled to legislative function, dramatically expanding the functions and powers of the Standing Committee of the NPC.[46]

However, after the functions and powers of the Standing Committee of the NPC are expanded, especially after both the NPC and the Standing Committee of the NPC have gained legislative power, does the constitutional status of the Standing Committee of the NPC equate or juxtapose with that of the NPC? The answer is negative. In the 3rd Plenary Session of the Committee for Revision of the Constitution of the People's Republic of China in the afternoon of April 12, 1982, Secretary-General Hu Qiaomu clearly pointed out that this amendment of the Constitution "strengthens the status and roles of the Standing Committee of the NPC; however, the Standing Committee of the NPC cannot be completely equated with the NPC."[47] Therefore, in terms of the constitutional status, the NPC is the supreme body of state power that exercises the supreme state power, while the Standing Committee of the NPC is only a permanent organ that is different from the NPC in respect of nature, thus it cannot be regarded as the supreme organ of state power.[48] The difference in the constitutional status determines that the NPC and the Standing Committee of the NPC are organs of different natures.

Third, their constitutional functions and powers are different. As state organs, the functions and powers of the NPC and the Standing Committee of the NPC are expressly stipulated in the *Constitution*. The functions and powers of the NPC are mainly provided for in Article 62 of the *Constitution*, and the functions and powers of the Standing Committee of the NPC are mainly provided for in Article 67 of the *Constitution*. There are more than 14 provisions concerning the functions and powers of the NPC in the *Constitution*, among which those more important ones are the power of amending the *Constitution*, the power of enacting and amending basic laws, the power of supervising the *Constitution*, etc. In addition, a miscellaneous provision is specifically added: "to exercise such other functions and powers as the highest organ of state power should exercise." Compared with the extensive functions and powers of the NPC, the functions and powers of the Standing Committee of the NPC are stipulated in a more detailed way in the *Constitution*. There are 21 related provisions, including a miscellaneous provision added specifically: "to exercise such other functions and powers as the National People's Congress may assign to it." In the enumeration of the functions and powers of the two as well as their miscellaneous provisions, it can be found obviously that neither the nature nor the limits of the functions and powers of the two are the same; whether in terms of the rank of effectiveness or the limits of functions and powers, the NPC is superior to the Standing Committee of the NPC. This difference is most obviously manifested in the miscellaneous provisions on their functions and powers. As for the functions and powers of the NPC, the miscellaneous provision in the *Constitution* prescribes that "to exercise such other functions and powers as the highest organ of state power should exercise," which is actually an expansion of the NPC's authority in a general manner. As long as the NPC holds that it "shall" exercise a power, it can exercise this power, which is the embodiment of the full authority and supremacy of the NPC. As for the functions and powers of the Standing Committee of the NPC, its miscellaneous provision in the *Constitution* prescribes that "to exercise such other functions and powers as the National People's Congress may assign to it," which is also an enabling clause, however, its subject that assigns powers can only be the NPC. From this comparison, it can be seen that the functions and powers exercised by the NPC and the Standing Committee of the NPC are different in nature. If they are the same organ, it will be unnecessary to distinguish their functions and powers in the *Constitution* and stipulate the different scope of them; meanwhile, it is even less necessary to make the provision that the NPC assigns functions and powers to the Standing Committee of the NPC.

Fourth, their legislative procedures are different. In accordance with the provisions of China's *Constitution*, both the NPC and the Standing Committee of the NPC exercise the legislative power; however, their legislative procedures are different from each other. As for this difference, two sections of the *Law on*

Legislation are expressly used to stipulate it: The legislative procedure of the NPC is prescribed from Article 12 to Article 23, and the legislative procedure of the Standing Committee of the NPC is prescribed from Article 24 to Article 41, which indicates that basic laws and non-basic laws are different in terms of the legislative process. The legislative procedures of the NPC and the Standing Committee of the NPC are quite distinct from each other in respect of the procedure of introducing a bill, deliberating a bill, voting a bill, and promulgating a law. It is generally believed that legislative results of the NPC are called "basic laws," while legislative results of the Standing Committee of the NPC are called "general laws," "ordinary laws," or "non-basic laws." Their differences in legislative procedures and legislative results also confirm the judgment that the NPC and the Standing Committee of the NPC are different organs.

The rank of effectiveness between basic laws and non-basic laws

The term "basic law" is a legal concept clearly defined in the 1982 Constitution; its textual basis is Paragraph 3 of Article 62 of the *Constitution* which provides that "The National People's Congress exercises the following functions and powers:... (3) to enact and amend basic laws governing criminal offences, civil affairs, the state organs and other matters..." Since the concept of basic law is too simply defined in the *Constitution*, there has been much debate on its connotation and denotation in the jurisprudential field. In terms of the definition of basic law, there are generally three viewpoints in the field, namely "subject-orientated standard," "content-orientated standard," and "double standards."

The view of "subject-orientated standard" holds that the only basis for judging basic law is the enacting subjects. Since China's *Constitution* stipulates that the NPC has the power of enacting basic laws, laws enacted by the NPC will be basic laws without exception. For example, some scholars have argued that the NPC has the power of formulating laws concerning fundamental and global relations of some aspect of state affairs, namely basic laws in China. "The NPC is the only subject exercising the power of enacting and amending basic laws, any other state organs, including the permanent organ of the NPC, namely the Standing Committee of the NPC does not have this power."[49]

The view of "content-orientated standard" supports that the primary standard of judging basic laws is the importance of basic laws and their content; only those laws with important content concerning the overall situation of the state can be classified into the category of basic law. In this sense, the so-called basic laws refer to "the laws with overall significance regulating the political, economic, and social life of the state,"[50] or "important laws governing criminal offences, civil affairs, state organs and other matters." "Other" here mainly refers to "legislation on citizens" basic rights and obligations, important legislation on economy and legislation on the system of civil servants, and the system of administrative and judicial procedures;" while non-basic laws refer to "the other laws except for the above-mentioned aspects."[51] It should be noted that "other" mentioned here needs to be strictly limited, "other" here takes "criminal offences, civil affairs, and state organs" as the reference, basic laws that are not listed should be homogeneous with "criminal offences, civil affairs, and state organs" in content, and this homogeneity cannot be found in other normative documents or legislative forms.[52] In line with the content-orientated standard, the NPC as the enacting subject is not a sufficient condition for a law to be classified into "basic law." This can be convincingly found in the self-judgment of the NPC, for not all laws enacted by the NPC are defined as "basic laws." Although many laws regarded as "important laws" or even not defined should fall into the category of "basic law," on the basis of the standard that whether or not stipulations are made on important issues concerning the overall situation of some domain of political, economic, and social life of the country, some laws enacted by the NPC obviously fail to be regarded as "basic laws."

The viewpoint of "double standards" holds that the judgment of basic laws should include not only the important condition that the enacting subject of this law is the NPC, but also the importance of the contents it adjusts and the relations involved. For some scholars believe that basic laws refer to "those laws enacted and amended by the NPC, regulating or adjusting relations that are fundamental and comprehensive in some aspect in state affairs and social life...basic laws are generally involved with citizens' rights and obligations, adjust the political and social life of the country, and are concerned with the fundamental interests of people of all nationalities, therefore, the power of enacting and amending these laws has to be exercised by the NPC."[53] In this sense, the standard of judging basic laws should be "the importance of the law in itself in addition to the enacting subject. In specific operation, when we make a judgment about whether a law belongs to the scope of basic law, the importance of the law in itself should be taken as the mainstay and the enacting subject should also be considered."[54]

Compared with the other two viewpoints, we believe that the viewpoint of "double standards" is more rational; to be specific, whether a law belongs to the category of basic law is determined by its enacting subject in terms of the form, but determined by the importance and comprehensiveness of social relations that it regulates in terms of the content. "Basic laws" should refer to those laws with fundamental significance, of which the rank of effectiveness is preceded only by the *Constitution*. According to the classification and analysis of laws enacted by the NPC, what "basic laws" regulate are important affairs concerning the overall situation in some domain of the national political, economic, and social life. In a word, "basic laws" are those laws enacted by the NPC, regulating important affairs concerning the overall situation in some domain of the state's political, economic, and social life, which are subordinate only to the *Constitution*, but superior to other laws.[55] The viewpoint of "double standards" actually establishes two standards for judging basic laws: One is the subject-oriented standard, which is a restriction on basic laws in terms of the form, requiring that the enacting subject of basic laws should only be the NPC rather than other state organs, including the Standing Committee of the NPC; the other is the content-oriented standard, which is a restriction on basic laws in terms of the substance, requiring that the content of basic laws should be concerned with criminal offences, civil affairs, state organs, and other matters with the characteristics of importance and comprehensiveness.[56]

In the analysis of the legal system, some scholars believe that the NPC "occupies the most important position in China's system of legislative authority;" laws enacted by it "enjoy the highest position in China's whole system of laws and the forms of laws. Since the legislation of the NPC enjoys the highest status, then the NPC have the supreme authority."[57] As for maladies such as indefinite subjects, vague nature, and obscure authority found between basic laws enacted by the NPC and non-basic laws by the Standing Committee of the NPC, it is advocated to resolve them by scientifically defining "the title of the law." It is proposed that the titles of China's laws should be simplified into nine kinds of titles, including the *Constitution*, basic law, law, statute, regulation, authorization regulation, rule, amendment, detailed implementation rule, etc., among which, basic laws can only be adopted by the NPC. Laws enacted by the NPC except for the *Constitution* are generally called "Basic Law on ______________ of the People"s Republic of China," and those laws originally called "basic laws" remain their original titles, such as "The Basic Law of the Hong Kong Special Administrative Region of the People's Republic of China." Those laws originally called "law" or other titles are renamed as "basic law." For example, the *Criminal Law of the People's Republic of China* can be renamed as the *Basic Law on Criminal Offences of the People's Republic of China*. All the titles of basic laws adopted by the NPC should include the words "basic law" so as to distinguish them from other laws adopted by the Standing Committee of the NPC. And the laws passed by the Standing Committee of the NPC are generally called the "Law on ______________ of the People's Republic of China;" all of the titles of laws adopted by the Standing Committee of the NPC should include the word "law" so as to distinguish them from basic laws adopted by the NPC as well as regulations and rules.[58]

Although the NPC's power of enacting basic laws is clarified in China's *Constitution*, in practice, there are numerous situations in which basic laws ought to be enacted by the NPC are actually enacted by the Standing Committee of the NPC. In identifying the enacting subject of specific laws, there is a certain arbitrariness among legislators. From the perspective of legislation, sometimes laws ought to be enacted by the NPC are actually enacted by the Standing Committee of the NPC, which causes confusion in the logic of the legal system. In legislative practice, the connotation and denotation of the power of enacting basic laws should be strictly defined, the constitutional principle that the NPC exercises the power of enacting basic laws should be adhered to, and the formalization of the power of enacting basic laws should be prevented. In the construction of the legal system, the NPC's dominant position in legislation should be insisted on and the functions and powers of the NPC and the Standing Committee of the NPC should be divided in strict accordance with the provisions of the *Constitution*.

Guaranteeing the balanced development of the legal system on the basis of the *Constitution*

In the construction and development of the legal system, the balance or consistency of the legislation is a very important issue. In general, the legal system of the country is an organic unity. If there is no unified planning and long-term goal in the construction of the legal system, the state legislation will become utilitarian and temporary, unable to adapt to the long-term development of the society. The balance and consistency of the legal system are mainly reflected in the proportion of various legal branches in the legal system as well as the proportion of the content of legislation in the legal system.

The balance of the state legislation is first of all reflected in the proportion of various legal branches in the legal system. According to the white paper of "*The Construction of the Rule of Law in China*" released in 2008, China's legal system consists of seven legal branches: the Constitution and the Related Laws, civil and commercial laws, administrative law, economic law, social law, criminal law, procedural and non-procedure laws. According to the data provided by this white paper, the proportion of various legal branches in China's legal system is shown in Table 2.5.

Table 2.5 The proportion of the legal branches in the legal system (229 laws in total)

Legal branch	Quantity	Proportion (%)
The Constitution and the Related Laws	39	17.0
Civil and commercial laws	32	14.0
Administrative law	79	34.5
Economic law	54	23.6
Social law	17	7.4
Criminal law	1	0.4
Procedural and non-procedural laws	7	3.1

As shown in the above table, the development of different legal branches is extremely unbalanced: The number of administrative laws is 79, which is the largest and accounts for more than one-third of the total; the number of economic laws is 54, which is the second largest and accounts for nearly one-fourth; the number of social laws is 17, which is relatively small and accounts for about 7.4% of the entire legal system.

In terms of the content of legislation, the development of China's legal system is also unbalanced. According to the difference in the content of legislation, the legislation can be roughly divided into several types, including economic legislation, political legislation, cultural legislation, social legislation, etc. The classification of the content of legislation is based on the statement that "In accordance with the overall arrangements for the cause of socialism with Chinese characteristics, we will promote all-round economic, political, cultural, and social development" in the report to the 17th CPC National Congress, dividing state legislation into four types in terms of the content, namely legislation on economic development, legislation on political development, legislation on cultural development, and legislation on social development. The proportion of the content of legislation in the legal system is shown in Table 2.6.

Table 2.6 The proportion of the content of legislation in the legal system (229 laws in total)

Content of legislation[59]	Quantity	Proportion (%)
Legislation on economic development	114[60]	49.9
Legislation on political development	80[61]	34.9
Legislation on cultural development	4[62]	1.7
Legislation on social development	31[63]	13.5

As shown in the above table, in the development of China's legal system, legislation on economic development occupies the absolute leading position, accounting for half of the state legislation. The fact that legislation on economic development is the largest in number is related to the state policy of focusing on economic development. In contrast, the amount of legislation on cultural and social development is relatively small and the sum of the two accounts for only about 15% of the entire legal system. In terms of the content of China's legal system, legislation on political development occupies an important position, accounting for more than one-third of the entire national legal system.

In the construction of the legal system, we should adopt an integrated idea of social development, maintaining a reasonable proportion of the state legislation and the balanced development of the legal system. In order to continue strengthening the basic position of the *Constitution* in the legal system, it is necessary to show the *Constitution*'s function of consistency, so as to change the original pattern of economic legislation and political legislation into a pattern in which political, economic, cultural, and social legislation receive equal attention. To protect human rights, the *Constitution* has to champion rights and people's livelihood should be regarded as the foci of the *Constitution*. Therefore, it is essential to enhance the intensity of social legislation, to change the original pattern in which economic legislation is particularly emphasized so as to maintain a balance in the content of China's legal system.

In the early times of China's reform and opening up and legal construction, too much emphasis is placed on the role of economic legislation, and the value of social legislation is ignored. In the 1980s, due to the emphasis of constitutional construction as well as the trend of economic development in China, economic legislation had been given priority in legislation to facilitate the economic construction. According to statistics, in the 20 years of the 6th, 7th, 8th, and 9th Session of the NPC, the NPC and its Standing Committee altogether enacted 341 sets of legislation, among which, there were 107 pieces of economic legislation, accounting for 31.4%; while there were 16 pieces of social legislation, accounting for only 4.7%. To be more specific, the Standing Committee of the 6th NPC enacted 37 sets of legislation, including 22 sets of economic legislation and one piece of social legislation; the Standing Committee of the 7th NPC enacted 62 pieces of legislation, including 21 sets of economic legislation and five sets of social legislation; the Standing Committee of the 8th NPC enacted 118 sets of legislation, including 35 sets of economic legislation and six sets of social legislation; the Standing Committee of the 9th NPC enacted 124 sets of legislation, including 29 sets of economic legislation and four sets of social legislation. In the *Legislation Plan of the Standing Committee of the Tenth National People's Congress* promulgated on December 17, 2003, it is prescribed that during the term of office of the current NPC, 59 draft laws are going to be deliberated, including 14 draft laws of economic legislation, and six draft laws of social legislation; 17 draft laws are going to be drafted and then deliberated, among which there are six draft laws of economic legislation but no draft law of social legislation. In March 2008, when the term of office of the 10th National People's Congress and its Standing Committee was finished, there were 73 laws deliberated and adopted, among which, social laws included the *Labor Contract Law*, the *Employment Promotion Law*, and the *Labor Dispute Mediation and Arbitration Law*, of which the proportion is relatively small compared with the totality of legislation. As for this situation of unbalanced legislation, in the seminar of "Academic Dialogues of the Constitution and Social Laws" held by Renmin University of China on December 29, 2007, some scholars have pointed out that in China's legal system, social legislation mainly is aimed at regulating labor relations, social security, social welfare, and protection of interests and rights of particular groups has lagged far behind for a long time, which gradually evolved into a institutional bottleneck in the establishment of a harmonious society. With the social and economic development, issues on society and people's livelihoods are increasingly prominent at present, thus the imbalance between economic legislation and social legislation starts to be corrected to a certain extent. In recent years, legislation on the society and people's livelihood is increasing; moreover, in the report to the 17th CPC National Congress, it is clearly stated that social development focused on improving people's livelihoods should be accelerated so as to expand the original trinity of economic, political, and cultural development into a pattern of economic, political, cultural, and social development. In this regard, the participants of the seminar believe that social legislation springing up comprehensively will not only perform the practical task of resolving issues on people's livelihood and social contradictions, but will also gradually become the core issue of China's society, contributing to a prosperous era.[64]

For a long period of time, social law has been the weakest branch in China's legal system. From the perspective of social development, through 30 years of reform and opening up, China has basically met the livelihood needs of the people and has begun to fight for a better living standard. Since the 1990s, with the rapid development of the reform, a series of "social maladies" such as the widening income gap between the rich and the poor, the "Three Rural Issues," unemployment, labor conflicts, unauthorized collection of fees by educational institutions, inadequate and expensive medical treatment, food and drug safety, and industrial accidents, began to appear. Thus, the lack of social legislation has caused the institutional bottleneck in the construction of a harmonious society.[65] In the twenty-first century, various issues such as the diversification of interests and the widening of the gap between the rich and the poor are also emerging; therefore, the social justice and the guarantee of people's livelihoods should be regarded as the foci of the government policy, to safeguard social fairness and justice and to enable all citizens to share the achievements of reform and development.

It is also necessary to review and arrange existing economic and social legislation. In this regard, some scholars believe that three factors need to be considered in the review and arrangement:

(1) In accordance with the requirements of the scientific standpoint on development and the construction of a harmonious Socialist society, it is important to review whether the existing economic and social legislation conforms to these requirements;

(2) Since the current level of economic development and comprehensive national power have been significantly improved, the country has gained favorable factors to improve the level, standard, and capacity of economic and social legislation, it is essential to perfect some existing economic and social laws;

(3) As the respect and protection of human rights have become constitutional principles, various laws, regulations, local regulations, and government rules should be consistent with the amended *Constitution* and need to be promptly added, amended, and improved. Special attention should be paid to finding and resolving problems of the infringement of human rights, social conflicts, and mass incidents caused by or likely to be caused by economic and social legislation.[66] While the provision "the state respects and preserves human rights" is included in the *Constitution*, the state legislation plan should comply with the spirit of human rights of the *Constitution* and the reality of protecting human rights, which actually provides value targets for the state legislation and proposes requirements for the improvement of the state legal system.

Improving the system of the national legislation plan on the basis of the *Constitution*

In the construction of the legal system, the legislation plan made by the state legislature plays an important role. On the one hand, the introduction of the state legislation plan can contribute to the improvement of the state legal system; on the other hand, through the state legislation plan, the state can strengthen the legislation of specific domains so as to maintain the integrity and consistency of the legal system in a better way. Compared with other branch laws, the *Constitution* is fundamental, holistic, and comprehensive, thus it can be in line with the basic trend of social development in a better way. Consequently, when introducing the state legislation plan, the legislature should take the *Constitution* as the foundation and constitutional principles, values, and spirit as the foci, rather than taking certain characteristics of branch laws as the basis.

In the *Legislation Plan of the Standing Committee of the NPC* passed in the 15th Meeting of the Chairmen of the Standing Committee of the 11th NPC on December 15, 2008 and amended in line with the spirit of the 2nd Session of the 10th NPC on March 23, 2009, it is stated that in the legislative work of the Standing Committee of the NPC in 2009, we should fully implement the spirit of the 17th National Congress of the CPC, the 3rd Plenary Session of the 17th CPC Central Committee and the No.15 (2008) of the CPC Central Committee, take Deng Xiaoping Theory, and the important thought of "Three Represents" as our guide. It is significant to thoroughly follow the perspective of scientific development, to focus on the kernel work of the party and the state, to achieve the target and accomplish the task of ensuring that the Socialist legal system with Chinese characteristics will be established and constantly improved in 2010, to persist in scientific and democratic legislation, to press ahead with the formulation of laws that play the role of bolstering the Socialist legal system with Chinese characteristics, is urgently needed and when legislative conditions are relatively mature, to timely amend those laws which are incompatible with economic and social development, to promptly organize the regulations, to participate actively in the formulation of supportive regulations, the publicity, and the legal training so as to be well-prepared in the establishment of the Socialist legal system with Chinese characteristics and to provide forceful legal protection to the promotion of economic, political, cultural, and social development as well as the development of ecological civilization in China.

Just with the textual expressions, it is hard to figure out the role of the *Constitution* in the *Legislation Plan of the Standing Committee of the NPC*. Yet, the impact of the Constitution can actually be found everywhere in the *Legislation Plan of the Standing Committee of the NPC*. First of all, the guideline of the legislation plan is to "fully implement the spirit of the 17th National Congress of the CPC, the 3rd Plenary Session of the 17th CPC Central Committee and the No.15 (2008) of the CPC Central Committee, take Deng Xiaoping Theory and the important thought of "Three Represents" as our guide," and in the Preamble of the *Constitution*, Deng Xiaoping Theory and the thought of "Three Represents" are also regarded as the guideline of the Constitution. The two are connected with each other. Therefore, the *Legislation Plan of the Standing Committee of the NPC* should also be drafted on the basis of constitutional provisions in addition to adhering to Deng Xiaoping Theory and the thought of "Three Represents." Secondly, as the *Legislation Plan* is adopted to "fulfill the target and task of ensuring that the Socialist legal system with Chinese characteristics will be established and constantly improved in 2010;" if we want to improve China's legal system, it is necessary to stick to the *Constitution* in the legislative process. Therefore, the goal of establishing and constantly improving the Socialist legal system with Chinese characteristics in itself indicates that the legislation plan should be carried out on the basis on the *Constitution*.

Settling the relations between the formulation, amendment, and interpretation of law

The improvement of the Socialist legal system cannot be separated from large-scale legislation in the state. Under the circumstances in which the Socialist legal system has been improved and the legal system has been basically formed, on the one hand, the formulation of laws should continue in a planned way; on the other hand, the interpretation and specific application of laws should also be attached with great importance. Ensuring that laws already enacted are conscientiously and effectively implemented in practice after the legal system is basically formed is the work that we should pay more attention to. At present, China's Socialist legal system has been improved; large-scale legislation in the state becomes no longer the kernel task of the construction of the legal system, and the current key issue is the improvement of law enforcement mechanisms. There are two forms of the improvement of law enforcement mechanisms: One is amendment, while the other is interpretation. The amendment of laws is considered to be convenient and efficient; however, frequent amendments would undermine the stability of laws and the authority of the legal system. In comparison, legal interpretation is a more important way to improve laws. The legislature has realized the importance of legal interpretation, for example, in the *Legislation Plan of the Standing Committee of the NPC* in 2009, it was prescribed that "in accordance with the arrangement, requirements, and schedule of the Standing Committee of the NPC, relevant organs should sort out, analyze, and research into those obviously incompatible and unsuitable regulations of existing laws, distinguish between different situations, and timely make necessary adjustments and improvements through amendment, repeal, interpretation, etc. According to the progress of sorting out laws and actual needs, a package of measures can be taken, concentrating on the amendment or repeal of a number of obviously outdated provisions."

Constitutional interpretation corresponds with legal interpretation. It is an activity of exploring the objective connotation of constitutional norms, of which the aim is to pursue the rationality and legitimacy of interpretation and the stability of constitutional order. Since constitutional norms and constitutional provisions are featured with ambiguity, abstraction, openness, and extensiveness, almost all of the constitutional provisions need to be objectively illustrated through constitutional interpretation so as to achieve the goal of actualizing constitutional norms. The significance of exploring the connotation of constitutional norms lies in objectively understanding the constitutional phenomena and seeking the value of the *Constitution* in a variety of social problems; on the one hand, the discovery of the constitutional issues, on the other hand, the judgment and determination of the constitutional issues. Through regular constitutional interpretation, we can standardize people's understanding of constitutional norms, establish and expand the common basis of the value system of the *Constitution*, and provide reasonable support for the improvement of the operation mechanism of the *Constitution*, enabling the *Constitution* to realize its value of openness in its continuity and variety. In particular, there is a lack of constitutional tradition in China, thus, through activities of constitutional interpretation, we can disseminate constitutional ideas and knowledge in an active, specific and common form so that people can grasp a sense of constitutional values in their daily lives and establish the belief in maintaining the authority of the *Constitution*. For subjects of the society, the benefits brought by activities of constitutional amendment are different from that brought by activities of constitutional interpretation; activities of constitutional interpretation are more beneficial for people to experiencing, understanding, and applying the *Constitution* in actual interest relations.

China is now experiencing social transformation. In this special and critical period, constitutional interpretation has irreplaceable significance for the fulfillment of constitutional functions: to contribute to the consistency and balance of diversified values; to contribute to resolving potential conflicts in the social life through convincing constitutional interpretation; to contribute to forming the awareness of social community and consensus through constitutional interpretation and establishing the society's core value system so as to provide conditions for the formation of the minimum value system of the society; to contribute to disseminating constitutional knowledge in the whole society and promoting the socialization of constitutional norms; to contribute to reasonably determining the boundary between personal and public interests.

As for the situation in China, the current *Constitution* of 1982 has been amended four times, adapting to the political and social development to a certain extent. However, not all kinds of inconsistency between constitutional norms and social reality can be alleviated only through constitutional amendment; interpreting the *Constitution* is also an important tool. Compared with the revision of the *Constitution*, the interpretation of the *Constitution* is more flexible and more conducive to saving the cost of legislation and maintaining the stability and authority of the *Constitution*. Moreover, constitutional amendment to a great extent only indicates that the *Constitution* passively adapts to changes in social life, and it fails to adequately reflect the *Constitution*'s effectiveness in regulating and controlling the society; while constitutional interpretation has both the function of developing the *Constitution* and enabling it to adapt to social development and the function of enforcing the *Constitution* and enabling it to regulate and control the society. Meanwhile, as the fundamental law of the state, this nature of the *Constitution* requires establishing a diversified system of the enforcement of the *Constitution*, including the system of constitutional interpretation, rather than making the *Constitution* passively adapt to changes in the social life. Only if we guarantee the stability of the *Constitution* and play the actual effects of the *Constitution* through interpretation, can we maintain the authority of the *Constitution* more effectively. Of course, when some provisions of the *Constitution* or systems fail to obtain the legitimacy by interpreting the *Constitution*, the *Constitution* also needs to be amended. However, even if the *Constitution* is amended, the system of constitutional interpretation cannot be abandoned.

After examining the history of the implementation of the *Constitution* of 1982, it can be found that the CPC Central Committee has been very concerned about how to fulfill the function of constitutional interpretation, and has repeatedly raised this issue in different historical circumstances and backgrounds. For example, in the *Instructions on the Proposal to Amend Part of the Constitution* in 1993, the CPC Central Committee pointed out that "This revision of the *Constitution* is not a comprehensive one, the issues not in an urgency to be revised should not be altered, and some of the issues can be resolved in the future through constitutional interpretation;" meanwhile, "constitutional interpretations should be put on the concrete content of the socialist market economy when it is necessary." In 1999, in the "Forum on the Constitutional Amendment," Li Peng also pointed out that the amendment of the *Constitution* is extremely significant, we should only amend a part of well-established content that needs to be amended; as for the content which does not need to be amended, as well as controversial issues, amendment is unnecessary. The *Constitution* entitles the Standing Committee of the NPC to the power of constitutional interpretation, thus some issues can be resolved in the future through the constitutional interpretation made by the Standing Committee of the NPC."[67] On December 4, 2002, Hu Jintao, in his speech at the Meeting Celebrating the 20th Anniversary of the Promulgation and Implementation of the Constitution in all social circles in Beijing, pointed out that "the NPC and its Standing Committee... should effectively assume the duty of supervising the implementation of the *Constitution* and resolutely correct unconstitutional acts; should effectively perform the function of constitutional interpretation and give necessary interpretations and explanations of problems found in the implementation of the *Constitution* so as to implement the provisions of the *Constitution* in a better way." On September 15, 2004, in the Meeting Celebrating the 50th Anniversary of the Founding of the

National People's Congress, Hu Jintao pointed out that "governing the country by law is prior to governing the country by the *Constitution*, and exercising the state power by law is prior to exercising the state power by the *Constitution*," "all members of the CPC, all civil servants and people of all nationalities should conscientiously study the *Constitution*, abide by and uphold the *Constitution*, and ensure the implementation of the *Constitution* in the whole society." On October 15, 2007, in the Report to the 17th CPC National Congress, Hu Jintao again stressed the need to "strengthen the implementation of the *Constitution* and other laws… maintaining the consistency, dignity, and authority of the socialist legal system."

It can be found that "exercising the state power according to the *Constitution*" and "governing the country according to the *Constitution*" have become the basic ideas of the CPC. Targeting at the enforcement of the *Constitution*, the leaders of the CPC all attached great importance to the interpretation of the *Constitution* at different periods. However, the proposition to give prominence to the constitutional interpretation has failed to become the will of the state or be changed into the legal system. There is neither the concrete practice of constitutional interpretation, nor the legislation on constitutional interpretation; the power of constitutional interpretation has long been in a state of "ineffectiveness." From the perspective of the constitutional text, Article 67 of the *Constitution* only briefly provides the power of "constitutional interpretation" of the Standing Committee of the NPC. Thus, we cannot find the procedures or foundations of constitutional interpretation directly from the constitutional text. Since the constitutional provision is too general, once we start to make constitutional interpretations, we will encounter the problem of the uncertainty of subjects and procedures, and there is lack of specific textual foundation as to how to carry out activities of constitutional interpretation. In order to maintain the dignity of the *Constitution*, safeguard the integrity of the socialist legal system and regulate activities of constitutional interpretation, it is important to enact a "Constitutional Interpretation Procedure Law." Such a law can ensure that all aspects of the interpretation of the *Constitution* are specified, there are laws to abide by for the interpretation of the *Constitution* and normative and scientific constitutional interpretation can be made. In addition, although there are different views on whether constitutional interpretation can be initiated in China's constitutional system in the circle of the Constitution, most of the domestic research is focused on the subject of constitutional interpretation, trying to provide conditions for the initiating of constitutional interpretation in China through demonstration of the power of constitutional interpretation of other subjects, in particular, that of the court.[68] However, as for the issue of establishing the operating mechanism of the *Constitution* which attaches equal importance to constitutional interpretation and constitutional amendment, there is broad consensus in the circle of the constitution studies. Through theoretical research into constitutional interpretation in recent years, the basic categories and methodological system of constitutional interpretation have been generally established in theory, providing necessary theoretical support to the practice of constitutional interpretation.

The Constitutional Interpretation Procedure Law is a set of legislations on the enforcement and supervision of the *Constitution*; whether it can be effectively enforced is directly related to the destiny of the *Constitution* and its future development. It is necessary for us to clarify the basic attributes of this law. Firstly, it is a basic law. The reason why we legislate rather than formulating a set of internal rules is that the activity of constitutional interpretation is concerned with the fundamental law of the state, thus this interpretation has legal validity. More importantly, the activity of constitutional interpretation is not internally valid, but will affect the overall operation of state power and the protection of citizens' basic rights. Secondly, this piece of legislation aims to make it possible for constitutional interpretation to operate on the one hand, and cause no unnecessary influence on the state's legal order and social life on the other hand. Thus, conditions for submitting plans of constitutional interpretation and procedures of deliberating constitutional interpretation should be strictly prescribed in this law. Thirdly, the framework of this law should be designed in accordance with the process of constitutional interpretation, namely, the proposal of constitutional interpretation, the acceptance of proposals for constitutional interpretation, the deliberation of bills of constitutional interpretation, and the passing of bills of constitutional interpretation. Fourthly, this law is mainly a procedural law, thus it should attach importance to procedures of constitutional interpretation and try to make various provisions operable.

In the future legislation plan and construction of the legal system, we should further straighten out relations of legal formulation, legal amendment, and legal interpretation, taking legal interpretation as a means to improve the *Constitution* as important as legal formulation and legal amendment, perfecting the law and diversifying forms of legal development through interpretation.

Improving the constitutional review system with Chinese characteristics

China has basically established a constitutional supervision system with Chinese characteristics, playing a positive role in the construction and development of the legal system. However, it should also be noted that the constitutional supervision system is also facing many problems and challenges. The current *Constitution* has been amended four times after its promulgation and enforcement to adapt to the social life; and the respect for the *Constitution* starts to become the fundamental value of the country. However, generally speaking, the authority of the *Constitution* has not been fully established and unconstitutional phenomena are still fairly severe. The poor performance of the enforcement of the *Constitution* has been not only a major problem of the constitutional practice in China, but also the social issue that the public is most concerned about. As shown by the "Investigation of Chinese citizens' Awareness of the *Constitution*" carried out by the Research Center of the Constitution and Administrative Laws of Renmin University of China in 2002, the public is not satisfied with the overall performance of the enforcement of the *Constitution*. Among the respondents to the question "your evaluations of the performance of the enforcement of the *Constitution*," those believing that the performance is "good" or "relatively good" accounted for 45%, and those believing the performance is "relatively poor" accounted for 26%, and those believing the performance is "poor" accounted for 17%. In addition, over 20% of the respondents were unable to comment on the enforcement, for they did not understand the meaning of enforcing the *Constitution* or did not know the standard of evaluating the performance of the enforcement of the *Constitution*. Among the respondents to the question "If the *Constitution* will be amended again in China, which part do you think needs to be improved the most?" (with 10 options listed), most of the respondents held the opinion that the constitutional supervision system should be improved, indicating that the public has concerns and expectations about the constitutional supervision system. In 2007, in order to know the citizens' awareness of the *Constitution* and the social effects of the *Constitution* after five years, the research team of the Research Center of the Constitution and Administrative Laws of Renmin University of China, focusing on citizens' awareness of the *Constitution*, again conducted a survey of citizens' awareness of the *Constitution*. Among the respondents to the question "Your evaluations of the performance of the enforcement of the *Constitution*," those believing the performance is "poor" or "relatively poor" accounted for 45%, those believing the performance is "good" or "relatively good" accounted for 40%, and 15% of respondents had no idea of the performance of the enforcement of the *Constitution*. The enforcement of the *Constitution* is a very important factor of measuring the enforcement of the law, having an important impact on the enforcement of the law of the whole state. However, more than 45% of the citizens in this survey believed that the enforcement of the *Constitution* in China was not satisfactory, which indicates that there is still a big gap between the textual provisions of China's *Constitution* and reality.

In order to improve the constitutional review system with Chinese characteristics, we should first actively change our perception and further improve the understanding of the status and functions of the *Constitution*. In 2004, in his speech delivered at the Meeting Celebrating the 50th Anniversary of the Founding of the National People's Congress, Hu Jintao explicitly pointed out that "governing the country by law is prior to governing the country by the *Constitution*, and exercising the state power by law is prior to exercising the state power by the *Constitution*." At the national meeting of political and legal work in 2008, Hu Jintao further issued an important statement: "The cause of the party, the people's interests, and he *Constitution* and the law are of supremacy." These statements make no better summary of the nature of the Socialist concept of the rule of law, and they are also the enrichment and development of the concept that governing the country by the *Constitution* and exercising state power by the *Constitution*.

To improve the constitutional review system with Chinese characteristics is an important condition for building a well-established, consistent, and harmonious Socialist legal system, an important mechanism for building a Socialist country under the rule of law and an important guarantee for establishing a stable order of the *Constitution*. In order to further improve the constitutional review system with Chinese characteristics, we should strengthen the work in the following respects.

Firstly, the CPC's leadership should be upheld in the enforcement of the *Constitution*, and organizations of the party at all levels and all the party members should follow and enforce the *Constitution*. In respect of the construction of the constitutional review system in China, the experiences and lessons are very important. The history of New China's *Constitution* shows that when the party determines a correct political line and respects the *Constitution*, the implementation of the constitutionalism will be guaranteed and the *Constitution* will pose positive social effects; and when the party deviates from a correct political line and does not attach importance to the authority of the *Constitution*, the constitutional ideal and the reality will inevitably come into conflict. For example, although the 1954 *Constitution* is satisfactory, yet it was not achieved in real life, and eventually it could only become ineffective. The key to governing the country by law is governing the country by the *Constitution*, which means to govern the country according to the *Constitution*, to establish the authority of the *Constitution*, and to make the *Constitution* the supreme criterion for all state organs, social groups, and activities of political parties. If the authority of the *Constitution* cannot be maintained, it is impossible to lay a foundation for the country under the rule of law, and the process of building a country ruled by law will be hampered.

Secondly, the actual situation of China should be taken into consideration in the improvement of the constitutional review system with Chinese characteristics. It is also necessary to draw on foreign experience for reference, and choose the constitutional review system suitable for China's actual conditions. The different modes of constitutional review systems reflect the different actual conditions of various countries and different constitutional cultures. When choosing a specific constitutional supervision system, all countries will generally pay attention to the coordination between the system and culture. In improving the constitutional supervision system, we should first take full account of the specific economic, political, and cultural characteristics of Chinese society and make full use of local resources without indiscriminately copying foreign experience. Especially in the context of economic globalization, we should not only consider our own actual conditions, but also prudently draw on valuable foreign experience for reference and give full play to the institutional strengths, so as to promote the development and improvement of the constitutional safeguard system with Chinese characteristics.

Thirdly, we should further improve the procedures of the constitutional review, make full use of institutional resources within the existing framework, safeguard the dignity of the *Constitution* and ensure the consistency and unity of the legal system. The *Law on Legislation* and the *Working Procedures for the Record and Review of Regulations* make some stipulations on the review procedures after those initiating subjects applied to the Standing Committee of the NPC for initiating constitutional review, which provides the institutional basis for the establishment of constitutional review in China. However, we should also notice that these two laws only prescribe the procedures of initiating the constitutional review after submitting applications, but fail to prescribe the procedures of taking the initiative to review those filed regulations or specify the procedures of accepting applications, reviewing organizations, and reviewing procedures and the legal authority after the review. In respect of the initiating subjects of the constitutional review, the *Law on Legislation* and the *Working Procedures for the Record and Review of Regulations* provide a relatively wide range for initiating subjects: Any individual citizen is entitled to initiate the constitutional review, in other words, to have covered almost all of the social subjects; however, they do not prescribe issues such as whether the citizens' applications should be responded to and how to respond to them. Moreover, the original intention of stipulating that any citizen has the power to apply for the constitutional review is to protect individual rights; however, in view of the actual operation of the system, the application of constitutional review without any conditions is inclined to induce organs for constitutional review to be negligent of their duties. As for the objects of constitutional review, the *Constitution* and the *Law on Legislation* define three kinds of objects, including administrative regulations, local regulations, and autonomous regulations as well as separate regulations; in other words, whether these three kinds of regulations contravene the *Constitution* will be reviewed, while acts conducted by state organs in accordance with the law are only the objects of legal review and they cannot be directly reviewed according to the *Constitution*. In addition, the *Law on Legislation* does not prescribe whether laws and judicial interpretations will be reviewed.

Fourthly, in respect of the trend of development, it is necessary to establish a specific organ of constitutional review in the system of people's congresses, so as to make the constitutional review become a professional and regular activity. The NPC and the Standing Committee of the NPC are organs of constitutional review in China, and the power of constitutional review exercised by the Standing Committee of the NPC is regular, authoritative, and practical. However, the NPC only convenes a meeting annually and each meeting lasts for over 10 days, matters needed to be discussed and decided are great in both quantity and importance, thus it is objectively impossible for it to be engaged in the specific work of the constitutional review. In addition, although the Standing Committee of the NPC convenes one meeting every two months and there are also Meetings of Chairmen, however, since it is confronted with the huge pressure of legislative tasks and the work of supervising and examining the enforcement of the law, it is also impossible for it to have adequate time and effort to make a judgment about the constitutional review. At present, the Legislative Record and Review Office set up by the Commission of Legislative Affairs of the Standing Committee of the NPC assumes certain functions of constitutional review, but fail to fully undertake the important task of constitutional review as expected due to constraints on rank, personnel, and institutional design. Under such circumstances, there is an objective necessity to establish a specific organ of constitutional review under the system of NPC. We believe that the establishment of a specific organ of constitutional review in the system of the NPC is a solution that is feasible and practically operational. The Committee of Constitutional Supervision is exclusively in charge of matters of constitutional review, directly subordinate to the NPC and responsible to the NPC and its Standing Committee, and has relative independence.

Notes

Overview: Framework of the Socialist Legal System with Chinese Characteristics

1. Deng Xiaoping, *Deng Xiaoping wen xuan*, 146.
2. Ibid., 147.
3. For example, Professor Sun Guohua believes that China's legal system can be divided into 10 branches, namely the constitutional law (the state law), administrative law, civil and commercial laws, marriage and family laws, economic law, fiscal and financial laws, labor and social security laws, ecological (environmental) law, criminal law, and procedural law, among which the five branches of the constitutional law, civil and commercial laws, administrative law, criminal law, and procedural law are the basic branches; while the other five, including marriage and family laws, economic law, fiscal and financial laws, ecological law, and labor and social security law are derivative branches created by division and integration. All these 10 branches also fall into three major categories, namely the public law, the private law, and the social law (Sun Guohua, *Zhongguo tese shehui zhuyi falü tixi yanjiu*, 164–71).
   Professor Shen Zongling holds that China's legal system can be divided into branches of constitutional law, administrative law, civil law (civil and commercial laws), economic law, labor and social security laws, laws on education, science, arts, and health, resources and environmental protection laws, criminal law, litigation law, and economic law (Shen Zongling, *Falixue*, 336–41).
   Based on the relevant reports drafted by the National People's Congress Standing Committee, Professor Zhang Wenxian divides the Socialist legal system with Chinese characteristics into the Constitution and the Related Laws, civil and commercial laws, administrative law, economic law, social law, criminal law, procedural and non-procedural laws (Zhang Wenxian, *Falixue*, 130–4).
4. Ulpianus is generally regarded as the father of the distinction between public law and private law, He discussed the classifications of legal branches in *The Digest of Justinian*, He expressed that some of them were beneficial to public interests, while some were beneficial to individuals. Public law could be found in religious affairs, religious institutions, and state administrative organs (see Bonfante, *Luoma fa jiaokeshu*, 7).
5. Justinian, *Faxue zonglun*, 5–6.
6. Karl Marx and F. Engels, 1965, 523.
7. Karl Marx and F. Engels, 1971, 488.
8. S.S. Alekseev, 1988, 258.
9. Li Long and Fan Jinxue, *Fa de yiban lilun*, (5).
10. Xu Xianming and Qu Xiangfei, "Renquan de tixi yu fenlei."
11. Morris Cohen, "Property and Sovereignty," 470; Robert L. Hale, "Bargaining, Duress and Economic Liability," 603; Ibid., "Coercion and Distribution in a Supposedly Non-Coercive State," 470.
12. See Chicago v. Wilson, 75 III, 2d 525 (1978).
13. John Henry Merryman, *Dalufa xi*, 95–105.
14. Roberta M. Unger, *Xiandai shehuizhong de falü*, 186–96.
15. Harold J. Berman, *Falü yu geming*, 39–49.

Notes

16. Sun Guohua and Yang Sibin, "Gongsifa de huafen yu fa de neizai jiegou," (4).
17. Jiang Ming'an, "Chuanqiuhua shidai de xin xingchengfa."
18. Although the three laws mentioned simultaneously acquire natures of administrative law, civil and commercial laws, economic law, and social law, these provisions do reflect administrative guidance.
19. Plea bargain refers to the procedure that the defendant in a criminal case negotiates with the public prosecutor (through the counsel) and makes a mutually acceptable agreement. The first case of plea bargaining in China is an intentional injury case heard by the Railway Transportation Court of Mudanjiang on April 11, 2002. Defendant Meng Guanghu with another five or six fellows beat Wang Yujie and caused serious injury to the victim. After the crime, all the other suspects were at large, for this reason the criminal who causes serious injury to the victim cannot be identified specifically. In order to settle the case as soon as possible, the public prosecution organ reached an agreement with the counsel and then submitted an application for plea bargain to the court. The Railway Transportation Court of Mudanjiang adopted the plea bargain and sentenced Meng Guanghu who committed the crime of intentional injury to a three-year imprisonment and a three-year probation. This case cost only 25 minutes from beginning a court session to pronouncing the sentence (see Wang Lixin et al., "Kaiting zhiyong ershiwu fenzhong").
20. Criminal reconciliation refers to the institution that in criminal litigations, after the reconciliation between the offender and the victim is reached, the criminal responsibility of the offender will not be investigated and he may be exempted from punishment or given a mitigated punishment. Criminal reconciliation is different from a plea bargain, restorative justice, mediation, and "private settlement." This concept is regarded as a "reconciliation between the offender and the victim" in the West — Victim Offender Reconciliation, VOR for short (see Chen Guangzhong and Ge Lin, "Xingshi hejie chutan," [5]).
21. Article 37 of the *Criminal Law* (1997) provides that "if the circumstances of a person's crime are minor and do not require criminal punishment, he may be exempted from it; however, he may, depending on the different circumstances of the case, be reprimanded or ordered to make a statement of repentance, offer an apology or pay compensation for the losses, or be subjected to administrative penalty or administrative sanctions by the competent department."
22. Jürgen Habermas, *Gonggong lingyu de jiegou zhuanxing*, 179.
23. Ibid.
24. David M. Walker, *Niujin falü da cidian*, 21.
25. Ji Weidong, *Fazhi zhixu de jiangou*, 14.
26. It is composed of procedural due process and substantive due process, and the substantive one is not just the derivative from the procedural one (see John Orht, *Zhengdang falü chengshi jianshi*).
27. There are a great number of relevant cases; Re Cohn's case (61 LQR 340 [1945]) is one of the cases. A mother and her daughter both had habitations in Germany, but they lived in England. They lost their lives in an air raid in London, but it was impossible to determine the time order of their death. In accordance with the will of the mother made when she was alive, the daughter would be eligible to inherit her personal property if and only she lived longer than the mother. According to the Conflict of Laws of England, the inheritance of personal property is dominated by domicile law and its procedure is dominated by lex fori. As for the time order of their death, the mother was presumed to die first pursuant to Article 184 of the *Law of Property Act 1925*, while the two are presumed to die simultaneously pursuant to Article 20 of the *German Civil Code* (Bürgerliches Gesetzbuch). Therefore, whether the presumption of death (in

England and Germany) was identified as substantive or procedural issues, would cause the adjudication to be totally different. The judge, Augustus Andrewes Uthwatt, finally adjudicated that the presumption made in England was substantive and it would not be accepted; while the presumption made in Germany was also substantive, and yet it would be accepted. However, there may be other circumstances. For example, if the judge believes that Article 184 is procedural and Article 20 is substantive, or vice versa, or if the judge holds that both Article 184 and Article 20 are procedural, the adjudication will be more complicated (See J.H.C Morris, *Daixi he molisi lun chongtufa*, 52–53).

28. David M. Walker, *Niujin falü da cidian*, 1082.
29. More about the International Criminal Court and the *Rome Statute* can be found in: Li Shiguang, Liu Daqun, and Ling Yan, *Guoji xingshi fayuan luoma guiyue pingshi*; William A. Schabas, *Guoji xingshi fayuan daolun*; Wang Xiumei, *Guoji xingshi fayuan yanjiu*.
30. Chu Huaizhi, "Zaishuo xingshiyitihua."
31. Karl Marx and F. Engels, 1995, 287.
32. Wu Bangguo 吳邦國, "Quanguo renmin daibiao dahui changwu weiyuanhui gongzuo baogao" 全國人民代表大會常務委員會工作報告 (Report on the Work of the Standing Committee of the National People's Congress), *Renmin ribao* 人民日報 (People's Daily), March 24, 2008.
33. According to *Legislation Statistics of the People's Republic of China* (2008), there were a total of 229 effective laws in China by March 2008; since then to the end of August 2009. The NPC and its Standing Committee have formulated or amended another 14 laws, including four new laws, namely, the *Circular Economy Promotion Law*, the *Law on the State-Owned Assets of Enterprises*, the *Law on the Mediation and Arbitration of Rural Land Contract Disputes*, and the *Law on the People's Armed Police Force*. In June 2009, the Standing Committee of the NPC issued the decision on the abolition of various laws, of which four laws, i.e. the *Police Stations Organic Regulations*, the *Urban Neighborhood Offices Organic Regulations*, the *Regulations on Overseas Chinese's Application for the Use of State-Owned Barren Hills and Wasteland*, and the Standing Committee of the NPC's *Ratification of the State Council's Resolution on the Measures of Overseas Chinese's Donation for School* as well as the *Methods of Overseas Chinese's Donation for School* were included in the *Legislation Statistics of the People's Republic of China*. Thus, in China, there were still 229 laws currently in effect up to August 2009. On October 31, 2009, the Standing Committee of the NPC passed the *Diplomatic Personnel Law*, and in December 26, 2009, it passed the *Tort Law* and the *Island Protection Law*.
34. It is by no means merely an academic issue but has a close relationship with judicial practice. For instance, the civil law system is divided into public law and private law, accordingly, in its court system there exist administrative courts to resolve disputes concerning public law and ordinary courts to handle disputes concerning private law. The common law system is divided into common law and equity, accordingly, in its court system there are general courts and courts of equity. Law of the United States is divided into federal law and state law, accordingly, there are federal courts and state courts in its court system. It is not necessary to impart the theoretical knowledge on the division of legal systems to people since these have already been a part of the daily legal lives.
35. Surely, such an idea is only with relative significance, because the systematization of law, in the final analysis, is determined by the systematization of the social relations that law adjusts, and the systematization of the social relations is determined by the degree of the stability of the society itself. However, a major

symbol differing the modern society from the traditional one exactly lies in its rapid development, due to the frequent changes of social relations; the efforts to systematize them often become bubbles. The phenomenon – "the code is outdated as soon as it is just enacted" – has become a portrait of our times. In fact, this is exactly the problem confronted by China's reform and opening up at present. Legislation is very practical as it needs to normalize people's experience of adjusting and solving the practical problems they confront. The systematization of law will be achieved naturally at the right time. Thus, if the society itself is instable and frequently changes, a forced codification will be difficult to make improvements or even labor in vain.

The Constitution and the Related Laws

1. See Zhang Wenxian, *Falixue*, 78.
2. Tang Yaoguo, "Zhongguo falü tixi jiang ruqi xingcheng," (11).
3. The *Law on Diplomatic Personnel Stationed Abroad* was passed at the 11th Session of the 11th National People's Congress on October 31, 2009. The *Tort Law* and the *Island Protection Law* were enacted at the 12th Session of the 11th National People's Congress on December 26, 2009. The *National Defense Mobilization Law* was passed at the 13th Session of the 11th National People's Congress on February 26, 2010, The number of law in effect has reached 233.
4. He Qinhua, "Feichu guomindang liufa quanshu."
5. Xu Chongde, *Zhonghua renmin gongheguo xianfashi*, 46.
6. Zhang Shengguang, "Quanguo renda ji qi changweihui lifa quanxian guanxi jiantao," (3).
7. Han Dayuan and Liu Songshan, "Xianfa wenben zhong 'jiben falü' de shizheng fenxi," (4).
8. Hu Jinguang, *Zhongguo xianfa wenti yanjiu*, 208.
9. Chen Xinmin, *Deguo gongfaxue jichu lilun*, Vol. 2, 362.
10. Liu Chunmao, *Zhongguo falü tixi yu faxue yuanli*, 3.
11. Xie Weiyan, "'Mufa' guannian shidu," (5).
12. Hu Jinguang and Han Dayuan, *Zhongguo xianfa*, 137.
13. Lin Laifan, *Cong xianfa guifan dao guifan xianfa*, 308.
14. Xie Weiyan, "'Mufa' guannian shidu," (5).
15. Jiang Ming'an, *Xinzhengfa yu xingzheng susongfa*, 52–53.
16. Abe Teruya, *Xianfa*, 43.
17. Lin Laifan, *Cong xianfa guifan dao guifan xianfa*, 308.
18. Xiao Weiyun, *Lun aomen jibenfa*, 164–66.
19. Jiao Hongchang, "Aomen tebie xingzhengqu jibenfa rouganwenti yanjiu," (1).
20. Jiang Zhaoyang, "Lun jibenfa zai guojia falü tixi zhong de falü diwei," (1).
21. Zou Pingxue, "Xianggang jibenfa jieshi jizhi de fayuan guifan tanxi," (1).
22. State Council Information Office 國務院新聞辦公室, *Zhongguo de minzu zhengceyu ge minzu gongtong fanrong fazhan* 中國的民族政策與各民族共同繁榮發展 (White Paper of "China's Ethnic Policy and Common Prosperity and Development of All Ethnic Groups), September 2009.
23. Ibid.
24. Wu Zongjin and Zhang Xiaohui, *Zhongguo minzu faxue*, 400.

25. State Council Information Office 國務院新聞辦公室, *Zhongguo de minzu zhengceyu ge minzu gongtong fanrong fazhan* 中國的民族政策與各民族共同繁榮發展 (White Paper of "China's Ethnic Policy and Common Prosperity and Development of All Ethnic Groups), September 2009.
26. Wang Weicheng 王維澄, "Dijiujie quanguo renda falü weiyuanhui guanyu lifafa caoan shenyi jieguo de baogao" 第九屆全國人大法律委員會關於立法法草案審議結果的報告 (Report by the Law Committee of the 9th National People's Congress on the results of the deliberation of the Legislation Law [Draft]), *Renmin ribao* 人民日報 (People's Daily), March 15, 2000.
27. Li Xiaodong and Ou Can, December 1, "Woguo junshi fagui tixi riyi wanshan, fazhi jianshe kaichuang xinjumian."
28. Deng Xiaoping 鄧小平, *Guanyu zhonghua renmin gongheguo quanguo renmin daibiao dahui ji defang geji renmin daibiao dahui xuanjufa* 關於中華人民共和國全國人民代表大會及地方各級人民代表大會選舉法 (Explanation of the Draft of the Electoral Law for the National People's Congress and Local People's Congresses), reported at the 22nd Meeting of the Central People's Government Committee on February 11, 1953.
29. Chen Hongyi, "Lun lixian zhuyi," (3).
30. Liu Zuoxiang, *Falixue*, 105.
31. Xu Chongde, *Xianfa*, 9.
32. Hu Jinguang, *Zhongguo xianfa wenti yanjiu*, 122.
33. Hu Jinguang and Han Dayuan, *Zhongguo xianfa*, 29.
34. Lin Laifan, *Cong xianfa guifan dao guifan xianfa*, 308.
35. Liu Wanghong, "Ershi shiji zhongguo renquan de xianfa baozhang huimou," (1).
36. Xu Bing, "Weixian shencha."
37. Wu Jiaqing, "Ershiyi shiji woguo xianfa bianqian de jiazhi quxiang," (11).
38. Zhu Fuhui, Cong xianquan dao kongquan — xianfa gongneng fazhan yanjiu," (5).
39. Lin Laifan, *Cong xianfa guifan dao guifan xianfa*, 306.
40. Jiang Ming'an, *Xinzhengfa yu xingzheng susongfa*, 18.
41. Mei Qiyong 梅啟勇, and Ouyang Guowen 歐陽國文, "Lüshifa shishi de wenti yuce ji jiejue lujing" 律師法實施的問題預測及解決路徑 (The Forecast of the Implementation of the Lawyers Law and the Solutions), *Renmin fayuan bao* 人民法院報 (People's Court Daily), July 22, 2008.
42. See "Xin lüshifa yu xingshi lüshifa zai xiugai de xianjie yu hudong" 新律師法與刑事律師法再修改的銜接與互動 (Summary of the Symposium on the Connection and Interaction between the Amendment of the New Law on Lawyers and Criminal Procedure Law), http://www.ahlawyer.org.cn/show_new.aspx?id=3218)
43. For example, Professor Chen Guangzhong, Professor Fan Chongyi of China University of Political Science and Law, and Tian Wenchang who is a lawyer of the Criminal Operations Committee of the All China Lawyers Association all advocate this viewpoint.
44. Jiao Hongyan 焦紅艷, and Chen Hongwei 陳虹偉, "Xingshi bianhu lüshi repan lüshifa xingsufa shixian wufeng duijie" 刑事辯護律師熱盼律師法刑訴法實現無縫對接 (Criminal Defense Lawyers Expects the Consistency Between the Lawyers Law and the Criminal Procedure Law), *Fazhi ribao* 法制日報 (Legal Daily), February 3, 2008.

45. Cui Min, "Guanyu dui jiben falü de xiugai xukequan wenti," (4).
46. Xu Chongde, *Zhonghua renmin gongheguo xianfashi*, 512.
47. Xu Chongde, *Zhonghua renmin gongheguo xianfashi*, 669. The 1982 Draft Constitution once prescribed that "the NPC and the Standing Committee of the NPC are the supreme organs exercising legislative power," in this regard, Rong Yiren believes that it is inappropriate to regard the NPC and the Standing Committee of the NPC as juxtaposed supreme organs exercising legislative power (ibid., 650).
48. Article 57 of the present *Constitution* stipulates that "The National People's Congress of the People's Republic of China is the highest organ of state power. Its permanent body is the Standing Committee of the National People's Congress." In accordance with the provisions in the text, only the NPC is "the highest organ of state power" and the NPC and the Standing Committee of the NPC together exercise the legislative power of the state.
49. Jiao Hongchang, *Xianfaxue*, 329.
50. Mo Jihong, *Xianfaxue*, 388.
51. Cai Dingjian, *Zhongguo renmin daibiao dahui zhidu yanjiu*, 239.
52. Lin Yan 林彥, "Quanguo renda changweihui jiben falü xiugaiquan shijian fenxi" 全國人大常委會基本法律修改權實踐分析 (Analysis on the National People's Congress Standing Committee's Amendment Authority of Basic Laws), *Huadong zhengfa daxue shuoshi lunwen* 華東政法大學碩士論文 (Masters Dissertation of the East China University of Political Science and Law), 2003.
53. Wei Dingren, *Xianfaxue*, 326.
54. Zhang Zhen, "Jiben falü yihuo xianfaxing falü?" (5).
55. Han Dayuan and Liu Songshan, "Xianfa wenben zhong 'jiben falü' de shizheng fenxi," (4).
56. Basic laws concerning other matters mainly include the laws concerning basic rights and obligations prescribed in the *Constitution*, the important laws concerning economy, the laws concerning rights and obligations of civil servants, and the laws concerning judicial systems (see Han Dayuan, *Xianfaxue jichu lilun*, 345–47).
57. Zhou Wangsheng, *Lifaxue jiaocheng*, 129.
58. Zhou Wangsheng, *Lifafa*, 336–38.
59. According to the classification of the content of legislation in the *Report to the 17th CPC National Congress*, issues concerning science and technology, rural development, environmental protection, macro-control, fall into the category of economic development, therefore legislation on these issues is all classified as legislation on economic development; issues concerning autonomy at the grassroots level, the reform of judicial system, and the reform of the administrative system fall into the category of political development, therefore legislation on judicial system and part of administrative laws are classified as legislation on political development; issues concerning media, publication, broadcasting, film, sports development, historical relics, and cultural heritage fall into the category of cultural development, therefore laws concerning these aspects are classified as legislation on cultural development; issues concerning education, employment, social security, health care, emergency management fall into the category of social development, therefore laws related to these aspects are classified as legislation on social development.
60. The legislation includes 32 civil and commercial laws, 54 economic laws, and 28 administrative laws.
61. The legislation includes 39 laws in the Constitution and the Related Laws, one criminal law, seven procedural and non-procedural laws, and 33 administrative laws.

62. The legislation includes the *Protection of Cultural Relics Law of the People's Republic of China*, the *Archives Law of the People's Republic of China*, the *Law of the People's Republic of China on Physical Culture and Sport*, and the *Law of the People's Republic of China on the Standard Spoken and Written Chinese Language*.
63. The legislation includes 17 social laws and 14 administrative laws.
64. Ruan Zhanjiang 阮占江, "2008nian woguo shihui lifa jiang quanmian tuijin, jiang you 44xiang zhiduo" 2008年我國社會立法將全面推進，將有44項之多 (The Number of Social Legislation Would Be Further Increased in 2008 to Reach 44 Sets of Law), *Fazhi ribao* 法制日報 (Legal Daily), January 10, 2008.
65. A Ji, "Zhongguo shehui lifa quanmian qihang," (8).
66. Li Lin, "Tongchou jingji shehui fazhan de jige lifa wenti," (9).
67. *Renmin ribao* 人民日報 (People's Daily), February 2, 1999.
68. Wang Lei, "Shilun woguo de xianfa jieshi jigou;" Fan Jinxue, "Xianfa jieshi zhuti lun;" Zhou Wei, "Woguo xianfa jieshi jiguan yanjiu."

References

Overview: Framework of the Socialist Legal System with Chinese Characteristics
Translated materials:

Arup, Christopher. "Quanqiuhua yu fa — yige xingchengzhong de jiaojiedian" 全球化與法 — 一個形成中的交接點 (Globalization and Law — A Developing Connection). Translated by Sun Chao 孫潮, and Shen Wei 沈偉. *Nanjing daxue falüe pinglun* 南京大學法律評論 (Nanjing University Law Review), (1) (1997).

Alekseev, S.S. *Fa de yiban lilun* 法的一般理論（上冊）(The General Theory of Law Vol. 1). Translated by Huang Liangping 黃良平, and Ding Wenqi 丁文琪. Beijing: Law Press, 1988.

Berman, Harold J. *Falü yu geming* 法律與革命 (Law and Revolution). Translated by He Weifang et al. 賀衛方等. Beijing: Encyclopedia of China Publishing House, 1993.

Bonfante, Pietro. *Luoma fa jiaokeshu* 羅馬法教科書 (Roman Law). Translated by Huang Feng 黃風. Beijing: China University of Political Science and Law Press, 2005.

Durkheim, David Émile. *Shehui fengong lun* 社會分工論 (The Division of Labor in Society). Beijing: Joint Publishing, 2005.

Friedman, Lawrence M. "Lun falü yu fazhan" 論法律與發展 (On Legal Development). In *Fazhi xiandaigui yanjiu (di 3 juan)* 法制現代化研究（第3卷）(The Study on Legal System Modernization Vol. 3). Nanjing: Nanjing Normal University Press, 1997.

Habermas, Jürgen. *Gonggong lingyu de jiegou zhuanxing* 公共領域的結構轉型 (The Structural Transformation of the Public Sphere). Translated by Cao Weidong et al. 曹衛東等. Shanghai: Xuelin Press, 1999.

Justinian I. *Faxue zonglun – faxue jieti* 法學總論 — 法學階梯 (The Institutes of Justinian). Translated by Zhang Qitai 張企泰. Beijing: The Commercial Press, 1989.

Kawashima, Takeyoshi 川島武宜. *Jindaihua yu fa* 近代化與法 (Modernization and Law). Beijing: China University of Political Science and Law Press, 1994.

Maine, Henry Sumner. *Gudai fa* 古代法 (The Ancient Law). Beijing: The Commerical Press, 1984.

Marx, Karl, and F. Engels. *Makesi Engesi quanji* 馬克思恩格思全集 (Collected Works of K. Marx and F. Engels Vol. 21). Beijing: People's Publishing House, 1965.

———. *Makesi Engesi quanji* 馬克思恩格思全集 (Collected Works of K. Marx and F. Engels Vol. 37). Beijing: People's Publishing House, 1971.

———. *Makesi Engesi quanji* 馬克思恩格思全集 (Collected Works of K. Marx and F. Engels Vol. 1). Beijing: People's Publishing House, 1995.

Merryman, John Henry. *Dalufa xi* 大陸法系 (The Civil Law Tradition). Translated by Gu Peidong 顧培東, and Lu Zhengping 祿正平. Beijing: Law Press, 2004.

Morris, J.H.C., ed. *Daixi he molisi lun chongtufa* 戴西和莫里斯論衝突法 (Dicey and Morris on the Conflict of Laws). Translated by Li Shuangyuan et al. 李雙元等. Beijing: Encyclopedia of China Publishing House, 1998.

Nonet, Philippe, and Philip Selznick. *Zhuanbianzhong de falü yu shehui* 轉變中的法律與社會 (Law and Society in Transition). Beijing: China University of Political Science and Law Press, 1994.

Orth, John V. *Zhengdang falü chengshi jianshi* 正當法律程式簡史 (Due Process of Law: A Brief History). Translated by Yang Mingcheng 楊明成, and Chen Shuangling 陳霜玲. Beijing: The Commercial Press, 2006.

Schabas, William A. *Guoji xingshi fayuan daolun* 國際刑事法院導論 (An Introduction to the International Criminal Court). Translated by Huang Fang 黃芳. Beijing: Chinese People's Public Security University, 2006.

Seidman, Ann, and Robert B.Seidman. *Fazhan jinchengzhong de guojia yu falü* 發展進程中的國家與法律 (State and Law in the Development Process). Beijing: Law Press, 2004.

Tigar, Michael E., and Madeleine R. Levy. *Falü yu zibenzhuyi de xingqi* 法律與資本主義的興起 (Law and the Rise of Capitalism). Shanghai: Xuelin Press, 1996.

Trubek, David M. "Lun dangdai meiguo de falü yu fazhan yundong" 論當代美國的法律與發展運動 (Law and Development Movement: What We Know and What We Do Not Know Today). *Bijiaofa yanjiu* 比較法研究 (Journal of Comparative Law), (2) (1990).

———. "Falü yu shehui yundong huigu" 法律與社會運動回顧 (Back to the Future: The Short, Happy Life of the Law and Society Movement). *Waiguofa yiping* 外國法譯評 (Global Law Review), (3) (1993).

Unger, Roberta M. *Xiandai shehuizhong de falü* 現代社會中的法律 (Law in Modern Society). Nanjing: China University of Political Science and Law Press, 1994.

———. Xiandai shehuizhong de falü 現代社會中的法律 (Law in Modern Society). Translated by Wu Yuzhang 吳玉章, and Zhou Hanhua 周漢華. Nanjing: Yilin Press, 2001.

Walker, David M. Niujin falü da cidian 牛津法律大辭典 (The Oxford Companion to Law). Translated by Li Shuangyuan et al. 李雙元等. Beijing: Law Press, 2003.

Weber, Max. *Jingji yu shehui* 經濟與社會 (Economy and Society). Beijing: The Commercial Press, 1997.

Zweigert, Konrad, and Hein Kotz. *Bijiaofa zonglun* 比較法總論 (An Introduction to Comparative Law). Guiyang: Guizhou People's Publishing, 1992.

Non-Chinese materials:

Cohen, Morris. "Property and Sovereignty." *Cornell Law Review*, (13) (1923).

Freedman, Lawrence M. "On legal development." *Rutgers Law Review* 24 (1969).

Glanter, Marc. "Modernization of Law." In *Modernization: The Dynamics of Growth*. New York: Basic Books, 1996.

Hale, Robert L. "Coercion and Distribution in a Supposedly Non-Coercive State." *Political Science Quarterly*, (38) (1923).

———. "Bargaining, Duress and Economic Liability." *Columbia Law Review*, (43) (1943).

Kennedy, Duncan. "Laws and Development." In *Contemplating Complexity: Law and Development in 21st Century (Cavendish)*, 2003.

Santos, Boaventur de Sousa. *Towards a New Common Sense, Law, Science and Politics in the Paradigmatic Transition*. New York: Routledge,1995.

Trubek, David M. *Law and Development Then and Now*. 90ASIL Proc, 1996.

Watson, Alan. *Legal Transplants: An Approach to Comparative Law*. Virginia: University of Virginia Press, 1974.

Chinese materials:

Chen Guangzhong 陳光中, and Ge Lin 葛琳. "Xingshi hejie chutan" 刑事和解初探 (Primary Research into Criminal Settlement). *Zhongguo faxue* 中國法學 (China Legal Science), (5) (2006).

Chu Huaizhi 儲槐植. "Zaishuo xingshiyitihua" 再說刑事一體化 (Reconsidering the Integration of Criminal Justice). *Faxue* 法學 (Law Science), (3) (2004).

Deng Xiaoping 鄧小平. *Deng Xiaoping wen xuan* 鄧小平文選 (Selected Writings of Deng Xiaoping Vol.2). Beijing: People's Publishing House, 1994.

Guo Daohui 郭道暉. *Zhongguo lifa zhidu* 中國立法制度 (China's Legislative System). Beijing: People's Publishing House, 1998.

Hao Tiechuan 郝鐵川. *Zhongguo shehui zhuyi chuji jieduan yifa zhiguo yanjiu baogao* 中國社會主義初級階段依法治國研究報告 (Research Report on the Primary Stage of Socialist Rule of Law in China). Beijing: Law Press, 2004.

Ji Weidong 季衛東. *Fazhi zhixu de jiangou* 法治秩序的建構 (Rule of Law Order Construction in China). Beijing: China University of Political Science and Law Press, 1999.

Jiang Ming'an 姜明安. "Chuanqiuhua shidai de xin xingchengfa" 全球化時代的新行政法 (Analysis about the New Administrative Law at the Age of Globalization). In *Chuanqiuhua shidai de zhongguo fazhi xiandaihua xueshu yantaohui lunwenji* 全球化時代的中國法制現代化學術研討會論文集 (Papers of the Modernization of China's Legal System in the Age of Globalization Conference). Nanjing: Legal System Modernization Research Center of Nanjing Normal University, 2009.

References

Legislation Planning Office of the Commission of Legislation Affairs of the National People's Congress Standing Committee 全國人大常委會法工委立法規劃室, ed. *Zhonghua renmin gongheguo lifa tongji* 中華人民共和國立法統計 (Legislation Statistics of the People's Republic of China). Beijing: China Democracy and Law Publishing House, 2008.

Li Buyun 李步雲. "Yifa zhiguo: jianshe shehui zhuyi fazhi guojia" 依法治國：建設社會主義法治國家 (Rule of Law: Construction of a Socialist Country Ruled by Law). *Zhongguo faxue* 中國法學 (China Legal Science), (2) (1996).

Li Lin 李林. *Lifa lilun yu zhidu* 立法理論與制度 (Theory and Practice of Legislation). Beijing: China Legal Publishing House, 2005.

Li Long 李龍, and Fan Jinxue 范進學. "Lun zhongguo tese shehui zhuyi falü tixi de kexue goujian 論中國特色社會主義法律體系的科學構建 (On the Scientific Construction of the Socialist Legal System with Chinese Characteristics). *Fazhi yu shehui fazhan* 法制與社會發展 (Law and Social Development), (5) (2003).

Li Shiguang 李世光, Li Daqun 劉大群, and Ling Yan 凌岩. *Guoji xingshi fayuan luoma guiyue pingshi* 國際刑事法院羅馬規約評釋 (Evaluation of the Rome Statute of the International Criminal Court). Beijing: Peking University Press, 2006.

Liu Hainian 劉海年, and Li Lin 李林, eds. *Yifa zhiguo yu falü tixi jiangou* 依法治國與法律體系建構 (Rule of Law and the Construction of Legal System). Beijing: China Legal Publishing House, 2001.

Qiao Xiaoyang 喬曉陽. "Quanyu zhongguo tese shehui zhuyi falü tixi de goucheng tezheng he neirong" 關於中國特色社會主義法律體系的構成、特徵和內容 (The Construction, Characteristics, and Content of the Socialist Legal System with Chinese Characteristics). In *Quanguo renda ganbu peixun jiangyi* 全國人大幹部培訓講義 (Training Handouts for the Officials of National People's Congress). Edited by Training Center of National People's Congress 全國人大培訓中心. Beijing: China Legal Publishing House, 2004.

Shen Zongling 沈宗靈, ed. *Falixue* 法理學 (Jurisprudence). Beijing: Higher Education Press, 2004.

———. "Dangdai zhongguo jiejian waiguo falü de shili" 當代中國借鑒外國法律的實例 (Factual Cases on Contemporary China's Learnings from the Foreign Laws). *Zhongguo faxue* 中國法學 (China Law Science), (5), (6) (1997).

Special Branch of General Office of the National People's Congress Standing Committee 全國人大常委會辦公廳研究室課題組. "Zhongguo tese shehui zhuyi falü tixi ruogan wenti yanjiu 中國特色社會主義法律體系若干問題研究 (Various Issues on the Socialist Legal System with Chinese Characteristics). *Lilun qianyan* 理論前沿 (Theoretical Frontiers), (3) (1999).

Sun Guohua 孫國華, and Yang Sibin 楊思斌. "Gongsifa de huafen yu fa de neizai jiegou" 公私法的劃分與法的內在結構 (The Division of Public Law and Private Law and the Internal Structure of Law). *Fazhi yu shehui fazhan* 法制與社會發展 (Law and Social Development), (4) (2004).

Sun Guohua 孫國華, ed. *Zhongguo tese shehui zhuyi falü tixi qianyan wenti yanjiu* 中國特色社會主義法律體系前沿問題研究 (Research on the Key Issues of the Socialist Legal System with Chinese Characteristics). Beijing: China Democracy and Law Publishing House, 2005.

———. *Zhongguo tese shehui zhuyi falü tixi yanjiu – gainian lilun jiegou* 中國特色社會主義法律體系研究 — 概念、理論、結構 (Research on the Socialist Legal System with Chinese Characteristics — Concept, Theory, and Structure). Beijing: China Democracy and Law Publishing House, 2009.

Wang Chenguang 王晨光. *Renmin daibiao dahui ershinian fazhan yu gaige*人民代表大會二十年發展與改革 (20-Year Development and Reform of the National People's Congress). Beijing: China Procuratorial Publishing House, 2001.

Wang Lixin et al. 王立新等. "Kaiting zhiyong ershiwu fenzhong" 開庭只用25分鐘 (25-Minute Court Case). *Renmin fayuan bao* 人民法院報 (People's Court Daily), April 21, 2002.

Wang Xiumei 王秀梅. *Guoji xingshi fayuan yanjiu* 國際刑事法院研究 (Research on the International Criminal Court). Beijing: China Renmin University Press, 2002.

Wu Bangguo 吳邦國. "Quanguo renmin daibiao dahui changwu weiyuanhui gongzuo baogao" 全國人民代表大會常務委員會工作報告 (Report on the Work of the Standing Committee of the National People's Congress). *Renmin ribao* 人民日報(People's Daily), March 24, 2008.

———. "Wei xingcheng zhongguo tese shehui zhuyi falü tixi er fendou" 為形成中國特色社會主義法律體系而奮鬥 (To Strive to Construct the Socialist Legal System with Chinese Characteristics). *Renmin ribao* 人民日報 (People's Daily), February 1, 2004.

Xin Chunying 信春鷹. "Zhongguo guoqing yu shehui zhuyi fazhi jianshe" 中國國情與社會主義法治建設 (China's Conditions and the Legal Construction of Socialism). *Fazhi ribao* 法制日報 (Legal Daily), June 29, 2008.

Xu Xianming 徐顯明, and Qu Xiangfei 曲相霏. "Renquan de tixi yu fenlei"人權的體系與分類 (System and classification of human rights). In *Yifa zhiguo yu falü tixi chonggou* 依法治國與法律體系重構 (Rule of Law and the Reconstruction of Legal System). Edited by Liu Hainian 劉海年, and Li Lin 李林. Beijing: Social Sciences Academic Press, 2008.

Zhang Hengshan 張恒山. *Fazhi yu dang de zhizheng fangshi yanjiu* 法治與黨的執政方式研究 (Research on the Rule of Law and the Reign of the Party). Beijing: Law Press, 2004.

Zhang Wenxian 張文顯, ed. *Falixue* 法理學 (Jurisprudence). Beijing: Higher Education Press, 2007.

Zhou Wangsheng 周旺生. *Lifaxue* 立法學 (Legislative Studies). Beijing: Law Press, 1998.

———. "Lifa pinzhi yu pinzhi lifa" 立法品質與品質立法 (Legislation Quality and Qualified Legislation). In *Lifa yanjiu* 立法研究 (China Legislation Review). Edited by Zhou Wangsheng 周旺生. Beijing: Law Press, 2000.

The Constitution and the Related Laws

Translated materials:

Abe, Teruya 阿部照哉. *Xianfa* 憲法 (Constitution). Translated by Zhou Zongxian 周宗憲. Beijing: China University of Political Science Law Press, 2006.

Ghestin, Jacques, and Gilles Goubeaux. *Faguo minfa zonglun* 法國民法總論 (General Introduction to French Civil Law). Beijing: Law Press, 2004.

Kelsen, Hans. *Fa yu guojia de yiban lilun* 法與國家的一般理論 (General Theory of Law and State). Beijing: Encyclopedia of China Publishing House, 1996.

Nobuyoshi, Ashibe 蘆部信喜. *Xianfa* 憲法 (Constitution). Beijing: Peking University Press, 2006.

Non-Chinese materials:

Favoreu, Louis, Patrick Gaïa, Richard Ghevontian, Jean-Louis Mestre, Otto Pfersmann, André Roux, and Guy Scoffoni. *Droit constitutionnel*. Paris: Dalloz, 2008.

Chinese materials:

A Ji 阿計. "Zhongguo shehui lifa quanmian qihang" 中國社會立法全面啟航 (A full-scale beginning of social legislation in China). *Gongmin daokan* 公民導刊 (Citizen Magazine), (8) (2007).

Cai Dingjian 蔡定劍. *Zhongguo renmin daibiao dahui zhidu yanjiu* 中國人民代表大會制度研究 (Research on the System of the National People's Congress of China). Beijing: Law Press, 2003.

Chen Hongyi 陳弘毅. "Lun lixian zhuyi" 論立憲主義 (Discussion on Constitutionalism). *Shijiao (zhongwen ban)* 視角（中文版）(Perspectives [Chinese edition]), (3) (2002).

Chen Xinmin 陳新民. *Deguo gongfaxue jichu lilun* 德國公法學基礎理論 (Fundamental Theory of Public Law of Germany). Jinan: Shandong People's Publishing House, 2001.

Cui Min 崔敏. "Guanyu dui jiben falü de xiugai xukequan wenti" 關於對基本法律的修改許可權問題 (On the Issues of the Amendment Authority of Basic Laws). *Renda yanjiu* 人大研究 (People's Congress Studying), (4) (2007).

Ding Zunian 丁祖年, and Lu Qunxing 盧群星. "Guanyu jiaqiang shehui lifa ruogan wenti de sikao" 關於加強社會立法若干問題的思考 (Various Issues on Strengthening Social Legislation). *Fazhi yanjiu* 法治研究 (Study the Rule of Law), (10) (2007).

Fan Jinxue 范進學. "Xianfa jieshi zhuti lun" 憲法解釋主體論 (Theory of Constitutional Interpretation Subject). *Zhongguo faxue* 中國法學 (China Legal Science), (6) (2004).

Gong Xiangrui 龔祥瑞. *Bijiao xianfa yu xingzhengfa* 比較憲法與行政法 (A Comparison between the Constitution and the Adminstrative Law). Beijing: Law Press, 2003.

Han Dayuan 韓大元, and Liu Songshan 劉松山. "Xianfa wenben zhong 'jiben falü' de shizheng fenxi" 憲法文本中"基本法律"的實證分析 (A Positive Analysis of "Basic Law" in the Text of the Constitution). *Faxue* 法學 (Legal Science), (4) (2003).

Han Dayuan 韓大元. "You wuquanfa de zhenglun xiangdao de rougan xianfa wenti" 由物權法的爭論想到的若干憲法問題 (Various Constitutional Issues from the Conflicts of the Property Law). *Faxue* 法學 (Legal Science), (3) (2006).

———. *Xianfaxue jichu lilun* 憲法學基礎理論 (Fundamental Theory of the Constitutional Studies). Beijing: China University of Political Science Law Press, 2008.

He Qinhua 何勤華. "Feichu guomindang liufa quanshu" 廢除國民黨六法全書 (Abolishing Kuomintang's Complete Literatures on Six Laws). *Xinmin wanbao* 新民晚報 (Xinmin Evening News), July 12, 2009.

Hu Jinguang 胡錦光, and Han Dayuan 韓大元. *Zhongguo xianfa* 中國憲法 (China's Constitution). Beijing: Law Press, 2004.

Hu Jinguang 胡錦光, ed. *Zhongguo xianfa wenti yanjiu* 中國憲法問題研究 (Research on the Issues of China's Constitution). Beijing: Xinhua Publishing House, 1998.

Jiang Ming'an 姜明安, ed. *Xinzhengfa yu xingzheng susongfa* 行政法與行政訴訟法 (Administrative Law and the Administrative Procedure Law). Beijing: Peking University Press, 2005.

Jiang Zhaoyang 蔣朝陽. "Lun jibenfa zai guojia falü tixi zhong de falü diwei" 論基本法在國家法律體系中的法律地位 (Discussion on the Legal Status of Basic Law in the State Legal System). In *"Yiguo liangzhi" yanjiu* "一國兩制"研究 (Academic Journal of One Country Two Systems), (1) (2009).

Jiao Hongchang 焦洪昌, ed. *Xianfaxue* 憲法學 (Constitutional Studies). Beijing: Peking University Press, 2006.

———. "Aomen tebie xingzhengqu jibenfa rouganwenti yanjiu" 澳門特別行政區基本法若干問題研究 (Studies of Several Issues on the Basie Law of the Macao Special Administrative Region). *Zhengfa luntan* 政法論壇 (Tribune of Political Science and Law), (1) (1999).

Li Buyun 李步雲, ed. *Xianfa bijiao yanjiu* 憲法比較研究 (Comparative Constitutional Studies). Beijing: Law Press, 1998.

Li Lin 李林. "Tongchou jingji shehui fazhan de jige lifa wenti" 統籌經濟社會發展的幾個立法問題 (Various Legislative Issues on the Coordination of Socio-economic Development). *Faxue* 法學 (Legal Science), (9) (2005).

Li Xiaodong 李小東, and Ou Can 歐燦. "Woguo junshi fagui tixi riyi wanshan, fazhi jianshe kaichuang xinjumian" 我國軍事法規體系日益完善，法制建設開創新局面 (A New Era of the Legal System with the Improving Military Regulations). *Jiefangjun bao* 解放軍報 (People's Liberation Army Daily), December 1, 2008.

Lin Laifan 林來梵. *Cong xianfa guifan dao guifan xianfa* 從憲法規範到規範憲法 (From Constitutional Regulation to Regulating Constitution). Beijing: Law Press, 2001.

Liu Chunmao 劉春茂, ed. *Zhongguo falü tixi yu faxue yuanli* 中國法律體系與法學原理 (China's Legal System and the Principles of Jurisprudence). Beijing: Law Press, 1997.

Liu Wanghong 劉旺洪. "Ershi shiji zhongguo renquan de xianfa baozhang huimou" 20世紀中國人權的憲法保障回眸 (Review on the Constitutional Protection of China's Human Rights in the 20th Century). *Weishi* 唯實 (Truths and Facts), (1) (2004).

Liu Zuoxiang 劉作翔, ed. *Falixue* 法理學 (Jurisprudence). Beijing: Social Sciences Academic Press, 2005.

———. "'2010 nian xingcheng you zhongguo tese falü tixi' de sikou" "2010年形成有中國特色法律體系"的思考 (Thoughts on the Establishment of the Socialist Legal System with Chinese Characteristics in 2010). *Shanghai shizhengfa guanli ganbu xueyuan xuebao* 上海市政法管理幹部學院學報 (Law Journal of Shanghai Administrative Cadre Institute of Politics and Law), (5) (2001).

Mo Jihong 莫紀宏, ed. *Xianfaxue* 憲法學 (Constitutional Studies). Beijing: Social Sciences Academic Press, 2004.

———. "Lun falü tixi jiangou de feifazhihua qingxiang" 論法律體系建構的非法治化傾向 (Discussion on the Tendency of Non-Legalization of the Construction of Legal System). *Shehui kexue* 社會科學 (Journal of Social Sciences), (8) (2000).

State Council Information Office 國務院新聞辦公室. *Zhongguo de minzu zhengceyu ge minzu gongtong fanrong fazhan* 中國的民族政策與各民族共同繁榮發展 (White Paper of "China's Ethnic Policy and Common Prosperity and Development of All Ethnic Groups), September 2009.

Tang Yaoguo 湯耀國. "Zhongguo falü tixi jiang ruqi xingcheng" 中國法律體系將如期形成 (China's Legal System Would Be Formed as Scheduled). *Liaowang xinwen zhoukan* 瞭望新聞週刊 (Outlook Weekly), (11) (2007).

Wang Lei 王磊. "Shilun woguo de xianfa jieshi jigou" 試論我國的憲法解釋機構

(Discussion on the Consititutional Interpretation Organ in China). In *Xiandai xianfa jieshi jiben lilun* 現代憲法解釋基本理論 (Fundamental Theory of Modern Constitutional Interpretation). Beijing: China Democracy and Law Publishing House, 2006.

Wang Mincan 王珊燦, ed. *Xingzhengfa gaiyao* 行政法概要 (Introduction to the Administrative Law). Beijing: Law Press, 1983.

Wang Weicheng 王維澄. "Dijiujie quanguo renda falü weiyuanhui guanyu lifafa caoan shenyi jieguo de baogao" 第九屆全國人大法律委員會關於立法法草案審議結果的報告 (Report by the Law Committee of the 9th National People's Congress on the Results of the Deliberation of the Legislation Law [Draft]). *Renmin ribao* 人民日報 (People's Daily), March 15, 2000.

Wei Dingren 魏定仁, ed. *Xianfaxue* 憲法學 (Constitutional Studies). Beijing: Peking University Press, 2005.

Wu Jialin 吳家麟, ed. *Xianfaxue* 憲法學 (Constitutional Studies). Beijing: Qunzhong Publishing House, 1983.

Wu Jiaqing 吳家清. "Ershiyi shiji woguo xianfa bianqian de jiazhi quxiang" 21世紀我國憲法變遷的價值取向 (The Changing Value of China's Constitution in the 21st Century). *Jianghan luntan* 江漢論壇 (Jianghan Tribune), (11) (2001).

Wu Zongjin 吳宗金, and Zhang Xiaohui 張曉暉. *Zhongguo minzu faxue* 中國民族法學 (Chinese Legal Science). Beijing: Law Press, 2004.

Xiao Weiyun 蕭蔚雲. *Lun aomen jibenfa* 論澳門基本法 (Discussion on the Basic Law of Macau). Beijing: Peking University Press, 2003.

Xie Weiyan 謝維雁. "'Mufa' guannian shidu" "母法"觀念釋讀 (The Explanation of the Concept "Mother Law"). *Sichuan daxue xuebao* 四川大學學報 (Journal of Sichuan University), (5) (2005).

Xu Bing 徐炳. "Weixian shencha" 違憲審查 (Examination of Unconstitutional Issues). In *Xianfa bijao yanjiu* 憲法比較研究 (Comparative Constitutional Studies). Beijing: Law Press, 1998.

Xu Chongde 許崇德, ed. *Xianfa* 憲法 (The Constitution). Beijing: China Renmin University Press, 2004.

———. *Zhonghua renmin gongheguo xianfashi* 中華人民共和國憲法史 (The History of the Constitution of the People's Republic of China). Fuzhou: Fujian People's Publishing House, 2005.

Xu Xianghua 徐向華, and Lin Yan 林彥. "Woguo lifafa de chenggong he buzu" 我國《立法法》的成功和不足 (The Strength and Deficiency of the Law on Legislation of China). *Faxue* 法學 (Legal Science), (6) (2000).

Xue Zuowen 薛佐文. "Lun 'jiben falü' he 'falü' de xingzhi he diwei" 論"基本法

律"和"法律"的性質和地位 (Discussion on the Nature and Status of "Basic Law" and "Law"). *Xinan zhengfa daxue xuebao* 西南政法大學學報 (Journal of Southwest University of Political Science and Law), (2) (2003).

Zhang Shaoyu 張少瑜, ed. "Yifazhiguo yu falü tixi jiangou xueshu yantaohui zongshu" 依法治國與法律體系建構學術研討會綜述 (Summary of Rule of Law and the Academic Conference of the Construction of Legal System). *Faxue yanjiu* 法學研究 (Chinese Journal of Law), (5) (2000).

Zhang Shengguang 章乘光. "Quanguo renda ji qi changweihui lifa quanxian guanxi jiantao" 全國人大及其常委會立法權限關係檢討 (Review on the Legislative Authority of the National People's Congress and its Standing Committee). *Huadong zhengfa xueyuan xuebao* 華東政法學院學報 (Journal of the East China University of Politics and Law), (3) (2004).

Zhang Wenxian 張文顯, ed. *Falixue* 法理學 (Jurisprudence). Beijing: Higher Education Press, 1999.

Zhang Zhen 張震. "Jiben falü yihuo xianfaxing falü?" 基本法律抑或憲法性法律？(Basic Law or Constitutional Law?). *Neimenggu shehui kexue* 內蒙古社會科學 (Inner Mongolia Social Sciences), (5) (2007).

Zhou Wangsheng 周旺生, ed. *Lifaxue jiaocheng* 立法學教程 (Course on Legislative Studies). Beijing: Law Press, 1995.

———. *Lifafa* 立法法 (Law on Legislation). Beijing: Law Press, 2004.

Zhou Wei 周偉. "Woguo xianfa jieshi jiguan yanjiu" 我國憲法解釋機關研究 (Research on the Constitutional Interpretation Organ in China). *Gongfa yanjiu* 公法研究 (Public Law Research), (1) (2005).

Zhu Fuhui 朱福惠. "Cong xianquan dao kongquan — xianfa gongneng fazhan yanjiu" 從限權到控權 — 憲法功能發展研究 (From Limitation to Regulation — Research on the Development of Constitutional Functions). *Xiandai faxue* 現代法學 (Modern Law Science), (5) (1999).

Zou Pingxue 鄒平學. "Xianggang jibenfa jieshi jizhi de fayuan guifan tanxi" 《香港基本法》解釋機制的法源規範探析 (Analysis of the Legal Source of the Interpretation of the Basic Law of Hong Kong). *"Yiguo liangji" yanjiu* "一國兩制"研究 (Academic Journal of One Country Two Systems), (1) (2009).

Index

Index